2000

how we talk

AMERICAN REGIONAL ENGLISH TODAY

ALLAN METCALF

HOUGHTON MIFFLIN COMPANY

Boston   New York

Library of Congress Cataloging-in-Publication Data

Metcalf, Allan A.
    How we talk : American regional English today / Allan Metcalf.
        p. cm.
    Includes indexes.
    ISBN 0-618-04363-2 (cloth) – ISBN 0-618-04362-4 (paper)
    1. English language—Spoken English—United States. 2. English language—
United States—Pronunciation. 3. English language—Variation—United States.
    4. English language—Dialects—United States. 5. Americanisms. I. Title.

PE2808.8 M48 2000
427'.0973—dc21

                                                                    00-059777

Manufactured in the United States of America

MP 10 9 8 7 6 5 4 3 2 1

For Susanna Elizabeth Metcalf
Now you're talking!

Contents

Introduction

Americans have different ways of speaking. About 270 million of them, to be precise.

That's 270 million Americans, of course, not ways of speaking. But you could make the argument that since no two people speak alike, there really are 270 million different ways of speaking in our country.

We usually don't make such a fine point of it, however. When we ask ourselves how many different ways of talking American there are, we generally think of just a few. Maybe two, like South and North. Maybe three, adding the Midlands or the West. Maybe half a dozen or so, including some of our bigger cities. Or maybe just one.

That one would be American English itself. From coast to coast, old and young, rich and poor, whatever our ethnic group or religion, all Americans who speak English have some things in common. Our American language sets itself apart from the English of England, for example, so much that when a book is published in both countries it often is edited for the special vocabulary of each. An American character may hold a *flashlight* and a *wrench* in an *elevator*, while a British one holds a *torch* and a *spanner* in a *lift*. An American will see a *soccer* match that someone from England sees as *football*. In America, you wear *braces* to straighten your teeth; in England, you wear *braces* (Americans would call them *suspenders*) to hold up your pants. Ailing Americans are *in the hospital*, while residents of the United Kingdom would be *in hospital*. And an American will *have gotten* what the British will *have got*.

There are significant pronunciation differences too. Americans have many different ways of pronouncing their vowels and consonants, but it's a rare American, for example, who would say *hot*, *pot*, or *dog* with the rounded lips and deep-throated vowel of the British. And Americans have a distinctly un-British way of pronouncing "t" — when it comes in the middle of a word, that is, and the next syllable isn't emphasized. To the British, the "t" sound in *latter* is the same as that in *table* or *tea*, but for almost all Americans, *latter* has a "d" sound in the middle. The same goes for the middle "t" in words like *waiting*, *letter*, *butter*, and *kitten:* Americans make them sound like "wading," "ledder," "budder," and "kidden."

How does it happen that we speak differently than the people in the land that gave us our language? Two reasons: First, there is even more variety in British English than there is in American — they had a thousand-year head start, after all. So the English language brought to American shores wasn't all one kind. These initial differences started the variety we still experience in American English.

Second, we've had more than two centuries to develop American English independent of British. Without particularly trying, we've developed new things to talk about, new ways of talking about old things, and new attitudes, all of which have taken our language further from that of the island we left behind.

In fact, American English is different enough from all other varieties — British, Canadian, Australian, South African, to name a few — that you could write an entire book just about those differences. Happily, there are such books. Here, however, we will take a closer look at our own ways of speaking.

Looking at varieties of the American language is like looking at varieties of the American climate: How many we find depends on how closely we look. The United States, we could say, has a temperate climate, neither tropical nor arctic. But then there's the semitropical South and Hawaii; arctic Alaska; the arid Southwestern desert; the rainy Pacific Northwest; the Mediterranean climate on the California coast; and so on down to particular microclimates. Likewise, in the language climate of the United States, you could say that Americans generally pronounce the "r" sound in every word that's spelled with an *r*, and enjoy a *milk shake* made with ice cream, even if it's *expensive;* but in some parts of the country the *r* after a vowel is silent, and in a few places that particular ice cream beverage is a *frappe* or a *cabinet*, and there are Americans who might say it's *spendy*. This book will look at the generalities of American English, but also its specialties, the words and pronunciations that give a distinctive flavor to the way we speak.

Of course, language isn't climate or food. The way we speak doesn't depend on temperature or humidity, as evidenced by the fact that our particular ways of speaking don't change from summer to winter. The greatest influence of climate on our language is that we may have names for special local kinds of weather, like the *Santa Ana wind* of southern California or the *blue norther* of Texas. The way we speak also doesn't depend on the food we eat, except to the extent that we have local preferences in food not found elsewhere, like the *horseshoe* and *pony* sandwiches of central Illinois or the *fry sauce* of Utah.

For that matter, our language doesn't depend on who our parents were or the shape of the mouth we inherited. Whatever our color, size, and shape, we grow up speaking the way people around us speak. That is why our most notable differences in language are usually differences from place to place; we talk most like those we talk with, and those are usually our neighbors.

So how many ways of speaking do we have, then? What do we notice?

Well, there's Southern, for certain. And there's the proper — oops, "propah" — talk of certain folk in eastern New England. There's "Noo Yawk Tawk," in our face. There's "Minnesohta" and "Wi-SCON-sin." Texas too might want a place of its own. There are the Yats of New Orleans, the practitioners of Utahnics, the surfer dudes and Valley Girls of California. There is the "Spoken Soul" developed by African Americans and the distinctive kinds of English spoken by our Latino communities. There is Gullah, on the Sea Islands of South Carolina, and Pidgin in Hawaii. Though language varieties generally don't respect state boundaries, there's something to be said about every state, and there are matters of language that are significant to an entire state, like the *Hoosiers* of Indiana, or the *pickles* of Nebraska.

Thanks to powerful tools like the Hubble telescope, astronomers are learning that the universe is stranger than anyone had imagined. Thanks to increasingly powerful studies of our language, we are learning that the universe of American English is stranger and more complicated than anyone had imagined.

That doesn't mean we no longer see the Big Dipper, Orion, and the Milky Way when we look at the night skies. The constellations are still there for the naked eye, even though we know their constituents are complex. Likewise, as we listen to Americans speaking, we still hear what we might expect within the broad familiar categories: Southern accents, and those of New York City, Texas and New Orleans; the distinct vowels of northern Wisconsin and the Yoopers; and the grand sweep of Western talk and the smooth Pacific coast. All are audible to the naked ear; it's just that now we know their constituents are complex indeed.

Does that make half a dozen varieties, then, or maybe two dozen, or one for each of the 50 states and then some? Yes indeed. All those answers are possible and even necessary for an appreciation of the variety of our language. They will all be on display here.

Also of interest and importance is the leftover, the residue, the common core, something that has been called "General American." It could just as well be called "Generic American": neutral speech, closest to that of parts of the North and much of the West, but without a sense of place. To say it has no accent isn't fair; it has an accent, just one that doesn't tell where you're from. It's what remains when we remove the local flavor, the language we use in order to sound educated and professional and businesslike.

It's the language also of national broadcasts and publications and thus is familiar to almost all Americans. Many of us are able to put it on and take it off like business clothes. We wear it in the formal world of business or education, but change to local ways of talking when at home and among friends.

At the start of the twentieth century, America had a variety of cultivated accents: Boston Brahmin, New York aristocrat, Southern Plantation, and the near-British of actors and orators, for example. At the start of the twenty-first century, few traces of those cultivated accents remain. Setting ourselves up in suburban enclaves detached from established local communities, we have developed a neutral norm for the middle class nationwide that their offspring then bring to colleges and universities. The neutral speech of the Midwest and West has become the norm for almost all educated persons, for the boardrooms of business and the consulting rooms of professionals as well as the vast suburban middle class. And there is no longer much of an inclination toward the British, no matter what your level of education or authority.

But the lower-status local and regional accents have stayed on. By default, with the diminution of cultivated accents, the lower-status ones have become the principal indicators of the distinctive language of a community. And so those seeking a local identity through language embrace what previously they would have shunned as vulgar.

Years ago the well-educated made a point of avoiding local ways of speaking as too provincial. Nowadays, educated or not, we're more inclined to have our cake and eat it too (with *frosting* or *icing*, depending on where we're from). That is, while we may speak a version of "General American" at work, at home we enjoy putting on and even showing off our local ways of speaking. We proudly and with good humor offer lessons for outsiders in "How to Speak" Texan, or Philadelphian, or Pittsburghese.

To continue the analogy with clothes: Nowadays we can choose our style of speaking as we choose our wardrobe, with choices we didn't have in earlier times. As late as the mid-twentieth century there was a standard of dress for both men and women. Hemlines on women's dresses went up and down from year to year as if by ukase, though it was merely the pronouncement of fashion designers. But during the 1960s this uniformity of dress broke down. Perhaps it was the hippie rebellion, when for the first time young people did not want to look and act like grownups. Perhaps it was the disillusionment of the Vietnam War. Perhaps, in the case of women's fashions, it was the absurd brevity and exposure of the miniskirt. Whatever the cause, since the 1960s there have been multiple standards of dress rather than a single norm. It's not anarchy; nobody wears a toga or a bearskin to anything but a costume party. But we can choose to look businesslike, creative, casual, or comfortable. The same holds true for speech. Although we may grow up talking the local talk, as adults we don't have to talk that way, nor do we have to talk like college professors, network broadcasters, or our favorite role models from Hollywood. We can choose.

Not that putting on a new way of speaking is as easy as changing a T-shirt for more formal attire. It's a whole new wardrobe, and it can take some effort to wear it naturally. But the choice is there.

Perhaps we enjoy our local speech more nowadays because we have that choice. Thanks to modern mobility and the broadcast media, fewer and fewer of us are stuck with only one way of speaking. So if we do talk in Hawaiian Pidgin, or Brooklynese, or Texan, it's probably not because we don't know any better but because we're having fun.

That development makes it harder to be categorical about how someone is likely to speak. You'll find residents, even natives, of Atlanta with hardly a trace of a Southern accent; Bostonians who sound like Coloradans or Californians; Minnesotans who could be from Ohio. Radio host Garrison Keillor, for example, tells the News from Lake Wobegon with small-town Minnesota character but with barely a hint of a Minnesota accent.

So there are national ways mixed in with local ways of speaking almost everywhere you go. Nevertheless, out of pride or out of a wish not to be just like everywhere else, local ways of speech are thriving, even if we put them on just for fun. Sometimes we literally put them on. On Ocracoke Island, North Carolina, for example, you can buy a T-shirt celebrating the Ocracoke Brogue. Nowadays we celebrate our diversity of cultures, customs, and cookery, and as we do so we are inclined to celebrate our diversity of accents as well.

This book is a trip around the United States, all 50 of them, looking for and listening to local ways of speaking. It begins in the South, the first part of our country settled by English speakers and still the region with the greatest sense of distinctive language. The trip then takes us north to New England, the second place settled by English speakers and until recent times our standard of high culture. We stop at the port of New York, then follow our language as it makes its way westward, gradually becoming more "General American" but continuing to have its local distinctions.

The tour concludes with ethnic American accents, because our sense of place involves not just geography but the groups we affiliate with. And then we go to the movies, considering how our accents are echoed there and who does them best.

The aim of this tour is not to be comprehensive but to offer a comprehensive overview of varieties of American English. To do that, it has to be selective. There's something from every region and every state, often many things, but by no means everything you could find.

Whatever place you call home, you're likely to find it underrepresented in its depth, breadth, and subtlety. While trying to think globally, a visitor just can't capture the full flavor of speaking locally. But this book can offer at least a glimpse of the riches of local American English. If it encourages you to go and listen more, it has succeeded.

Note on Sources

Three major projects have provided the greatest amount of information for this book: the enterprise known as the Linguistic Atlas of the United States and Canada, the *Dictionary of American Regional English*, and the *Atlas of North American English*.

The "Linguistic Atlas" studies came first, starting in New England in the 1930s and continuing to the present day. Their findings as of the 1960s were summarized in Carroll E. Reed's *Dialects of American English* (World, 1967) and for the Atlantic states in three books published by the University of Michigan Press: Hans Kurath's *Word Geography of the Eastern United States* (1949); E. Bagby Atwood's *Survey of Verb Forms in the Eastern United States* (1953); and Kurath and Raven I. McDavid, Jr.'s *Pronunciation of English in the Atlantic States* (1961). There are also detailed atlases for individual regions, beginning with Kurath's *Linguistic Atlas of New England* (3 volumes, Brown University Press, 1939–43) and including Harold B. Allen's *Linguistic Atlas of the Upper Midwest* (3 volumes, University of Minnesota Press, 1973–76) and Lee Pederson's *Linguistic Atlas of the Gulf States* (7 volumes, University of Georgia Press, 1986–92).

The great study of our vocabulary is the *Dictionary of American Regional English (DARE)* edited by Frederic G. Cassidy and Joan H. Hall (Harvard University Press, 1985–   ). Three volumes with 30,000 entries for the letters *A* through *O* have been published, along with indexes by region to those entries: *Publication of the American Dialect Society* 77 (1993) and 82 (1999). Although *DARE* is concerned with vocabulary, the "Guide to Pronunciation" in its first volume gives a detailed overview of the different sounds of American English, based on 1,843 taped interviews. Craig M. Carver's *American Regional Dialects: A Word Geography* (University of Michigan Press, 1987) is based on the *DARE* files.

In the 1990s, American pronunciations were studied in detail for the Telsur Project at the University of Pennsylvania. The results were published as the *Atlas of North American English: Phonetics, Phonology and Sound Change* edited by William Labov, Sharon Ash and Charles Boberg (Mouton de Gruyter, 2000). The book has 200 maps and includes a CD-ROM with sound clips. Methods and examples of gathering information about American English are given in two recent books: *American English: Dialects and Variation* by Walt Wolfram and Natalie Schilling-Estes (Blackwell, 1998) and *Language Variation in North American English* edited by A. Wayne Glowka and Donald M. Lance (Modern Language Association, 1993). More information on American pronunciation appears in the 12th edition of a book by that name, John Samuel Kenyon's *American Pronunciation*, expanded by Donald M. Lance and Stewart A. Kingsbury (George Wahr, 1994). Our slang receives full treatment in J.E. Lighter's *Random House Historical Dictionary of American Slang* (Volumes 1–2 covering *A* through *O*, 1994–1997). American English as a whole has often been written about but never so eloquently as in *The American Language* by H.L. Mencken, revised by Raven I. McDavid, Jr. (Knopf, 1963).

All those books cover the whole United States or at least large parts of the country. In addition, there are thousands of studies focused on particular places or particular vocabulary, pronunciation, and grammar. Many of them appeared in the American Dialect Society's journal *American Speech;* many others are books like E. Bagby Atwood's *Regional Vocabulary of Texas* (University of Texas Press, 1962), John Gould's *Maine Lingo* (*Down East Magazine*, 1975), and Walt Wolfram and Natalie Schilling-Estes' *Hoi Toide on the Outer Banks: The Story of the Ocracoke Brogue* (University of North Carolina Press, 1997).

There are dictionaries of African American English like Geneva Smitherman's *Black Talk: Words and Phrases from the Hood to the Amen Corner* (Houghton Mifflin Company, revised edition 2000) and books like John Russell Rickford and Russell John Rickford's *Spoken Soul: The Story of Black English* (John Wiley, 2000). Studies of other ethnic varieties are not so plentiful, but there are for example Joyce Penfield and Jacob L. Ornstein-Galicia's *Chicano English: An Ethnic Contact Dialect* (John Benjamins, 1985) and William L. Leap's *American Indian English* (University of Utah Press, 1993).

To those and many other studies, too numerous to mention here, this book is indebted. It is also greatly indebted to the copious evidence of present-day American English among the billion pages of the World Wide Web, not just scholarly websites but popular ones like those for Utahnics and Seattlese, and ordinary sites whose comments and conversation provide evidence for local words like the Northwest's *spendy* or Boston's *cleansers*. You can hear the accents of American presidents, for example, going as far back as Grover Cleveland, on the website of the Vincent Voice Library at Michigan State University. On the Pittsburghese website, you can hear an authentic native pronunciation of "What yinz doin en at?"

Members of the American Dialect Society will recognize on the following pages many of their contributions to the society's "ADS-L" Internet e-mail discussion list as well as to its publications *American Speech* and *Publication of the American Dialect Society*.

Acknowledgments

With all these resources, I thought it would be easy. It was not. That this book exists at all is owing to the instigation and perseverance of Joseph Pickett, my editor at Houghton Mifflin. That it manages to cover as much as it does, with as much accuracy as it has, is owing to his careful reading, judicious questioning, and welcome suggestions for improvement. He helped me out of more mistakes than the reader will ever know.

Others at Houghton Mifflin also lent their expertise: Ben Fortson on his native New Orleans, David Pritchard and Jacquelyn Pope on the movies, and Steve Kleinedler, who braved the elements to do field research on the Vermonster. Margaret Anne Miles deserves credit for the illustrations. Freelancer Merryl Maleska Wilbur relentlessly and brilliantly copyedited the manuscript, saving me from a heap of trouble. Susan Chicoski did the proofreading.

Experts and friends — usually one and the same — willingly helped me when I had questions no published source could answer. I know a little of what they know because of the ready assistance of linguists David K. Barnhart, Ronald Butters, Joan Houston Hall, Allyn Partin Hernandez, Sonja Launspach, Allen Maberry, Peter McGraw, Dennis Preston, Erik Thomas, and Luanne von Schneidemesser. And there is no substitute for the first-hand local information I obtained from Tim Albertson of Vermont, Gerald Stone of Ohio, and Anne, John, and Sarah Hitt of Nebraska.

At MacMurray College I once again have Julian Hall colleagues Nadine Szczepanski and William DeSilva to thank for their hospitality and encouragement. The MacMurray College library has been my refuge and friend in need, with particular assistance from Mary Jo Thomas, Mary Ellen Blackston, and Penny Mitchell. More faculty colleagues and students than I can name advertently or inadvertently taught me about their native ways of speaking.

At home my wife Donna not only reminded me of my deadlines but looked with a reader's and designer's eye at the possibilities of the book and made it better in countless ways.

With all this help, there certainly remains room for improvement. If any reader can enlighten me on some matter that could be better explained, I'll be happy to acknowledge that help in a future edition.

Jacksonville, Illinois
March 2000

THE SOUTH

Hey, y'all!

In our search for authentic American English, the South might should be the place to start. (*Might should?* Might couldn't say that in the North!) Not only is Southern the best-known and most-discussed variety of American English; it is also closely associated with African-American English, which is spoken nationwide and influential in American popular culture. Moreover, American English had its beginnings in the South. The first permanent English-speaking outpost in North America — in Jamestown, Virginia — was established well over a decade before English speakers began to inhabit New England, let alone the middle colonies of New York and Pennsylvania.

Pure Elizabethan (or Jacobean)

In 1607 a ship from London made landfall on the coast of what we now call Virginia and established what would prove to be the first permanent English-speaking community in North America. The men and women in that ship came from different parts of England, speaking English with different accents a thousand years in the making. Forming a new community in a new land did not change their various accents much, because adults generally keep the habits of speech they learned growing up.

But children were born in Jamestown too, and as they grew and formed ties with others their own age they developed an accent of their own, not exactly that of any of their parents but something of an average or compromise. This was not a conscious decision but a natural development; people are inclined to share speech habits

> **I'm aware that** you have interpreters who translate the proceedings of this body [the United Nations] into a half-dozen different languages. And they have a challenge today, a very interesting challenge. As some of you may have detected already, I do not have a Yankee accent. (Laughter) I hope you have a translator here who can speak "Southern," someone who can translate words like *y'all* and *I do declare*. (Laughter) In any event, it may be that another language barrier will need to be overcome this morning.
>
> — U.S. Senator Jesse Helms of North Carolina,
> speaking to the U.N. Security Council in New York City, January 20, 2000

with peers rather than parents, and before adolescence their speech is flexible enough to adapt easily to others.

The Jamestown colony, founded on May 13, 1607, may be the source of the legend that there are still speakers of pure Elizabethan or Jacobean English in obscure corners of the South. Elizabethan refers to the reign of Queen Elizabeth, 1558–1603; Jacobean to the reign of King James, 1603–1625, remembered for sponsoring a translation of the Bible. The adventurers who populated Jamestown were all born into the Elizabethan era but in 1607 were talking and writing in Jacobean times, like their great contemporary William Shakespeare. The most famous leader of the Jamestown colony, Captain John Smith (1580–1631), writes like the born Elizabethan he was. Here he is describing events in November 1607:

> Their plenty of corne I found decreased, yet lading the barge, I returned to our fort: our store being now indifferently wel provided with corne, there was much adoe for to have the pinace goe for England, against which Captain Martin and my selfe, standing chiefly against it, and in fine after many debatings, pro et contra, it was resolved to stay a further resolution.

Nowadays no one in the South or anywhere in America talks or writes like this. But even in this early passage, Smith has already given an American meaning to an English word. *Corn* here means our American (or Indian) corn rather than wheat, as it would have in England — because *corn* referred to the principal grain, and that was different in America.

Jamestown 1607: "Now falleth every man to work" (John Smith). The first "plantation" of the English language in North America.

Smith and his fellow colonists also brought numerous Indian words into the English language to describe the exotic animals, plants, food, geography, and customs of the new continent: words like *raccoon*, *tomahawk*, and *swamp*.

It was still too early, however, to say that Jamestown had a Southern accent. But within a very short time — by the end of the first century of English-speaking settlement — the South *was* becoming distinctive. For example, *tote* instead of Northern *carry* is recorded as early as 1677. It may represent African influence, because it is notably similar to *tota* and *tuta*, words meaning "to pick up" or "to carry" in Bantu languages of western Africa. (Slave traders were bringing many Bantu speakers to the colonies along the South Atlantic coast.)

Not that there was any notion of a Southern accent back then. Each locality had its own local variety of English, distinctive though related to the others. To this day the South seems to have more local variation than any other part of the country. But in the nineteenth century, the growing conflict with the North over slavery, culminating in the Civil War, drew attention politically and culturally to the

South as a whole, as distinct from the North. Americans began to think of themselves as Northerners or Southerners and became conscious of North-South differences in speech that coincided with North-South differences in politics.

Thus emerged a "Southern accent," encompassing the states of the Confederacy from Virginia in the northeast to Texas in the southwest. And so we can find a Northern visitor in 1866, a year after the end of the Civil War, observing of the lawyers of New Orleans: "They were a fine-looking body of men, mostly of marked Southern accent and manner, very courteous." And an 1876 story of the Civil War described for Northern readers a country girl in Alabama: "Her voice was charmingly rich and sweet, and all her words seemed to wear trailing skirts of velvet, they came so slowly from her careless lips, and lingered so softly on the air. (Oh, the sweet voices of the South!)"

Some of the main features of present-day Southern English apparently weren't fully developed at the time of the Civil War. It was during the following century, when — not coincidentally — the region was developing its sense of itself as special, that certain fixtures of present-day Southern speech became widely used. For example, it was during this period that the Southern pronunciation of *I* as "ah," as well as the expressions "might could" and "fixin' to," became important fixtures of Southern speech.

The twentieth century brought many changes to the South, reducing its isolation from the rest of the country. Descendants of slaves migrated north and west, bringing Southern speech patterns to the rest of the country. Vacationers and retirees from the cold North flocked south, bringing Northern speech to southern Florida. National corporations established head offices in Southern cities like Atlanta and Dallas, bringing Northern-accented business speech to the region. CNN and the Weather Channel established national headquarters in Atlanta, and Disney and Universal Studios established national attractions in Orlando, likewise bringing in Northern speech norms.

But with all the opportunities for language assimilation, the majority of inhabitants of the Old South still pledge allegiance to some form of Southern English. In both North and South, the old stereotypes about Southern speech persist, strongly influencing our ideas about the land and people: that Southern speech is kinder, gentler, more intimate than the speech of the North, though also less educated and sophisticated.

Because of its distinctiveness and its political and social importance, Southern English is the most notable and talked-about style of American speech. A 1989 bibliography lists 3833 studies of the language of the South, and that number continues to grow. Further evidence of the distinctive importance of the South can be found in the *Dictionary of American Regional English*. The three volumes published as of 2000, covering American regional vocabulary from A through O, attribute far more vocabulary (2100 words) to the South than to any other part of the country. The next most frequent label is "South Midlands," an extension of the South, with about 1850 words. By comparison, only about 700 words are labeled "North." There are about 800 labeled "West" and 750 labeled "New England"; all other regions have even fewer.

The South is not only the most distinctive but also the largest of the distinctive areas of American speech, occupying the entire southeastern corner of the United States. More specifically, it stretches from Virginia to eastern Texas, including the Carolinas, Florida, Georgia, Alabama, Mississippi, and Louisiana. Its influence extends well beyond the boundaries of the old Confederacy to the area linguists call the Upper South or South Midland, stretching from Maryland to eastern Oklahoma and including Kentucky, Tennessee, Arkansas, much of Missouri, and the southernmost parts of Ohio, Indiana, and Illinois. In the *Dictionary of American Regional English*, the majority of words labeled "South" are also labeled "South Midland," and vice versa. Although there are some words limited strictly to the heart of the South, and some found only on the fringes, the majority of Southern vocabulary extends to those larger limits.

In fact, the language border between South and North, or between South and West, is not as clearly marked as the Mason-Dixon Line. Instead, there is a gradual change from South to North and from South to West. Texas, for example, is quite Southern on its eastern side and less so toward the west. To find the essence of a Southern accent we will look to the heart of Dixie — states like South Carolina, Georgia, Alabama, and Mississippi. And we had better be cautious of places like Atlanta, which has always been a newcomer

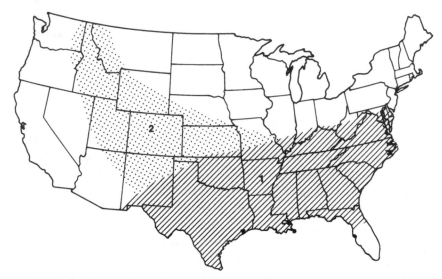

Hah Places: Diagonal stripes (1) indicate where the "long i" (in words like *by* and *high*) is often pronounced "ah" rather than "ah-ee." Dots (2) indicate where the "long i" (in words like *ride, mile,* and *fire*) is sometimes pronounced "ah" rather than "ah-ee." From the *Dictionary of American Regional English.*

among Southern cities and now exhibits an overlay of the business culture of the North. Similarly, southern Florida has had such an influx of Yankees that a Southern accent there is an exception.

In the end, geographical locations do not matter as much as mental ones. Like other kinds of American English, Southern has a definite geographical base, but linguistically it is a state of mind. If you speak Southern, you identify yourself to both friends and strangers as participating in Southern culture and the stereotypes that go with it: informal, friendly, personal, unhurried, family-oriented on the positive side; or unbusinesslike, slow, and clannish on the negative. The sounds and the words of the South conjure up images that Americans, South and North, have cultivated for at least two centuries.

Sounds of the South

Say "ah"   To be recognized as a Southerner, all you have to do is open your mouth and say "ah." That's the "ah" referring to yourself in the first person, as in "Ah'm fahn." If this "ah" is the same as the sound you make when showing your tonsils to your otolaryngologist, you're speaking Southern.

To be sure, all speakers of English say "ah" for *I* sometimes, rather than "ah-ee." In rapid casual conversation, nearly everyone says "Ah must go" rather than "Ah-ee must go." But if it's "ah" even when you're speaking real slow and careful, as in "Yes, it is ah," you're speaking Southern.

This "ah" is fundamental to Southern speech because it is so wahdspread in the Southern vocabulary. That is, it is heard not only in *I* but in other words that use the "long i" sound. Indeed, some Southerners say "ah" in all such words. If *nice white rice* comes out as "nahs whaht rahs," you have a Southern accent for sure. There is a joke about the Southerner who shocked his host at a party in the North by asking for a *piece of ice* using the Southern "ah" pronunciation.

Strangely, this "ah" is most pervasive at the upper edges of the South. In the heart of Dixie, Southerners tend to be more discriminating and pronounce "ah" or "ah-ee" depending on the sound that follows. They may say the Southern "ah" for *I*, "trah" for *try*, "tahm" for *time*, "tahr" for *tire*, "hahd" for *hide*, and "sahz" for *size*, for example, but for them *nice white rice* follows the Northern pattern, "nah-ees whah-eet rah-ees." These discriminating Southerners can't rhyme *I scream for ice cream*, because for them it comes out as *"Ah" scream for "ah-ee"ce cream.* For such people, consonants like *s*, *f*, *p*, *t*, and *k* make the difference; if the "long i" comes immediately before one of these "voiceless" sounds, in this variety of Southern speech it will sound like Northern "ah-ee." Nevertheless, even Southerners who make this exception will use plain "ah" in *sky*, *drive*, *child*, *pie*, *mind*, and countless other words with the "long i."

Those who study phonetics caution that the "ah" of *I*, whether Southern "ah" or Northern "ah-ee," isn't exactly the same as the "ah" of *father*, which is said with the tongue farther back. But for differentiating North from South, that distinction of "ah"s isn't important.

Count to tin   If the number that comes after nine sounds the same as the metal that makes a can, you're speaking Southern. If an ink-filled

Pen or Pin?

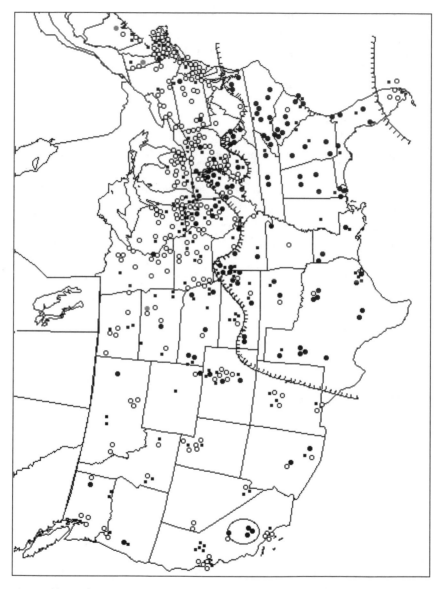

Pinpointing Pin and Pen: Each solid dot represents one person who pronounced *pin* and *pen* alike when interviewed for the *Atlas of North American English* created at the University of Pennsylvania. The lines enclose the large Southern and small California areas where such pronunciations predominate. Open dots represent those who pronounced the words differently, and solid squares represent intermediate situations.

writing instrument sounds the same as a little sharp-pointed metal object that holds fabric in place, same diagnosis. Counting to *tin* and writing with a *pin* mark you as Southern.

And if you have *tin pins* on your desk, instead of *ten pens*, chances are you will also use a "short i" pronunciation in all other words where "short e" is followed by *n*: *men, fence, tender*, and *mention* sound like "min," "fince," "tinder," and "mintion," for example. *Again*, which has the "short e" sound in the North, is "agin" in the South. And in the Southern pronunciation, "A penny for your thoughts" comes out as "A 'pinny'. . . ."

Non-Southerners might imagine that the similarity of sounds would cause problems. If *pen* sounds like *pin*, how does a Southerner know what to do when asked for a "pin"? But this hasn't resulted in an outbreak of accidental stabbings in the South. If the context isn't clear enough, a Southerner can always ask for an *ink pen*. In the rest of the country, *ink pen* sounds redundant. But that's exactly why *ink pen* is so useful in the South. Someone who says *ink pen* is likely to be someone who pronounces *pen* and *pin* alike.

If you do pronounce *pen* and *pin* alike, it doesn't mean you don't know the difference. Any literate Southerner will know which item is spelled *pen* and which is spelled *pin*. But in the South, the two words generally are homophones, written differently but sounding alike (as is the case, for example, with *to, too*, and *two* in all varieties of English). Here, for example, is a verse from "Arkansas, You Run Deep in Me," the state song of Arkansas, rhyming *wind* and *friend:*

Magnolia blooming, Mama smiling,
Mallards sailing on a December wind.
God bless the memories I keep recalling
Like an old familiar friend.

The map that shows the extent of sound-alike *pen* and *pin* drapes like a curtain over the old Confederacy and invades a little of Yankee territory too. Its northern folds weave up and down through Virginia, West Virginia, and Kentucky. The dividing line swings northward into Indiana, then south again as it goes westward through Illinois, Missouri, and Kansas. You'll find some people who say *pen* like *pin* in Nebraska and Colorado too. This sound-alike region also includes Oklahoma and Texas. But that's as far west as it goes.

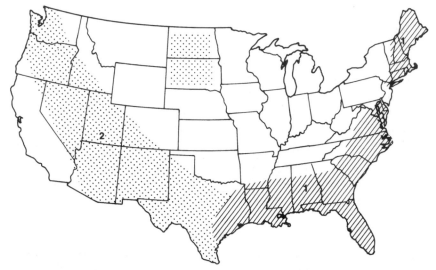

Where We R'nt: Diagonal stripes (1) indicate where R after vowels (in words like *course* and *work*) is sometimes not pronounced. Dots (2) indicate where R after the vowels is sometimes lightly pronounced. From the *Dictionary of American Regional English.*

Outside of the South and South Midlands, the only other place likely to rhyme *pin* with *pen* is the central valley of California (not to be confused with the San Fernando Valley of "Valley Girl" fame). In that central part of the state, especially around Bakersfield, *pen* and *pin* are likely to be rhyming words. It's not exactly the same rhyme as in the South, however. The Southern pronunciation of both *pin* and *pen* tends to be a drawn-out, emphatic vowel: "pih-un." The central California rhyme of *pin* with *pen* is a shorter, quicker sound, and therefore not so noticeable.

Back in the Southeast, there's also an exception to the pattern: southern Florida, including Miami, where the influx of discriminating Yankees has divided *pen* from *pin* in Northern fashion.

How we "r"   Most American speech is r-ful. Get the joke? If you do, your speech isn't as r-ful as the rest.

One of the most pronounced differences between types of American speech is the presence or absence of the "r" sound after vowels. Where it's absent, *r-ful* sounds like "ah-ful," which is pretty

The rhymes of Harry Macarthy's Confederate song "The Bonnie Blue Flag" suggest that "r-lessness" after vowels was characteristic of the South at the time of the Civil War. The song was first performed in Jackson, Mississippi, in the spring of 1861. One stanza ends with an "r-less" rhyme:

First, gallant South Carolina nobly made the stand;
Then came Alabama and took her by the hand;
Next, quickly Mississippi, Georgia, and Florida,
All raised on high the Bonnie Blue Flag that bears a Single Star.

And there is no "r" in the rhyme of the famous chorus:

Hurrah! Hurrah! for Southern rights hurrah!
Hurrah! for the Bonnie Blue Flag that bears a Single Star.

close to *awful*. Get it now, Northerners and Westerners? *R-ful* is *awful*.

Much of the South shares with eastern New England and New York City the distinction of being not so r-ful. The rest of the country pronounces the "r" sound everywhere it occurs in a word, but those three Eastern areas adopted the habit of dropping the "r" sound after a vowel when that became the British fashion in the eighteenth century. So, for example, *far* is "fah," *harm* is "hahm," and *bird* is "buhd." Sometimes, rather than simply eliminating the "r" sound, Southern speech will substitute an "uh" sound. So *rather* becomes "rath-uh" and *deer* becomes "dee-uh." The same can happen in *ear, care, sure,* and *four.*

Dropping the "r" sound happens only after a vowel, never at the beginning of a word or syllable. So the Southern pronunciation of *river* is "riv-uh," with the first "r" as loud and clear as it would be anywhere else and only the second "r" gone with the wind. Furthermore, even after a vowel, the "r" sound is not dropped when it comes before another vowel, as in *carry* or *miracle.*

And it's not the case that all Southerners drop the "r" sound after vowels. The outer areas of the South, like Kentucky and most of Texas, keep the "hard r" as much as anywhere else in the country. The difference has a historical explanation: dropping the "r sound" was an eighteenth-century innovation in British English. It spread to coastal areas that traded and kept in touch with England, but didn't reach places distant from British commerce and fashion.

Words to the y's   In most respects, Americans think of the Southern accent as less formal and businesslike than the Northern. But the news about the Southern accent is different when it comes to words like *news*. Southerners give an extra twist that sounds elegant and refined to Northern ears: they insert a "y" sound after the first consonant and before the vowel.

It isn't so different from what all speakers of American English, North and South, do in words like *few* and *music*. But the South does it in words that the North leaves alone, words beginning with *n, d* or *t*. So in the South, *news* is "nyews," *due* is "dyew," and *Tuesday* is "Tyewsday." It is one Southern style of pronunciation that is sometimes imitated with admiration in the North, notably by broadcasters presenting the "nyews". The prestige of the "y" pronunciation has an assist from the British, who insert a "y" sound after the first consonant or consonants in words like *new, due, student, assume, tune* and sometimes even *suit* and *Susan*.

From a Southern point of view, the North talks funny by leaving out the necessary "y." Those who think North Carolina's Duke University lacks Southernness mock it with the spelling *Dook*.

True Blue   But throughout the country, many Americans have developed a pronunciation for the "long u" of *news, due,* and *Tuesday,* as well as words like *blue, chew,* and *suit,* that overrides the *news* versus "nyews" distinction. Instead of the sound of "who," it is more like the "ee" of *tree*. In such circumstances, the "y" and the "ee" merge in a word like *news* to make it sound more like *knees*. Similarly, if you say *true blue* it sounds close to "tree blee."

This new pronunciation is by no means restricted to the South, but Southerners do have a distinctive twist for it. According to researcher Erik Thomas, in the area that includes Mississippi, Alabama, Georgia, South Carolina, North Carolina, Tennessee, Kentucky, West Virginia, and western Virginia, the pronunciation ends with a rising sound: "treey bleey" for *true blue*. The rest of the country, however, gives it a falling conclusion: "treew bleew." In the area that Thomas has identi-

fied, all "long u" words are affected, even *who* and *too*. "It's often especially obvious in *too*," Thomas notes, "because *too* tends to show up at
the end of a sentence, where it gets lengthened."

If you're one of the millions of subscribers to America Online,
you can hear a version of this vowel in the first word of "You've got
mail." It's pronounced by Elwood Edwards, a native of New Bern,
North Carolina, who has done that message for AOL since it began
carrying audio in 1989. As a professional radio and television broad-
caster, he gives it more of a Northern ending: "yeewve."

Pronounced Carefully   At the end of words, *y* in the South sometimes
has a short "ih" sound instead of the "ee" of the North. This affects
words like *carefully*, *happy*, and *elementary*. And the *i* before the final *y* has a "clear" sound made with the tongue in the front of the
mouth, heard easily in words like *easily* and *Billy*.

Oil Toil   *Oil*, *boil*, and *coil* often sound rather like *ol'*, *bowl*, and *coal* in
the South. The sound that is like the "oy" of *boy* becomes simplified to
the long "o" sound like that of *owe* when followed by the consonant *l*.

The Okay Way   Another change in the speech of some Southerners affects words with the "long a" sound as in *play*, *way*, or *okay*. These
Southerners say "ah" where Northerners say "ah-ee," in words like *I*
and *time*, but they put "ah-ee" to use in "long a" words, so they will
express agreement by saying "oh-kah-ee."

Dog Pen   Where the South reduces "ah-ee" to "ah" in words like *I*
and *pie*, it lengthens some vowels that in the North are short. So *dog*
is often "daw-ug" or *pen* "piy-un." (In the latter case the "short e" of
pen changes to a "short i" sound before it is lengthened.)

On Line on your Own Line   Southern speakers often use a long "oh" in
on, making it sound like *own*, as opposed to the short vowel of the
North and West. *On line* then is "own lahn."

Getting Greazy   One of the most clear-cut differences between North
and South occurs in the pronunciation of one little word: *greasy*.
Southerners give the last consonant a "z" sound, while in the North
and the West it's an "s." (The spelling *greasy* works for both,

because *s* between two vowels can be interpreted with either sound, as in *daisy* with a "z" and *ecstasy* with an "s.") The Southern "z" of *greasy* goes well up into the Midlands too, encompassing much of New Jersey, Pennsylvania, Ohio, Indiana, and Illinois. But New England, upstate New York, Wisconsin, Michigan, and most of the West use an "s" in that word.

There are Southerners who think the Northern "s" pronunciation sounds exceptionally greasy, and Northerners who do the same for the Southern "z." Way north in Minneapolis, for example, a popular band from 1995 to 1999 called itself Greazy Meal. They're featured in the 1998 independent movie *Funkytown*.

Strangely enough, the related word *grease* doesn't change its pronunciation at all. It has an "s" sound everywhere in the country.

There are many subtleties and variations in the pronunciations of the South, as there are in every region of the country. Books could be written on the subject, and indeed many have been. But it is the ones already mentioned, the "ahs" and "r"-dropping in particular, that characterize the South both to its residents and to outsiders.

And then there is the matter of vocabulary. As mentioned before, the South has far more distinctive words than any other region. And well, y'all, there's no doubt about which one should come first.

Words of the South:

Y'all   In the centuries after Jamestown, the South developed its most notable innovation in vocabulary, the polite and useful *you-all*. Y'all can hardly get along in the South without it.

Y'all came about as a matter of necessity, to distinguish between singular and plural, one and more than one, when talking to people. The English language used to do this by saying *thou* to one person, *you* to more than one. But we lost *thou* a couple of centuries ago, because *thou* didn't seem as polite as *you*. We'll tell that story when we discuss *you guys* in the language of the North. (In that sentence, notice how the plural *we* seems more polite than the singular *I*. It's nicer than saying, "*I*'ll tell that story when *I* discuss *you guys* in the language of the North." Same thing happened to the plural *you:* It sounded nicer than the singular *thou*.)

So the English language was left with only *you*. Since *you* was now both singular and plural, how could you make clear that you were speaking to more than one?

Most of the English-speaking world is still struggling with this problem. In the United States, the best the North can do is the casual *you guys*. But the South has found a comfortable solution: *y'all*.

To anyone who is not from the South, *y'all* may seem like nothing more than a contraction of *you all*, a two-word phrase heard everywhere English is spoken. But Southern *y'all* is no mere combination or contraction; in the South, the two words *you* and *all* have been fused into a unit. Clear evidence that *y'all* is one word instead of two is the possessive form *y'all's*. For example, Mamo's Garlic Sauce of Austin, Texas, posts on its website a collection of "Y'all's Recipes."

Y'all is the best known and most prevalent of Southernisms. You can hardly live in the South without adopting it, unless you choose to sound like a Yankee. But unless you're a Southerner, you may overuse it. To an outsider, it may seem that Southerners simply use *y'all* as a substitute for *you*, both singular and plural. That notion gets some Southerners hot under the collar. They reserve *y'all* for more than one, saying *you* when they mean just one person.

The misunderstanding about *y'all* as a singular comes about partly because of Southern notions of kinship. When one Southerner asks another, "How are y'all?" it is an inquiry about the well-being not just of the person spoken to, but also of that person's family. At a store it is proper to ask, "Do y'all have any more of these?" where *y'all* means not just the clerk but the whole company. "Y'all have a nice day" has the same extended meaning.

If you're not from the South, however, don't step in the way of an argument among Southerners about *y'all*. Some Southerners don't accept the explanation that *y'all* is the plural of *you*. They insist that *y'all* is just another way of saying *you*, with either singular or plural meaning. They contend that to make a plural, you must say *all y'all*. One website offering tongue-in-cheek instruction in Southern English recommends, "for the advanced Southerner, try the plural possessive *y'alls'es* as in 'BubbaJoe, BobbyRae, LulaFrank is that y'alls'es new truck?'"

If that's the case, it's a repetition of the development that led to *y'all* in the first place, several centuries ago. Perhaps the process will continue: some day *all y'all* may take the place of *y'all* in the singular as well as the plural, so to make a plural you will need to add another *all*, making it *all all y'all*. You can already hear that phrase in a 1996 song "Eyes of the Seeker" by Harry Connick, Jr.: "All . . . all ya'll, Try to push it further."

But for now many Southerners still would reject the notion that *y'all* can be properly applied to only one person. If you're a Northerner in the South, don't try it. On the other hand, go ahead and say *y'all* when you mean more than one. It's the courteous thing to do.

There are hundreds of other words peculiar to the South. Here are a few of the most distinctive ones.

hey   Hey, y'all! That has been a Southern greeting for some time. Without the *y'all*, in recent years *hey* has spread to the rest of the country too, serving as a friendly alternative to the neutral *hi* or *hello*. Its Southern use is illustrated in Harper Lee's *To Kill a Mockingbird*, which is set in Alabama: "Tell him hey for me, won't you?" . . . "I'll tell him you said hey."

In the 1950s, *hey* was enough of an oddity in the North that baseball star Willie Mays, from Westfield, Alabama, was nicknamed the "Say Hey Kid" because he used his Alabama "hey" as a greeting when he began to play for the New York Giants. The only "hey" known to the North at that time was a warning, as in "Hey, watch out!" but Willie obviously was being friendly. Half a century later the whole country was using the friendly "hey."

snack time   Another Southern term that has conquered the nation is *snack*. Between meals it used to be just Southerners who would eat *snacks*, while New Englanders would have a *bite* and other Northerners would have a *piece*. Now it's snack time everywhere in the country.

fixin'   Anywhere in the country Americans will be *fixing* things, from broken toys to traffic tickets, but only in the South is *fixing* a statement about the future. Make that *fixin'*, because one of the other characteristics of Southern speech is the "in" pronunciation of the suffix *-ing*. *Fixin'* involves intention and preparation, as in the

[**Linguist Michael**] **Montgomery** says Southerners use "fixin' to" in two ways — to convey physical activity and mental preparation. If someone is fixin' to leave, he may be packing a suitcase or he may be gathering his thoughts. Such distinctions can be difficult in the business world. Montgomery recounted the true story of a Southern secretary who told her Northern boss that she was "fixin' to" do something. Her boss became angry and said, "I can't see you're doing anything at all." "He thought she was being evasive," Montgomery said. "She thought she was addressing the problem."

— **Marsha Mercer, Media General News Service**

book *Fixin' to Be Texan* by Helen Bryant, written because "You don't just move here and immediately become a Texan, it takes training." Or there is the well-known blues song "Fixin' to Die" by Bukka White, an inmate at Parchman Prison Farm in Louisiana in 1938: "I'm lookin' funny in my eyes, And I believe I'm fixin' to die. . . . I've tried so hard to come home to die."

Only in the North and West, by the way, is *fixing* something the vet does to a dog or cat so it can't reproduce. So "I'm fixin' to have my cat fixed" is *not* a sentence you'll hear anywhere in American English.

Might could   If you might can talk like this, you might could be from the South. If you used to could talk like this, but might would likely avoid it nowadays, perhaps that's because you left the South for a cold Northern place where no more than one *might*, or *could*, or *may*, or *would* is allowed with any main verb. In the South, it's as many as three. Here are some real-life examples collected by linguists Michael Montgomery, Margaret Mishoe, and Gail Skipper at the University of South Carolina. Note how the second and third examples each use three of these auxiliaries in combination: *might will can* and *may might can*.

I reckon I might should better try to get me a little bit more sleep.

It's a long way and he might will can't come, but I'm going to ask.

Sorry, we don't carry them anymore, but you know, you may might can get one right over there at Wicks.

In Texas, linguist Mariana di Paolo found 25 different combinations of the *might could* kind, including *might oughta, musta coulda, oughta could, might supposed to,* and *might woulda had oughta.* Throughout the South, it's not the most common style of speaking, but if you get into a discussion with a Southerner you may might hear it.

It's a jungle out there   In the North, that's a saying about the world of business. In the South, that might could simply be the answer to a question about the view from an airplane window. That is, where the rest of the country begins a sentence with *There*, the South often uses *It*. So in the South you'll hear "It's plenty of time to get home" and "It's a silver lining to every cloud." William Faulkner's *Light in August* includes this sentence with a Southern *it* at the beginning: "I reckon it ain't any human in this country going to dispute them hens with you, lessen it's the possums and the snakes."

Those are some of the most important items of the Southern vocabulary. Here are more, in alphabetical order.

All the difference   In the South, it's *all the far* or *all the fast* I can go. In the North, except for New England, you can go *all the farther* or *all the faster.*

Someone once noted that a Southerner can get away with the most awful kind of insult just as long as it's prefaced with the words "Bless her heart" or "Bless his heart."

As in, "Bless his heart, if they put his brain on the head of a pin, it'd roll around like a BB on a six-lane highway." Or, "Bless her heart, she's so buck-toothed, she could eat an apple through a picket fence."

There are also the sneakier ones that I remember from tongue-clucking types of my childhood: "You know, it's amazing that even though she had that baby seven months after they got married, bless her heart, it weighed 10 pounds."

As long as the heart is sufficiently blessed, the insult can't be all that bad, at least that's what my Great-aunt Tiny (bless her heart, she was anything but) used to say.

— Celia Rivenbark in the *Sun-News,* Myrtle Beach, South Carolina

Bidness   In the South, instead of conducting business with a buzzing "z" sound in the middle, you can mind your own *bidness*. Or somebody else's. Molly Ivins wrote a 1997 column in the *Texas Observer* with the title "Bidness — As Usual" and comments like: "Bidness, as always, owned the Lege [Texas legislature]. Bidness pays to elect these folks, so bidness sets the agenda."

Blessing   The South is one part of the country where you may not want a *blessing*. The kind you don't want is usually called a *blessing out*, and it means a serious scolding. Likewise, if you *bless out* somebody, you're issuing a reprimand.

Branch water   If you order bourbon and *branch water*, you're from the South, where a branch is a stream.

Bucket   In the South, a round-sided flat-bottomed container for liquids has always been called a *bucket*. New England and the rest of the North used to call this a *pail*, but in recent times *bucket* has gone nationwide.

Butter beans   Even if you don't put butter on them, the flat beans known elsewhere in the United States as *lima beans* are *butter beans* in the South, especially if they are small.

Buzzard   If you hear of a person who hasn't enough sense to *bell a buzzard*, you're in the Southeast. *Belling*, of course, means "to tie a bell around the neck." Yankees might wonder who would be stupid enough to try to bell a buzzard, but evidently that's a different story.

Carry and tote   "Carry me back to old Virginny" begin the words of a hit song of 1878 that was declared the Virginia state song in 1940. "'There's where this old darkey's heart am long'd to go," it continues, and even though the composer and original performer was the African-American minstrel James Bland, it's understandable that the song was retired as "state song emeritus" in 1997. But the point of mentioning it here is to highlight the Southern meaning of *carry*.

Wherever you are, you can carry someone home, but in the South the operation is quite different from what it is in the North. The

Southern *carry* simply means "to accompany, escort, take or bring," while the Northern *carry* involves lifting. So "Carry me back to old Virginny" should not evoke a picture of someone lifting another up, but simply of having a traveling companion.

Because *carry* has a more general meaning, Southern speech often uses *tote* for the Northern sense of *carry*. African slaves brought *tote* to the South as far back as the 1600s. Bantu languages of western Africa have words like *tota* and *tuta* meaning "to pick up" or "to carry" (in the Northern sense) that were evidently the source of the Southern *tote*.

Here it is at the end of Stephen Foster's "My Old Kentucky Home":

A few more days for to tote the weary load.
No matter, 'twill never be light.
A few more days till we totter on the road,
Then my old Kentucky home, good night.

Chunk   Southerners will *chunk* rocks or wood, while Northerners will *throw* them.

Cold drink, Coke   America's favorite beverage is flavored carbonated water. In the South, some know that as a *cold drink* or just plain *drink*. In South Carolina it's often called *dope*. Atlanta, Georgia, is the home of the Coca-Cola Company, and Southerners are inclined to use *Coca-Cola* or the abbreviated *co-cola* to stand for any soft drink, even those made by other companies.

Evening and dinner   In the South, *evening* starts earlier than in the rest of the country. From Virginia to Texas, the evening begins at noon and continues till twilight.

In the South, *dinner* usually starts when evening does. Southerners generally reserve *dinner* for the name of a meal served at midday. The last meal of the day, the one served when the sun goes down, is most often *supper* in Southern speech.

Funny bone   Don't laugh — it hurts when you hit your funny bone. That's the usual Southern name for it, and it's also the usual name in some other parts of the country, especially New York State and

Michigan. Funny, though, it has a different name elsewhere in the North and West: *crazy bone.*

Gully washer   A *gully washer* is a really heavy rain — "more rain than a toad strangler," in one explanation. On the other hand, according to Phyllis Rossiter Modeland in *Ozarks Mountaineer* magazine, "a pour-down will flood the creeks certain sure. And a real goose drownder, which is worse than a gully washer but about the same as a toad strangler, will make them unfordable." However it's defined, there are gully washers throughout the South and South Midlands, and this is one Southern term that is well-known in the central Midwest as well, as far north as Nebraska, Iowa, and Wisconsin, and as far west as Colorado. But there aren't any gully washers in New England or the northernmost states, and the word is rare on the Pacific coast.

Icing on the cake   The South doesn't get much *icing* in its weather, but it does on its cakes. That's the preferred term not just in the South but as far north as New York State and as far west as Indiana, Illinois, and Michigan for the sweet covering of pastries.

Jackleg   You don't want to entrust your car to a *jackleg* mechanic or your soul to a *jackleg* preacher. The jackleg is at best incompetent, at worst a swindler. But why *jackleg*? The word comes from *jackleg knife*, an older word for what we now call a *jackknife.* Perhaps a jackleg worker was one who tried to do everything with no better tool than a jackknife.

Light bread   *Light bread* in the South is the same as *white bread* in the North. Southerners also know it as *loaf bread.*

Lightwood   The South has a special kind of kindling for fires. Well known in the Southern states from North Carolina to Alabama, but rare elsewhere, is *lightwood,* the knots or heartwood of a pine tree. In Florida and Georgia it is sometimes called *fatwood.*

Like to   When people "like to have died laughing" or "like to have got run over" or "like to done it," they're using the Southern way of saying that it almost happened, but not quite.

They *ment* it   If you have an attach*ment* to a compli*ment* or an argu-*ment*, emphasizing that last syllable *-ment;* if you might could even add a *-ment* (sounding like *mint*) to a plain old word to get *confuse-ment*, an *eatment* or a *devilment* of a *tanglement*, you'll be from the South.

Mash off, mash on   If you *mash* the button to *cut off* the lights, you're speaking Southern. Likewise if you mash it again to cut them on. You also mash the button in the elevator to take it to your floor.

The rest of the country would manipulate the light switch by pushing it.

You can do it in your car too. If you *mash* the brakes at a redlight, that's Southern.

Polecat   Northerners know it only as a *skunk*, but in the South its propensity to go after *poult*ry gives the odoriferous animal the name *polecat.*

Polecat, alias skunk

Redlight   In the rest of the country, the red-light district is a place no respectable person seeks out, or at least a place that no one seeks out when acting respectable. But in the South, respectable or otherwise, in any city you're bound to go through many *redlights*. That's because a Southern redlight is what the rest of the country calls a stoplight. Sometimes you stop at a redlight, sometimes you sail right through, depending on the color of the light. So, by Southern logic, a redlight can be green or yellow, as well as red.

In the sack   In the South, your groceries and your lunch go into a pa-per *sack*. In the North, it's a *bag*. There's a *poke* too, a term once widely used in the Upper Southern or South Midlands area, but now less well known.

During the President's Commission hearings on the assassination of John F. Kennedy, all three terms were used in this interchange during the questioning of Deputy Sheriff Luke Mooney, who helped search the sixth floor of the Texas School Book Depository in Dallas after the assassination.

MR. MOONEY: . . . And there was a little small paper poke.

MR. BALL: By poke, you mean a paper sack?

MR. MOONEY: Right.

MR. BALL: Where was that?

MR. MOONEY: Saw the chicken bone was laying here. The poke was laying about a foot away from it.

MR. BALL: On the same carton?

MR. MOONEY: Yes, sir. In close relation to each other. But as to what was in the sack — it was kind of together, and I didn't open it. I didn't put my hands on it to open it. I only saw one piece of chicken.

SENATOR COOPER: How far was the chicken, the piece of chicken you saw, and the paper bag from the boxes near the window, and particularly the box that had the crease in it?

Sick at the stomach   Stomachs get upset everywhere, but the central South is where it's *at:* that is, sick *at* the stomach, where Northerners would be sick *to* the stomach. Along the Atlantic coast from Florida north as far as Pennsylvania, it's also possible to be sick *on* the stomach, a choice of preposition possibly influenced by German in the Pennsylvania German and North Carolina German settlement areas.

Skillet   Frying pans are used everywhere, but Southerners cook in *skillets* too.

Spigot   Though Northern *faucets* have poured throughout the South thanks to mass Yankee merchandising, some of that water still flows through *spigots* in the South.

Furnished with Suits   In the South and its border areas, a furniture store will sell you a matching *suit* of furniture, perhaps a *bedroom suit*, that would be known in other parts of the country as a *suite*. Linguists Beth Lee Simon and Thomas Murray note that "suit" here is simply an older pronunciation for modern *suite*, but nowadays all around the English-speaking world *suite* generally rhymes with *sweet*, and even in the South the "suit" pronunciation is used only for furniture. So a Southerner might would put a *suit* of furniture in a *suite* of rooms. There are also those, North and South, who avoid the choice by saying *set* instead.

Wait on In the South, if you *wait on* someone, you're not necessarily a server in a restaurant. You may just be waiting till someone shows up. It's the same as waiting *for* someone, which we hear nearly everywhere, including in the South.

The Deep South: State by State

Despite the prominence of Southern American English as a whole, the South is also famous for its many *different* ways of speaking, ways that allow locals to distinguish themselves from outsiders and that provide plenty of material for scholars to try to record. We will sample some of these distinctive individual speechways, starting with the oldest English-speaking territory.

VIRGINIA

For more than a decade in the early 1600s Virginia was the only place in North America where English was spoken. That original colony of Jamestown was abandoned long ago, and present-day Virginia has changed its language considerably since King James' days. But Virginia still has its own version of the Southern accent, especially in the eastern or Tidewater region. There the vowel in *high* is sometimes neither the Southern "ah" nor the Northern "ah-ee" but an "uh-ee." The sound that is spelled *ou* in words like *out, house,* and *account* is sometimes "uh-oo" rather than the usual "ah-oo." You may hear the second syllable of *afraid* sounding like *Fred. Home* sometimes has the vowel sound of *book.* And eastern Virginia, along with eastern New England, is inclined to the British "ah" vowel in *aunt, chance* and *dance.*

There are also a few words distinctive to Virginia. *Curl* is a word recorded as long ago as 1638, referring to a bend in a river that is more than a bend, taking it in a nearly complete circle. To do well in a class at the University of Virginia also is to *curl,* though that *curl* is said to have an entirely different origin: the curls of elegant penmanship, according to one speculation, and the curling of a dog's tail when it is patted and praised, for another.

In Virginia, also, a tobacco plant that spirals up rather than spreading out is said to be a *frenchman. Batter bread,* pronounced "baddy-bread," is cornbread made with eggs and milk. A *come-here* is someone who moved to a community instead of being born there.

A *cranky* is not an annoyed native but a name for the great blue heron.

The second verse of Virginia's "retired" state song begins:

Carry me back to old Virginny,
There let me live 'till I wither and decay,
Long by the old Dismal Swamp have I wandered. . . .

The *Dismal Swamp* is an actual place, a large swamp encompassing southern Virginia and northern North Carolina. In Virginia and the Carolinas, such places have been called *dismals*.

In Virginia, as in Massachusetts, a small harbor or channel may be called a *hole*.

NORTH CAROLINA

Western North Carolina is Appalachian like eastern Tennessee. When you're *bad* here, you have an inclination or interest: *He's bad for smoking* means he is inclined to smoke. It's also where you can get a *gee-haw whimmey-diddle*, a notched stick with a spinner on the end that spins when you rub it with another stick.

A recent coinage in the vocabulary of western North Carolina is *halfback*, meaning "a Yankee who moves to Florida and then relocates to western North Carolina."

In the central and eastern part of the state, if you *go around your elbow*, you're taking (or talking) the long way around to get somewhere. And you might encounter *rock muddle*, a stew made with rockfish. You don't have to go to North Carolina to taste it; Carolina fish muddle is also served at Christiana Campbell's Tavern in Colonial Williamsburg, Virginia.

At school or college in North Carolina, you might be *on class* instead of in class. In North Carolina and Georgia, sometimes you'll have your picture *made* with a camera instead of taken.

When you go as far east as you can in North Carolina, you'll find lots of *Bankers*. They are not people who play with your money but residents of the long islands known as the Outer Banks. The term is used less by the Bankers themselves than by mainland residents referring to them.

There's a special way of speaking on some of those Outer Banks islands, whose residents have kept their distance from the mainland politically (they were mostly for the Union in the Civil War) and socially. Like Southerners, they say *y'all*. But like Northerners, and unlike many mainland North Carolinians, they pronounce the "r" sound in words like *hard* and *for*.

In other ways, their pronunciation is different from both South and North. Where mainland Southerners would pronounce the "long i" in words like *high tide* as "hah tahd" and Northerners would say "hah-ee tah-eed," residents of the Outer Banks often use a different pronunciation: "huh-ee tuh-eed." The closest phonetic spelling for this sound would be *oi*. For example, "high tide on the Sound side" would sound like "hoi toide on the Sound soide" (referring to the side of the island that faces the mainland). The Outer Banks pronunciation of the vowel sound in words like *out* and *house* is also distinctive, close to the "ah-ee" sound of the Northern pronoun *I*.

There are a few distinctive words on the Outer Banks as well. One is *quamished*, meaning "having an upset stomach." (It comes from *qualm*.) Another is *mommuck*, "to bother or harass." That word is widely known in the mainland South but with a somewhat different meaning, "to botch or confuse." On one of the Outer Banks islands, Ocracoke, linguists Walt Wolfram and Natalie Schilling-Estes found the unique terms *meehonkey*, "an island-wide game of hide and seek," and *scud*, "a ride in a car or boat."

SOUTH CAROLINA

In South Carolina the South gets truly Southern. Charles Town, now Charleston, was a center of wealth and influence in colonial days, thanks to the profits of the slave trade and slave labor. The city and the state have had more than three centuries to develop their ways of speaking.

Among the distinctive pronunciations heard in South Carolina and Georgia is "air" for *ear*, with the "r" sound often changed to the Southern "uh" so that it comes out as "A-uh."

One long-established tradition in South Carolina, and Georgia too, is to eat *hoppin' John* on New Year's Day. Doing so supposedly brings good fortune. The dish is a boiled combination of black-eyed peas, rice, and sometimes pork or bacon, properly served with collard greens. Its name, along with the dish itself, probably came from the West Indies. *Hoppin' John* is most likely a mispronunciation of the French term *pois pigeon* (meaning "pigeon peas"), but the current name has inspired people to imagine that hopping around the table was part of the original New Year's ritual.

South Carolina is where you'll find *artichoke pickles* and *artichoke relish*, but they have nothing to do with the artichokes grown in California. The Carolina versions are made from the roots of the Jerusalem artichoke, a kind of sunflower.

South Carolinians like *dope* — not hard drugs, but a cola-flavored soft drink. They sometimes call a pancake a *batter.* And the state is known for *okra soup*, made with okra and tomatoes, and *catfish stew* made with catfish and ingredients like ketchup, onions, and hot sauce.

Bog in South Carolina is not a place where cranberries grow but a rice dish or pilau made with meat. *Chicken bog* is a particular favorite.

A *cooter*, pronounced with the short "oo" of *cook*, is a turtle well known in South Carolina. *Bluebait* is a South Carolina term for earthworm.

To *cascade* is a polite way to vomit in South Carolina. To *joog* (pronounced with the short "oo" of *cook*) means "to poke with something sharp."

I beat the hound out of the big dog is a South Carolina way of letting it be known you really beat someone important.

A *bay* in North or South Carolina doesn't have to be an arm of a waterway. It can be a depression in the land, sometimes a swamp, sometimes just overgrown. In South Carolina a *hill* sometimes is just dry land in the middle of a swamp.

Along the Atlantic coast from New Jersey southward, a divided highway is often called a *dual highway*. In South Carolina, however, it's a *dual lane highway*.

Artichoke Relish

Place a spoonful of this southern delight alongside dishes of rice and pork. It is also great on burgers. This tart and sweet crunchy relish has uses limited only to one's imagination. Ingredients: Jerusalem Artichokes, bell peppers, onions, vinegar, sugar, flour, mustard seed, celery seed and turmeric.

—Rockland Plantation Pantry Collection

If you have a *case quarter* or a *case dime* in South Carolina, that means a single coin rather than change that adds up to a quarter or a dime. The term is especially well known among African Americans. And in South Carolina, a penny is sometimes called a *brownie.*

To put out a fire sometimes is to *outen* it, in South Carolina and also Pennsylvania.

For entertainment, some South Carolinians and Georgians *joggle* on a *joggling board,* a flexible board held up by posts at either end. Legend has it that the first one was constructed in 1803 according to a Scottish model to ease a lady's rheumatism.

Within all of the United States, to *lay out* is slang for lying in the sun. But in South Carolina and Georgia, and some neighboring places, to *lie out* is to loaf or skip work or school.

THE SEA ISLANDS: GULLAH

It's African, enty? On the Sea Islands of South Carolina and Georgia and the nearby coast, it is still possible to find a few speakers of a truly African variety of African-American English. This is the language and culture known as *Gullah.* Onto a base of English, Gullah grafted many words from West African languages spoken by slaves brought to America. In mainland African-American culture, almost all African words have died out through centuries of assimilation. But on the plantations of the Sea Islands, until recently there was little outside influence, even after the end of slavery.

The African-American linguist Lorenzo Dow Turner filled a book with Gullah words that could be traced to African origins. There is *buckra,* for example, a sometimes uncomplimentary word meaning "a white person or boss." It apparently comes from *mbakára,* a word with similar meaning in the Efik language of present-day Nigeria. *Benne* is a Gullah and thus also a South Carolina word for "sesame." It is derived from the Wolof language, spoken in Senegal, or the Bambara language, spoken in Mali. *Nyam,* "to eat," also derives from one or more West African languages. Dawn, or full daylight right after sunrise, in Gullah is known as *day clean,* probably an English translation of a similar phrase in Wolof. And to talk is to *crack teeth,* also a translation from the African.

However, not every Gullah word is African. For example, there's that exclamation *enty,* meaning "isn't it?" and apparently derived from *ain't he? Aw* is another exclamation, meaning "yes indeed." You can also hear *cubbitch*, meaning "stingy," derived from the English *covetous*. And *no-manners* is a way of saying someone is rude. A *basket name* is a nickname, often of African origin, given to a child at birth along with his or her "real" English name.

Gullah also has *bloodynoun*, a name for a bullfrog, apparently derived from the sound it makes. Try repeating it in a low slow voice: *bloodynoun, bloodynoun*. Then try *higguhri-hee*, which is supposedly the sound of an owl.

In addition to the vocabulary, the grammar of Gullah is distinctive. Instead of *be*, for example, Gullah can use *de* (pronounced "duh"). *Now dat de supm!* in Gullah means "Now that is something!" *I still de look* means "I am still looking." Gullah uses *been* to indicate past time, as in *We been see that man*, meaning "We saw that man." Gullah also uses *for* where others would say *to* before verbs. "If you don't know how to fix it, you have to wait till somebody comes to show you" in Gullah would be *You ain't know for fix 'em, you have to wait till somebody come for show you*. And in Gullah, *he* and *she* may be used for *his* and *her* as in *Scared of he shadow* and *She name is Bertha*.

GEORGIA

Georgia is a fully Southern state, without sharp boundaries distinguishing its speech from that of its neighbors. Businesslike Atlanta has recently acquired something of a Northern overlay, but even Atlanta remains basically Southern. Included in the "Translation of Atlanta for Visitors" website are these Southern features:

> *Sir* and *Ma'am* are used by the person speaking to you if there's a remote possibility that you're at least 30 minutes older than they are.
> *Sugar* is a more common form of address than *Miss*. So is *Honey*.

Language and customs are even more properly Southern in the venerable city of Savannah, Georgia. Jane Fishman of the *Savannah Morning News* was corrected by a friend:

> "In Savannah we like to say, Nice to see you. Not Nice to meet you. That way you cover all your bases in case it's not the first time you're meeting someone."
> Propriety is very important here. When you can't think of anything nice to add, you merely say, "I'm speechless" and that's that. . . .

"Deceased" or "passed" are both preferred to "died." The "miseries of the stomach" is a better way to say you have a "stomachache." And though I haven't been able to do it, remembering to add "sir" or "ma'am" to the end of your sentences will get you a long way. Just try to keep the sarcasm out of your voice. That gives you negative marks.

If you look hard enough, you can find a few culinary terms that distinguish Georgia from its neighbors. Cornbread made with eggs is known in Georgia as *egg bread*. An eggshell is sometimes called a *hull*. The stew known as *muddle* in North Carolina is *mull* in Georgia. You make it with rabbit, squirrel, turtle, or fish as a main ingredient.

And in Georgia, if you're sick at the stomach, you may *burk* what's in it.

If you're really poor, in Georgia you can be *poor as an owl*.

In Georgia's Okefenokee Swamp a *house* isn't a place to live in but an island of bushes and trees rising above water level. Also unique to the Okefenokee is the name *neverwet* for the floating plant otherwise known as *golden club*. It is called *neverwet* because even if you push it underwater, when it comes back up the leaves will be dry.

In Georgia and Florida, if you're looking for a *gopher*, you may be hunting a turtle instead of the mammal called by that name elsewhere. In the nineteenth century the Georgia turtle was called a *magopher*, a name that later was shortened to *gopher*. And in Georgia you can make tea with a shrub known as *gopher grass* or *gopher weed*, elsewhere called *wild indigo*.

Muck in Georgia and Florida can refer to farmland composed of rich, heavy soil.

FLORIDA

In the nineteenth century, Florida was a sparsely inhabited footnote to the South. In the twentieth, however, Henry Flagler's Florida East Coast Railway and later the Interstate highways brought Northern "sunbirds" in great flocks to towns like Palm Beach and Miami. So many New Yorkers have come to Miami, in fact, that the city and its environs have enclaves of New York speech. Northerners not lured by the sunshine and beaches were captivated later in the twentieth century by Disney World, soon joined by Universal Studios and Sea World, in mid-state Orlando of all places. Exiles from Castro's Cuba and other Latin Americans gave a Hispanic touch to the English of Miami and vicinity. At the start of the twenty-first century, Southern speech still dominates most of northern Florida, but Northern accents are becoming the norm in the south of the state.

Newcomers to Florida brought the abundant sunshine into their houses with a *Florida room*, an enclosed porch with large windows. Residents of other states also built Florida rooms to get the effect of a Florida climate without having to go there.

The natural features of Florida have left their mark on the state's language. In a Florida swamp you might find a *hummock*, a grove of big trees on land that stands out of the water. In Florida and Georgia, this hummock is also called a *head* or, if containing cypress trees, a *cypress head*. Seminole Indians used palmetto fans as the roof for a *chickee*, a house with a raised wood floor and open sides.

A Florida palm with an edible bud is known as a *cabbage palm* or *cabbage tree*. There is also a tree known as *inkwood*; it has hard wood and dark purple berries. A mahogany tree in Florida is sometimes called a *Madeira* or a *Madeira redwood*. And Florida has two trees known as *nakedwood* because their covering of bark sheds so easily.

Among the winged creatures of Florida are the *chizzywink* or *blind mosquito*, called *blind* not because it can't see but because it is stingless. Much more potent is the stinging scorpion known as *grampus*.

Key West was originally populated by people whose ancestors came from England via the Bahamas. To this day inhabitants of Key West are called *conchs* because those original settlers were skilled at diving for those shellfish.

In the highly competitive world of the Cuban sandwich, there are classic pitfalls. You have to avoid even the hint of gristle in your boiled ham. The roast pork must be moist and sliced thin. The cheese must be fresh. Too much pickle will overpower the entire creation. But the ingredient waiting to trip up most practitioners is the Cuban bread that envelops it all. It must be just the right thickness and must come out of the plancha (sandwich press) unburned and just crispy enough. Bread is to the Cuban sandwich what crust is to great pie.

— *Miami New Times*

One example of Latin American influence in southern Florida is the *Cuban sandwich*. It is made with sliced meats, cheese and pickles on Cuban bread — a version of what elsewhere might be called a *submarine*.

ALABAMA

From its location, it's obvious that Alabama is a truly Southern state. Here you will find the characteristics of Southern speech fully displayed and not strongly differentiated from the speech of neighboring states. In Alabama you might be able to find a *fiddle worm* for fishing, one that can be as much as a foot long. In Alabama or neighboring Georgia you might also pick up a *mellow bug*, a beetle named for having a "mellow" smell like a ripe apple. It's also known as a *whirligig beetle* because it floats on the water and spins around.

MISSISSIPPI

You've reached the deeps of the Deep South in Mississippi. In addition to sharing the general Southern pronunciations and vocabulary, it has a few distinctions of its own.

There's a traditional dessert known throughout the South but especially well known in Mississippi called *egg custard* — a pie made of eggs, flour, and milk.

Mississippi joins Louisiana in using *armoire* to refer to a piece of furniture that holds clothes: a large, elegant wardrobe. One that is

---

Well, I just seen red. I picked up a kaiser blade that was a layin' there by the screen door, some folks calls it a sling blade, I call it a kaiser blade. It's just a long handle like a axe handle with a long blade on it that's shaped kind of like a banana. Sharp on one edge and dull on the other. It's what the highway boys use to cut down weeds and whatnot. I went in the kitchen there and I hit Jesse Dixon up side the head with it and knocked him off my mother. I reckon that didn't quite satisfy me so I hit him again in the neck with the sharp edge and just plumb near cut his head off. Killed him.

— Billy Bob Thornton, *Sling Blade*

not necessarily so large and ornate, but is made of cedar, may be called a *cedar robe* in those states.

A tool known in Mississippi and vicinity as a *kaiser blade* gained national attention in Billy Bob Thornton's 1996 movie *Sling Blade*. That movie was titled after the tool's better-known name.

Thornton's character Karl Childers, like Thornton himself, is from Arkansas, where *sling blade* is the term generally used. Mississippi has the distinction of being the one state that commonly uses *kaiser blade*, a name that is said to be a direct import from Germany. During World War I, the story goes, some American prisoners of war were employed to cut brush along roads in Germany. They named the blade they were given the *Kaiser*, in mock tribute to the emperor of Germany. Apparently the prisoners were from Mississippi and brought the name with them when they returned from the war.

LOUISIANA AND NEW ORLEANS

With the exception of Hawaii and Alaska, no state is as rich in distinctive vocabulary as Louisiana. And in the rest of the country, except for Hawaii, English has overwhelmed the influence of other languages, but in Louisiana the French flavor remains strong to the present day.

Not that it's all French. There's also an admixture of Choctaw, African, and Spanish, making a lively blend in its own right.

The entire state of Louisiana is Southern, of course, but New Orleans speech is a thing unto itself. It includes many varieties, only some of which are stereotypically Southern. "Yeah, you right!" is a well-known New Orleans expression. Another is "Where y'at?" meaning "Hello, how are you?" That phrase is so well known that it has spawned the nickname *Yat* for a person belonging to a particular blue-collar section of the New Orleans population, and also for the language such a person speaks. Yats live mainly in the "Irish Channel," a less than elegant part of town that runs along the Mississippi upriver of the French Quarter.

Like working-class speech styles in other parts of the country, Yat has spread beyond the original boundaries of class and district to "become a symbol of identity" with increasing prestige, as a recent researcher notes. It is used to positive effect in radio and television

> **Yat** *n.* A member of a lower- and middle-class segment of the white population of New Orleans. 2. The variety of English spoken by these people, derived from Irish English.
> — *The American Heritage Dictionary of the English Language, Fourth Edition*

commercials. Bunny Matthews' Sunday cartoon in the *New Orleans Times-Picayune* features Yat-speaking Vic and Nat'ly, who also pitch products ranging from Barq's root beer to Leidenheimer's bread. Matthews' 1978 collection of cartoons was proudly titled *F'Sure!: Actual Dialogue Heard on the Streets of New Orleans*.

New Orleans Yat bears an uncanny resemblance to the speech of Brooklyn and other parts of New York City. The Yat pronunciation of *learn*, for example, is like New York "luh-in." And *boil* has the pronunciation "buh-il." The similarity has been attributed to similar groups of immigrants in both places: Irish, Italian, and German as well as French and Spanish. But New Orleans and New York weren't the only two cities with immigrants from those nationalities, so the similarities in sounds between the two cities still remain a mystery.

When the first Europeans arrived in what is now Louisiana and Mississippi, the language of the native inhabitants was Choctaw. *Bayou* and *bogue*, two Louisiana words for a slow-moving creek or river, come from Choctaw via French. The bowfin or cypress trout is known as *choupique*, a word ultimately from the Choctaw Indian language, sometimes Englishized as *shoe-pick* or *shoe-peg*.

After the Indians, the French had a century to develop Louisiana culture. The original American-born French-speaking population, called *Creoles*, was augmented by French speakers evicted from the Canadian province of Acadia, now Nova Scotia, by the British in 1755. These Acadians became known as *Cajuns*. To add to the confusion of Cajuns and Creoles, *Creole* has also been used to designate the combination of French or Spanish with African-American culture.

Thanks to the French language, Louisiana is the home of the *coulee*, a small stream or bayou. A swamp is a *marais*. A night heron is a *gros-bec*. A small green frog is a *grenouille*. And in New Orleans, a raised sidewalk can be called a *banquette*.

A stupid person is a *couillon*. To go to sleep is *go dodo* (from French baby talk, *faire dodo*, from *dormir*, to sleep) and the *fais-dodo* is a Cajun dance performed after the children have been put to bed. A cut or sore is a *bobo*.

Lagniappe in New Orleans is something extra, like the extra item in a baker's dozen. And since New Orleans has such influence, the term is known throughout southern Louisiana and Mississippi, and a bit in eastern Texas too. Usually it is pronounced "LAN-yap," with emphasis on the first syllable, though there are those who say "lan-YAP."

In Louisiana, *cha-cha-cha* is a call to cows or dogs to bring them home, and *kitty* is a call not to cats but to chickens. To call a cat, you say *minnie* or *minou*. Only the catcall can be blamed on the French; the others are of obscure origin.

Not all of the words distinctive to Louisiana are related to French. Some are plain English. In Louisiana, the *coast* can be the banks of a river. Soft river mud is known as *cowbelly*. The rest of the country puts their clothes in a closet; some residents of New Orleans and their neighbors put them in a *clothes locker*, which is the same thing. And the *krewe*, a social club that sponsors Mardi Gras festivities, gets its odd name from a deliberate misspelling of the simple word *crew*.

In Louisiana and southern Mississippi, *neutral ground* is the grassy median strip separating lanes of a divided street or highway.

West African languages are represented in the magical arts of *hoodoo* and *voodoo*, which are much spoken of in Louisiana. *Gris-gris*, an African word, is a voodoo charm.

New Orleans cuisine includes the *beignet*. It's something that New Orleanians also call a *donut*, but it's not the same as the doughnut known in the rest of the United States. A beignet is fried, like a doughnut, but it is rectangular, has no hole, and is covered with powdered sugar.

The city is famous for *jambalaya*, consisting of rice, tomatoes, onions, green peppers, and some kind of meat, poultry, or fish. It is also known for *dirty rice*, which is rice with chicken liver and gizzards and often many of the ingredients found in jambalaya. *Gumbo* comes from Louisiana, though it is now known far and wide. Ground sassafras leaves are *filé*. So *filé gumbo*, for example, is gumbo seasoned with ground sassafras, which is usually added just before serving.

Court bouillon (pronounced "coo-bee-YON") is a highly seasoned fish stew, and *daube* (which rhymes with *globe*) is a stew of beef or veal. There is *crawfish bisque,* a soup with stuffed crawfish heads, and *crawfish boil,* a party where boiled and highly seasoned crawfish is served. Crawfish (also called *crawdads* and *mudbugs,* but never *crayfish*) also often figure in the Cajun stew known as *étouffée.* And New Orleans is the home of the big round sandwich known as a *muffuletta,* invented at Central Grocery early in the twentieth century. Or you can have an *oyster loaf,* a small hollowed-out loaf of French bread filled with oysters and cream.

If you want to enjoy a beverage outdoors, you can get it in a plastic *go cup* at a New Orleans bar and take it with you. For safety's sake, it's against the law to drink out of a glass or a can on the streets.

Some of the distinctive New Orleans vocabulary is a reverse twist on French, an English translation of terms that other English speakers generally call by their French names. New Orleans sometimes speaks of *Fat Tuesday* for Mardi Gras and *coffee milk* for café au lait. French toast sometimes goes by the name *lost bread,* a translation of the French *pain perdu.* And instead of "going to the grocery store" you *make groceries,* based on the French *faire le marché.*

TEXAS

Texas is basically a Southern state. Its earliest English-speaking population came predominantly from other parts of the South, and it took the side of the Confederacy in the Civil War. But it is Western and Spanish-influenced too. It is the only Southern state that once was part of Mexico and that shares a border with that country. Its pronunciations exemplify the Upper South or South Midlands, with *pen* sounding like *pin,* for example, but the "r" sound is pronounced after vowels.

For nine years Texas was a country in its own right. Though that was long ago — from 1836 to 1845, to be exact — Texas still has a touch of independence in its vocabulary.

Thanks to Mexico, Texas is far more influenced by Spanish than the other Southern states. For example, there is a Texas bush called *amargoso,* a tree called *anacahuita,* and a pepper called *chilpitin.* Until recently *jalapeño* used to be a Texas term, too, but that hot

Texans are proudly self-conscious of their way of speaking and are happy to teach it to others. Here are two of their lessons. The reader of this book will notice that much of what they describe as "Texan" or "Texian" is true for the rest of the South as well.

Many one-syllable words in English have two syllables in Texan — car rhymes with drawer and yard roughly rhymes with toward. Another rule: Be careful not to enunciate the L in most words. Thus, the English help becomes the Texan "he'p." So if you hear a Texan saying "hep, hep . . . ," he is not fixinta finish the phrase with "hooray." He is asking for aid. Fixinta? Yes. That is Texan for "getting ready" or "preparing" to do something, perhaps to visit his "ain't" (an uncle's wife). . . .

When a Texan declares that he is going to the store "this e'ning to buy some white bread and sweet milk" on his way home, he means he is going to the store to buy bread and milk shortly after lunch. A Texan measures each day into three segments: morning, evening (from noon until 6 p.m.) and night (anything after about 6 p.m.). He eats his dinner at noon and his supper at about 6 p.m. The first meal of the day is "breffus," of course. Just ("Jist," in Texan) about any well-liked, respected, nice and personable person is, figuratively speaking, elderly. Well, not elderly . . . "ol'," as in "he's a good ol' boy."

— Chris Maxwell, *The Ludlum Report*

Texian is a combination of Southern patois, with touches of Spanish, Irish, and German, and a lot of mutation of its own. Ergo, don't depend upon phonetic pronunciation: mesquite *is pronounced "muh-SKEET",* tire *is "tar",* barbed wire *is "bob war." . . .* Waco *is likewise pronounced "WAY-co" instead of "Wacko," but the Branch Davidians and Baylor University made that point moot a long time ago.*

— Paul T. Riddell in *Tangent*

pepper is now known nationwide. The *mesquite* tree is native to Texas. And the grassy strip between lanes of a divided highway is sometimes called an *esplanade*.

And along with California, at the other end of the Mexican border, Texans tend to celebrate with a *fiesta* rather than the *fest* of Northern states.

But much of the distinctive Texas vocabulary is not particularly Hispanic. For example, in central Texas you can get food and drink at an *ice house*, a local name for a convenience store.

A *hoopy* is a Texas word for jalopy. Both Texas and northern Michigan share the term *headlighting* for hunting deer with a car's headlights.

Ever for *every* is especially common in Texas.

The *norther* or *blue norther* is a distinctive feature of the Texas climate, a north wind that will drop the winter temperature by thirty degrees or more. It is also known in Texas and points north as a *blue darter* and *blue whistler.* And in Texas you can also enjoy the sight of *Gulf clouds,* low and fast moving, that come from the Gulf of Mexico.

Texans have another use for *tank* besides its usual meaning of "a container for liquids." A Texas *tank* can be a pond, especially one for watering livestock.

There are Texas plants called *lazy daisy, mealy-cup sage,* and *Mexican hat,* and a Texas caterpillar called *asp* because it has poisonous stinging hairs. The *bluebonnet,* known outside of Texas as *lupine,* is the state flower.

Only in Texas will you hear of a *motte* or *mot,* a small grove of trees in the open prairie. The word was apparently introduced to Texas in the 1830s by Irish immigrants, who used the word for a similar feature in their homeland.

And *shinnery* is well known in western Texas. It means the native *shinnery oak* or *sand shinnery oak,* which also grows in western Oklahoma and eastern New Mexico. In Texas, *shinnery* can also refer to an area where shinnery oaks grow. Shinnery makes a good cover and tolerable forage for animals. Goats love it, deer accept it, but it makes cattle sick.

You can go hunting for Big Texas Hogs on the 2CK Ranch in Matador, Texas, which advertises that it "has it all — thick mesquite, open pasture, wheat fields, rolling sandhills, shinnery oak, plum thickets, and the beautiful Pease River." And Abilene Christian University's student literary magazine is the *Shinnery Review.*

Among African Americans in Texas, the 19th of June is *Juneteenth,* an annual celebration of the day in 1865 when Major General Gordon Granger of the U.S. Army took over the city of Galveston and issued General Order No. 3 proclaiming freedom for slaves. It was the last Confederate state to have its slaves freed, some two and a half years after the Emancipation Proclamation. Juneteenth is now a state holiday in Texas and Oklahoma, and Juneteenth celebrations have spread to hundreds of cities throughout the United States. The first annual National Juneteenth Celebration was held in Washington, D.C. in 1999.

The Upper South or South Midlands

Till now we have traveled the Deep South, from Virginia, capital of the Confederacy, to the heart of Texas. But Southern culture and speech extend north and west beyond those boundaries. The South climbs the mountains of Southern Appalachia and the Ozarks and comes down on the other side, even crossing the Ohio River into southern Ohio, Indiana, and Illinois. The "r" is no longer dropped after vowels in words like *charm* and *sugar* in these outlying territories of the South, but it still is the land of "ah" for *I*, *tin* for *ten*, and the greeting *y'all*.

Whether you call this true Southern speech depends on where you stand. To someone from farther north, like New York State, or from the West, like California, it sounds very Southern. To someone from the Deep South, like South Carolina or Mississippi, it isn't quite so Southern. Linguists who study dialects have used the name "South Midlands" for this territory on the inland side of the mountains. Just to the north of the South Midlands they find a corresponding "North Midlands" before they get to a true North at the upper edge of Pennsylvania, Ohio, Indiana, Illinois, and Iowa.

And it is useful to acknowledge a middle ground between South and North. East of the Rocky Mountains, where American English divides into South and North, our language does not change abruptly at Mason's and Dixon's Line. Instead, the transition is very gradual. In Illinois, for example, Cairo at the southern tip of the state has more of a Southern accent than Springfield in the middle, and Springfield has more of a Southern accent than Rockford or Chicago in the north. Residents of each place think that people a hundred miles south of them have more of a Southern accent, and they're right.

Midlands Pronunciation: warsh, marster

The Deep South often doesn't pronounce the "r" sound after vowels in words like *ward* or *marsh*. The Midlands generally pronounces that "r" and often adds an extra "r" for good measure in *wash* and

Washington. If you "warsh" your hands or your clothes and say that the capital of the United States is, "Warshington," you're likely from the Midlands.

You can also hear "marster" for *master* in the Midlands, but it's mostly confined to the Southern Appalachians.

Midlands Grammar: To be or not to be?

Another way in which Midlands speakers sometimes differ from their neighbors both South and North is their way of expressing *needs* and *wants.* Where deep Southerners and true Northerners require *to be,* the Midlands sometimes does without. So in the South and North Midlands, from Pittsburgh westward, you can hear statements like these:

The body is like an intricate watch. It needs repaired occasionally.

The walls need refinished. They need plastered, painted, and washed.

Just about everything needs done.

The cat wants fed.

Women want more respected in the business world.

The baby wants picked up.

My husband is a baby when he is ill. He wants waited on hand and foot.

To many (but not all) residents of the South Midlands and North Midlands, these sentences look perfectly fine. Southerners from farther south and Northerners from farther north, however, will expect "The walls need *to be* refinished" and "Women want *to be* more respected."

Midlands Grammar: anymore

"The only thing anymore about politicians is they're all crooked."

That will sound strange to someone from the southern South or northern North, not because of the opinion but because of the grammar. People in those regions would expect to hear instead:

"The only thing nowadays about politicians is they're all crooked".

Everyone — South, North, and middle — uses *anymore* when the context is negative: "Weekends aren't the same anymore." But only the Midlands uses *anymore* in a positive context: "Anymore we really enjoy the weekends." or "He used to take naps on the couch, but he sprawls out in that new lounge chair anymore."

Midlands Vocabulary

As the meeting place of South and North, the Midlands area has relatively little distinctive vocabulary of its own. One example, however, is *bedfast*, meaning "confined to bed or bedridden"; it's widely used in the Midlands but not in the South or North.

In the Midlands, people are likely to simply *want off* rather than *want to get off*.

And then there's an overgrown rodent, a kind of marmot, that has made a name for itself. Two names, in fact. In the far North, Deep South, and West, it's most often a *woodchuck*, famous for the philosophical riddle that begins "How much wood could a woodchuck chuck. . . ." In the Midlands, however, its name generally is more down-to-earth: *groundhog*. Perhaps it's no accident that the legend about the creature's emerging on February 2 to predict the arrival of spring comes from groundhog rather than woodchuck territory. After all, it is supposed to come out of the ground and look for its shadow on the ground; nothing to do with wood at all. The home of the famous forecasting rodent is Punxsutawney, well within the Midlands area in western Pennsylvania.

Finally, although both the South and North Midlands are not known for their tropical climate, that's where *mangoes* grow. These aren't the tropical fruit, though, but what are elsewhere called *green peppers*. They acquired the name *mango* because tropical mangoes used to reach the United States only as pickles; *mango* became a synonym for *pickle;* green peppers sometimes were pickled, and so they became known as *mango peppers* or just plain *mangoes*.

Southern Highlands

Within the South Midlands area, the Appalachian and Ozark Mountains have a variety of Southern speech that was once just called

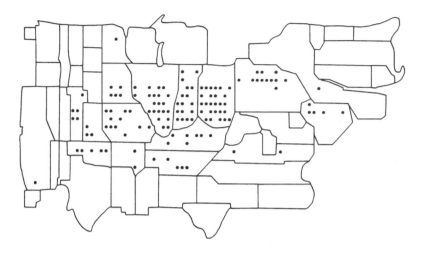

Mango Peppers: Each dot on this population-distorted map represents one person interviewed for the *Dictionary of American Regional English* who knew the meaning "green pepper" for *mango*.

"Scotch-Irish" because it carries some of the features of English as spoken in Scotland and Ireland. *Needs washed* and *wants picked up*, mentioned earlier, come from Scotch-Irish sources.

And if you're a-lookin' for a place where folks are still a-puttin' an *a* in front of verbs like *look* and *put*, you need go no farther than the Southern Highlands. You won't find everyone in Appalachia and the Ozarks a-talkin' this way, and you'll find folks in other Southern and Southwestern parts who go round a-speakin' like this, but other parts of the country that once had some fellers a-speakin' like this now find it almost extinct. Here is an example from a story told in 1929 to Ozark folklorist Vance Randolph:

> The marshal and his deputies rode their horses right into the crowd, and it looked like touch-and-go for a minute, as you could hear people a-cockin' pistols all over the place. But pretty soon the Yankees come to their senses, and went a-whoopin' back to the saloons and whorehouses where they belonged.

Even in those Southern hills, they are a-followin' strict rules about when they can put this *a* in front of words. The word has to be one that ends in *-ing*, and has to be a verb or adverb instead of a noun, and has to be accented on the first syllable. It also helps if the word starts with a consonant instead of a vowel. All these rules are followed regardless of whether the people who follow them have studied grammar in school or not, because it's not the grammar books that are a-makin' people talk the way they do, in the Southern mountains or anywhere else. People talk, and the makers of grammars figure out what rules they are a-usin', and write them down. Linguists Walt Wolfram and Natalie Schilling-Estes are among the experts who spent some time a-figurin' out just when folks use this *a*. They explain that you can say

"She was a-comin' home" because *comin'* is a verb, but not
    "He likes a-sailin'"
because in that sentence, *sailin'* is a noun. You can say
    "She was a-followin' me"
because the first syllable of *followin'* is the one that gets the emphasis, but not
    "I was a-discoverin' lots of new things"
because *discoverin'* has emphasis on its second syllable, not its first. All those examples have words that begin with consonants; it's unlikely to hear
    "She was a-eatin'"
because *eatin'* begins with a vowel.

Southern Highlands Pronunciations

Between the mountains and hills in Appalachia and the Ozarks there are many *hollows*. The word sometimes means "a stream in a valley." But whether it refers to the stream or just the valley, the Southern Highlands pronunciation is not "hollow." It's "holler" or "holla," depending on whether the speaker pronounces the "r" sound after vowels.

Likewise, *meadow* is "meader" in the Appalachians and Ozarks.

Southern Highlands Vocabulary

Cuckold is an example of an archaic English word still used in the Southern mountains. It is toned down from the days when it referred to a man whose wife was having sex with someone else. In Appalachia, sex isn't necessary to say one man *cuckolded* another, just that he spent some time with the other man's wife or girlfriend.

A treeless mountaintop is called a *bald*, pronounced "ball."

A *gum* can be a beehive or a trap for rabbits.

Something annoying, like a mosquito or a disagreeable person, is a *hateful*.

To *edzact* is to figure something out or make something exact.

Everly is always.

Everwhen is whenever, *everwhat* is whatever, *everhow* is however, *everwhich* and *everwho* are — well, you get the idea. That frees *whenever* to be used instead of *when*, as in

Whenever his Daddy died, he took over the farm.

That must have been whenever Jerry was a baby.

Whenever I was a gal, folks kept their clothes on, and the menfolks always wore the britches.

Appalachia

Appalachian Pronunciations

The Appalachian Mountains extend through the western parts of Maryland, Virginia, and the Carolinas; all of West Virginia; the eastern parts of Kentucky and Tennessee; as far south as northern Georgia and Alabama; and as far north as central Pennsylvania. Appalachian speech is generally Southern, but there are some exceptions. For example, in the southern Appalachians, *been* sometimes is pronounced the same as *bean*. *Push* and *bush* have the "long u" vowel sound of pool. *It* and *ain't* get an extra "h" sound at the beginning so that *it* sounds like *hit* and *ain't* becomes "hain't." *Chance* comes out as "chaince." Sometimes the letter *m* is pronounced like the word *elm*, as in "'Dial *Elm* for Murder' is on TV tonight." As mentioned above, *master* often has an extra "r" sound to make it "marster." And the southern Appalachians are where you most likely can hear *foreign* pronounced "furrin."

Appalachian Vocabulary

The *dulcimer* is one contribution from Appalachia to the musical culture and vocabulary of the whole country. It was little known outside Appalachia until the middle of the twentieth century.

A *gap* is a mountain pass. The word is known around the country, but is especially used in Appalachia. Among the best known is the Cumberland Gap where Virginia, Kentucky, and Tennessee come to-

gether. The Wilderness Road through
that gap was blazed by Daniel Boone in
1775, opening the way through the Appalachians for westward expansion of
what was soon to be the United States.

Dulcimer

On a smaller scale, a *milk gap* is a
place in a fence where cows and sometimes calves are let through at
milking time.

Least is the smallest or youngest, as in "Aunt Betty is Mamaw's
least child." (*Mamaw* is Grandmother.)

Kindly has the meaning "kind of" or "somewhat" as in "I'm feeling kindly sick."

If you say *I ain't much* when asked how you feel, you're not feeling so well.

You could find *flannel cakes* even at the Musso & Frank Grill in
Hollywood, California, but it's in Appalachia that you're most likely
to hear this name for what others call a *pancake*.

Instead of a bag or a sack, you might put your groceries in a *poke*.

If your hands are sticky or dirty, they're *gaumed up* or *gaumy*.

If you ask for the *check* in a restaurant, you might be served a
snack.

In the western United States, a *butte* is a hill or ridge that stands
out from its surroundings. In Appalachia, it's a *butt*.

Contemporary culture in the form of interstate highways, satellite TV and Wal-Marts has now moved into Appalachia and rendered
it less isolated; as a result, some of its distinctive vocabulary is
heard less frequently. Here are some words that survived into the
twentieth century but may be hard to find nowadays:

A *briggity* person had a high sense of self and a condescending
attitude toward others. It was a variant of *biggity*, which is still
widespread in the South. You could have expressed your opinion of
a briggity person by saying, "Hey briggity britches." Such a person
might have *feisted around*, acting provocatively or flirtatiously.

One day that person might have gotten a *quietus*, a punishment
sufficient to make him or her quiet.

A *moldwarp*, as in Shakespeare's time, was a stupid or worthless
person.

To *name* something was to mention it, as in "She named it to me."

To *discomfit* was to bother or discomfort someone.

A girlfriend was sometimes a *doney* or *doney-gal*.

An old-fashioned speaker in the mountains might have said *allers ago* or *allus ago*, that is, *always ago*, a long time ago.

To *brogue* was to walk around or hike. You might have also just *cootered around*, which was the same as wandering around. And if you were really doing nothing, you were *loafering*.

Something lasting a long time was *endurable* or *lasty*. A *hantle* was a handful, that is, a lot. On the other hand, a *little jag* was a small amount.

If you were getting worse instead of getting better, you were on the *down-go* or *drindlin' away*. And if you then *dropped off*, you would have died.

If you knew something *in reason*, you knew it for sure. And *knowing* meant "knowledgeable" or "aware," as in "I'm knowing to that."

A *hate* was a very little thing, so if you didn't care, you didn't give a hate.

A *budget* was a bundle or pack. A dinner table was an *eating table*.

A plant that elsewhere was known as a *burning bush* had the name *hearts-a-bustin'-with-love*. And a *hell* in Appalachia was a thicket of rhododendron or laurel, very thick indeed.

The Upper South: State by State

Though they have basic speech patterns in common, there is some diversity from state to state in the language of the South Midlands, just as there is in the Deep South. Here are some examples.

WEST VIRGINIA

The entire state of West Virginia belongs to Appalachia and shares Appalachian styles of speech.

In West Virginia you might call weeds *filth*. West Virginia associates itself with its western neighbor Ohio in using *berm* for the shoulder of a road and *belling* for the noisy celebration friends make for a newlywed couple.

KENTUCKY

In Louisville and elsewhere in Kentucky you might encounter a pronunciation of *house* with the "ah-ee" of Northern *mice*.

Here in the gleaming modern school where they gather from "up the holler," students suggested their dialect was prompting more pride and pleasure than shame. Kyre Bartz arose and, with an Appalachian flourish, offered "a handed-down story" that has been in her family for generations. It was replete with "crick" and "young 'uns" and "tomorry at sunrise" and "that ole woman stumblin' up that there hill with a poke and a pig walkin' right beside her."

— *New York Times* report from Allenboro, West Virginia

Set off by rivers and mountains, Kentucky has developed some distinctive vocabulary. There is *burgoo*, a spicy stew cooked outdoors in a kettle, which you can also get in central Illinois. For dessert in Kentucky you can eat a spicy *jam cake.*

Bourbon, Kentucky's famous beverage, is the sole or main ingredient of what is humorously called a *Kentucky breakfast.* But if you drink *lonesome water,* from a spring near your home, it is said you are sure to return home, no matter how far or how long you travel.

In eastern Kentucky, a voter or politician not tied to a political party is a *hogback.* If you're a hogback, you might not find it so easy to be designated a *Kentucky colonel,* an honor legally bestowed by the governor of the state.

A festival or fair can be called a *court day.*

If you offer something for sale at an *absolute auction* in Kentucky, you must accept the highest bid.

Where roads in other states have potholes, Kentucky has *chugholes,* steep-sided dips in the road that are often large.

Kentucky has a lot in common with its neighbor to the south, Tennessee. In both, *oodlins* meaning "a great amount" is heard oodlins of times. In both, you can eat a *dry-land fish,* which is a kind of mushroom. Your house can have several *houses,* that is, rooms, a term from the day of one-room houses. And *exercise* can be something you do not at a gym but at a religious revival, where your body moves of its own accord. This can include *falling exercise* and *barking exercise.*

In Kentucky and Tennessee, you might not want to be known as a *hunk,* which can mean the same as a hick elsewhere.

I am from Nashville and I say couldn, wouldn, shouldn, and I thank you get the point. People make fun of that all the time.

— Internet posting

In East Tennessee, farmers buy *fertilize* with which to fertilize their fields. . . . "The car is *kindly* a blue color" (instead of *kind of* or *sort of*).

When one is really close to reaching a destination or achieving a goal, the expression used is *purt near:* "We are purt near home" or "I'm purt near tuckered out."

My favorite story involved asking a new friend's daughter if she would baby-sit for me. She instantly responded, "I wouldn't care to." I thought that meant she didn't want to, and I was miffed. What she meant was, "I wouldn't mind to." We did get it straightened out!

— Internet posting

In West Tennessee, when someone is "in bed with the doctor" they are sick, not being naughty.

— Internet posting

TENNESSEE

Tennessee is Southern, and it shares Midland and Appalachian characteristics with Kentucky to the north. But the mountains kept Tennessee isolated enough to develop vocabulary of its own. To have the *weary dismals*, a somewhat old-fashioned term, is to be truly depressed. If you have too much of the dismals, you might be on the *drop edge of yonder,* elsewhere known as the *brink of death.*

A *hallway,* in Tennessee, may be the space between two buildings. Like the *neutral ground* of New Orleans, in Tennessee a *neutral strip* can be the grassy area in the middle of a divided highway or between sidewalk and curb.

The Ozarks

Where Arkansas, Missouri, and Oklahoma meet, you'll find the Ozark Mountains. The language of the folks who live there is Southern, and akin to Appalachian as well, but there are speechways unique to the Ozarks. Folklorist Vance Randolph explained in his book of Ozark folktales, *Who Blowed Up the Church House?* that he needed to make some translations:

> One storyteller told me that a character was "kind of *durgen.*" The word *durgen* is common in the Ozark backwoods, but readers elsewhere wouldn't understand it, so I wrote "kind of old-fashioned" instead. For the same reason I changed *chinch* to bedbug, *grub hyson* to sassafras tea, *ramp* to garlic, *mommix* to mess, *stinging-lizard* to scorpion, *tom-fuller* to hominy, and *woodscolt* to bastard.

Also in the Ozarks:

To *auger around* is to hang around or ramble. To *bush up* is to hide, especially where there is bush or woods to hide in.

Something that is really true is *black-actually* true.

To *draw* can mean to reach a conclusion. An old song has the lines, "He says you are a stranger, This idea I do draw."

ARKANSAS

Persons from Arkansas sometimes make a point of referring to themselves as *Arkansawyers* rather than *Arkansans* because the latter has too much of Kansas in it. For example: "Sondra is a native Arkansawyer, born and raised in the Mississippi River Delta region of eastern Arkansas."

The name of the state also makes a notorious verb. To *arkansaw*, in Arkansas as well as elsewhere in the Ozarks, is to take unfair advantage of your neighbor or the game you're hunting. And the

During the early days of statehood, Arkansas' two U.S. Senators were divided on the spelling and pronunciation. One was always introduced as the senator from "ARkanSAW" and the other as the senator from "Ar-KANSAS." In 1881, the state's General Assembly passed a resolution declaring that the state's name should be spelled "Arkansas" but pronounced "Arkansaw."

The pronunciation preserves the memory of the Indians who were the original inhabitants of our state, while the spelling clearly dictates the nationality of the French adventurers who first explored this area.

— Arkansas Secretary of State website

numeral *0*, for some Arkansawyers, is not zero but *ault*, a form of *aught*.

MISSOURI

How does a native of the state pronounce the name *Missouri*? That's right, with any of three possible endings, "ih," "uh," and "ee." The latter is increasingly the norm among the younger population, but Missour-"uh" still has strength in the northwest part of the state.

In rural Missouri, if you are *ornery* it doesn't necessarily mean you're bad tempered, just tired or not feeling well.

OKLAHOMA

Oklahoma has no mountain ranges to separate it from neighboring states, so it has little distinctive speech of its own. It shares vocabulary with Texas across the Red River to the south, terms like *bar ditch* as the name of the ditch along the side of a road, *blue whistler* as another name for the "blue norther" wind of Texas, and *boll weevil* as a nickname for an inexperienced or worthless worker. With Kansas, Oklahoma shares the name *Mexican sandburr* for a thorn strong enough to puncture tires that is otherwise known as a *puncture vine*.

The Midlands character of Oklahoma speech is reflected in this comment on the Internet: "Warsher is what we use in Oklahoma to warsh our clothes." And here is an Internet explanation from "Shawn" about Southern language in Oklahoma:

> A response to the person who lived in Oklahoma and picked up the use of *y'all: Y'all* refers to a collective group, as in "Y'all clean up your room." *All-o'-y'all* refers to a group of collected groups: "All o' y'all football teams head to your locker rooms." *Y'all's* is a possessive for a collective group: "Y'all's teacher's not going to be here today." *Y'all're* is a contraction: "Y'all're going to have a substitute." And, by the way, *fixin' to* is perfectly appropriate in the following sentence, "I'm fixin' to go to town." I should know; I've lived in Oklahoma for 21 years and I am doing my doctoral dissertation on speech patterns of native Oklahomans.

Oklahoma looks to the west too. In Oklahoma, when you talk about *Mexico*, you mean the neighbor state to the west of the Oklahoma panhandle, New Mexico to the rest of us. An Oklahoman will refer to the country of Mexico as *Old Mexico*.

MARYLAND

And then, back at the eastern edge of the South, there's Maryland. It's on the southern side of the Mason-Dixon Line, and separated only by the Potomac from Virginia. Its western counties are part of Appalachia. But it's not exactly like the rest of the South, either. Sandwiched between the Northern city of Philadelphia and the nationally-oriented city of Washington, D.C., Maryland has long felt Northern influences. That began at least by the time of the Civil War, when Northerners in the nation's capital saw to it that Maryland did not secede.

Spread out in such different geographic locations, from the Appalachian mountains to the Eastern Shore of Chesapeake Bay, Maryland participates in a variety of language patterns. And then there is Baltimore, a place of its own.

"WELCOME TO BAWLMER, HON"

Natives say that's the proper pronunciation of their city's name: "Bawlmer" or "Balamer."

Baltimore was the home of H.L. Mencken, a newspaperman and essayist who was a sharp social critic in the early twentieth century. His *American Language* is also one of the most important books on American English.

Nowadays "Hon" is a favorite term of endearment in Baltimore, as in "Howya doin', Hon?" Not that you won't hear "Hon" in other places, but Baltimore seems to have taken it to heart. The Baltimore Marketplace website has the greeting, "Welcome home, Hon." The Cafe Hon at 1002 West 36th Street in the Hampden neighborhood holds an annual "Hon-Fest" in June featuring a Bawlmerese contest, a Beach Blanket Bingo fashion show, and Bawlmer's Best Hon contest. The 1998 winner displayed a "bubble do" along with a tiger-striped stretch top and black lycra pants.

> **Hons are as much** a part of Baltimore's cultural landscape as crab cakes, the Orioles and Harborplace. They have earned their sociological niche for greeting friends and strangers alike the same way — "Howya doin', Hon?" — and speaking in "Bawlmerese," a dialect indigenous to the area and virtually unknown anywhere else.
>
> At the recent fifth-annual Best Hon contest, Ms. (Sharon) Gill, a 44-year-old legal secretary, defeated two other contestants with her quintessential Hon look: black stretch pants, faux tiger-skin shirt, high-heeled sandals and wildly teased hair that takes her as long as "two arries" — translation from Bawlmerese, two hours — to set properly in place.
>
> — *New York Times*

Hampden is the setting for John Waters' 1998 comic movie *Pecker* about a young photographer who takes pictures of his eccentric neighbors and makes a hit in the New York art world.

Baltimore is also known for its non-Arabian *Arabs* (pronounced "ay-rabs"): the city's street vendors. To *Arab* is to be a vendor, or just to roam the streets.

Baltimore is also one of the places where you can hear "zink" for *sink*. Other examples of that pronunciation have been found by the *Dictionary of American Regional English* in New York, Kentucky, Mississippi, Iowa, and North Dakota.

As is true of most places, not everyone is thrilled with the local ways of speech. Here's another commentator on the Internet: "I live in Maryland, and I don't have enough time in one day to tell you all the things the people here say that irritate me. I often wonder where these people learned this horribly unique dialect. It's worse than the sound of fingernails scraping a chalkboard! 'You's ain't done that yet?' 'We're goin' downa ocean the weekend.' They also put *ool* instead of oil in their cars, and have RA-diators instead of RAY-diators! I never correct anyone, yet they have the nerve to think I'm snobby because I speak properly!"

DISTRICT OF COLUMBIA

The capital city of the United States is historically Southern, but nowadays you'd hardly notice it — so many outsiders from the

A-rabbing is a Baltimore tradition — you probably won't find fruits and vegetables being sold from horse-drawn wagons in any other city in America — that ought to be maintained and even promoted. A-rabbing, with its street-hollerin' vendors and plumed ponies, is worth saving. Not because it's symbolic. Not because it's quaint. A-rabbing is real. It's a livelihood for men with colorful nicknames and hustle in their hearts.

— Dan Rodricks, *Baltimore Sun*

North and West have settled there. Actually, its "permanent residents" (people who may not be natives, but whose residency doesn't depend on the results of coming elections) come from such varied language backgrounds that you can find almost any American dialect, plus numerous foreign languages, well established in at least some pocket of D.C.

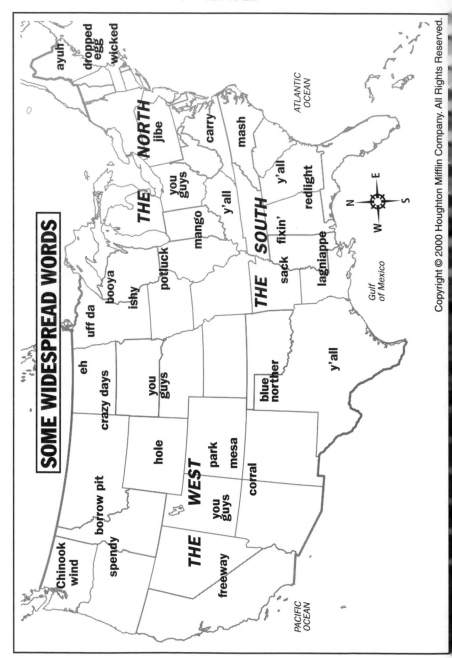

SOME WIDESPREAD WORDS

THE NORTH

The North is the opposite of the South. At least, that's what Americans decided in the nineteenth century as slavery divided the country to the point of civil war. In the latter part of the twentieth century and into the twenty-first, as American culture has become more national and less regional, the opposition between North and South has diminished. But the basic differences remain.

Where Southerners say "ah" for *I*, Northerners say "ah-ee." Where Southerners pronounce *pen* as if it were spelled *pin*, Northerners have kept it penned in with the "short c" vowel. Where Southerners often drop the "r" sound after vowels, Northerners rarely do, except for certain ones along the Atlantic coast. And where Southerners say *y'all*, Northerners say plain *you*, or the two words *you all* — or *you guys*.

The North won the Civil War. Its language also won the title of normal American speech, "General American." But that was a contest the South had no interest in winning. Though the South had to give up slavery, the "peculiar institution" on which its economy was based, white Southerners held all the more tightly to the other peculiarities of their culture, including ways of speaking that even in the more enlightened twenty-first century make the South markedly different from the rest of the country. For the most part, those who speak Southern know they are distinctive and are happy to have it that way.

Northerners, on the other hand, are happy to be — well, normal. To be sure, there are exceptions along the North Atlantic coast, in New York City and eastern New England where residents are quite aware of their distinctive speech, and in some inland Northern cities and states where people cultivate their local distinctions. But for the most part people in the North take it for granted that their way of speaking is at or close to the American norm.

In fact, as in the South, there is a good deal of variety in the speech of the American North, by which we very roughly mean everywhere north of the Mason-Dixon Line, continuing west to include the northern parts of Ohio, Indiana, and Illinois, crossing the Mississippi River to pick up Iowa and points north, then dipping down to include Kansas before blending into the West. All these different parts of the North have their distinctive qualities. But they also reflect an American norm articulated in the mid-twentieth century by a professor named John Samuel Kenyon (1874–1959), who just happened to be from northern Ohio.

Kenyon was born and raised in Medina, Ohio, thirty miles south of Cleveland, and became a professor of English at Hiram College in Hiram, Ohio, forty miles east of his birthplace. He studied the phonetics of American English and published two books that set the standard not just for dictionary makers but also for public figures like actors and broadcasters. His detailed book on the phonetics of American English, *American Pronunciation*, was first published in 1924 and had gone through eleven editions by 1950. That book had a great influence on makers of dictionaries. Even more direct was the influence of his *Pronouncing Dictionary of American English*, written with Thomas A. Knott and first published in 1944. Though that book was last revised in 1953, it remains the authority people will likely turn to when looking up the American pronunciation of a word.

The model of American pronunciation that Kenyon used for both books was his own speech. He was careful to acknowledge that there is no official standard for American pronunciation, and that one place will differ from another in its norms for cultivated speech. Yet however modestly he put it, his books made his own way of speaking the model for the whole country. He divided American dialects into "Southern," "Eastern," and "General American." His own, he said, was "General American."

Kenyon's implied endorsement of Medina, Ohio, as a norm for American speech reflected a westward shift from the previous Northern standard. Until well into the twentieth century, the ideal if not the norm for cultivated American speech was the speech of Boston and eastern New England. This was because it was closest to the speech of old England, the mother country. For example, New England followed the eighteenth-century English innovation of omitting the "r" sound after vowels (as in *far* and *hard*), a fashion that didn't catch on in the backwoods whose speakers later formed the backbone of Northern speech. Even after the United States attained political independence, many Americans continued to think of England as the prime meridian for the English language and the speech of eastern New England as the closest approximation to the real thing.

New England maintained its dominance for well over a century after independence, helped by the prestige of its writers. The New England lexicographer Noah Webster was also an important influence. Although he created Americanized spellings in his dictionary and spelling books, substituting *or* for British *our* and *er* for British *-re*, he took his Connecticut pronunciation as the norm for his books and therefore for the whole country. Until as late as the latter part of the twentieth century, actors and politicians often looked eastward and affected something of a New England if not British style.

But the experience of two world wars shifted the leadership of the English-speaking world from Britain to the United States, and not coincidentally brought to an end the sense of American cultural inferiority to England. The ideal form of our language moved westward from an Atlantic coast variety associated with England to a more independent inland variety. This one was also more widely spoken than the style of speech that stayed close to the shores of New England. Thus, the norm remained Northern, but moved closer to the heartland.

In general, then, to speakers of American English, the South is special, and the North is normal. That's the first impression. But on second thought, it's more complicated. The South is solid, the North is niches. We are comfortable with the notion of a "Southern accent," but a "Northern accent" isn't so easy to define. Though Northern speakers have much in common, they make the most of their regional and local differences. New England has its own speechways, and so does the upper Midwest. Maine is known for its "Down East" accent, and quite a few Northern cities and states are distinguished with -*an* or -*ese*: Bostonian, New Yorkese, Philadelphian, Pittsburgh-ese, Chicagoan, Minnesotan. And in recent years Northern cities from upstate New York to upstate Illinois have developed a distinctive urban pronunciation, characterized by vowels that change places as well as consonants that sometimes stand still.

Sounds of the North

The I's Have It   Everywhere in the North, the "long i" is the full two-part "ah-ee" diphthong, not the "ah" so characteristic of the South. *I, time, ride, nice* all have "ah-ee." Only before the "l" sound do Northerners tend to omit the "ee," so *I'll* comes out as "ahl" in the North as well as the South. But that's a limited exception to the prominent North-South difference.

Ten Pins and Tin Pens   In the South, it's often hard to distinguish *ten pins* from *tin pens* by the way they sound; in the North, it's easy. That's because, when a "short e" is followed by *n* in the South, it often shifts to become the same as a "short i." But the North maintains the "short e," even before *n*.

Furthermore, Southerners often stretch the short vowel and give it a twist: "tih-un mih-un" for *ten men.* Northerners keep the short vowels short.

Words of the North

you guys   Hey, you guys! Like Southerners with *y'all*, Northerners have long had ways of indicating the plural of *you*, namely *youse* and *you-uns*. These, however, are localized and often stigmatized. A hundred years or so after the South invented *y'all*, there was still a need in the North to develop a way to distinguish between one "you" and more than one, so that listeners would know whether the speaker was referring just to one person in particular or to the whole group. Towards the end of the twentieth century the North came up with its own solution: the plural *you guys.*

Like *y'all*, *you guys* is not actually new. We find it as far back as 1896 in a story by George Ade: "You guys must think I'm a quitter."

Old Guy: Guy Fawkes is a straw man in this 1805 English celebration of Guy Fawkes Day.

But in that early version, Ade was referring specifically to men, as *guy* still does. The word *guy*, in fact, traces back to *Guy Fawkes Day*, celebrated in England every November 5, the anniversary of the day in 1605 when the Gunpowder Plot to blow up the Houses of Parliament was discovered and successfully prevented. Guy Fawkes was leader of that plot, and festivities for Guy Fawkes Day include burning grotesque effigies of Fawkes. Those effigies led to the nickname *guy* for any odd-looking or strangely-dressed person.

In the nineteenth century, *guy* enlarged its meaning to include any man, odd-looking or otherwise. Finally, in the mid and late twentieth century *guy* became so neutral that *you guys* became a way of speaking to any group, even when the group included women as well as men, and sometimes even when it included only women. As long ago as 1942, an article in the *Journal of General Psychology* said that "*Guy* is used without regard to age or sex" and gave this example: "One girl to others, 'Come on, you guys.'"

You guys even seems to be invading the South. Celia Rivenbark, columnist for the *Sun-News* in Myrtle Beach, S.C., makes this complaint:

> The most grating example is found in restaurants and stores where nice, Magnolia-mouthed clerks now say *you guys* instead of *y'all*, as their mamas raised them up to say. I'd sooner wear white shoes in February, drink unsweetened tea and eat Miracle Whip instead of Duke's than utter the words *You guys*. Not long ago, I went to lunch with four women friends, and the waiter, a nice Southern boy, *you-guys*-ed all of us within an inch of our lives. "You guys ready to order? What can I get for you guys? Would you guys like to keep you guys' forks?"

Despite its widespread and frequent use in the North, however, *you guys* is not as fully accepted there as *y'all* is in the South. It is largely avoided in formal writing and speech, because for those purposes it has two strikes against it: masculine reference and slang. For those reasons, even a Northerner who regularly uses *you guys* in conversation may deny or at least regret saying it. But there is no question that it is now the normal Northern way of making a plural of *you*. And most of the time it is said without apology in informal contexts. Recently a distinguished professor recalled in print saying to others at a conference on college composition in Anaheim, California, in 1974, "If you guys will teach it, I'll put it together."

Like *y'all's*, *you guys'* can be used to show possession, as in the following examples from the Internet: "None of you guys' business"; "You guys' room is 201"; and "You guys' band is the greatest!"

One American dialect goes even further. Hawaiian Pidgin, our farthest-west dialect, takes *guys* to its logical extreme by using it as a plural not just for *you* but for any noun: *horse guys* for "horses" or *house guys* for "houses," for example.

Other Northern Vocabulary

The North is no match for the South in distinctive vocabulary, but it does have quite a few words you won't hear in the South. Most of these Northern words are familiar in the West as well.

armful   In the North, you're more likely to carry an *armful* than an *armload* of wood or groceries. The Northern word *armful* has spread to the Southern states too, but in the South Midlands states and Texas it's still more likely to be *armload*.

comforter   In the North and West, a thick covering for a bed is a *comforter*. The South calls it a *comfort*.

crazy bone   It's funny: the sensitive place on the elbow that Southerners call the *funny bone* is in most of the North and West the *crazy bone*. What's really crazy, however, is that in New York City and vicinity, New York State, and the state of Michigan, it's the Southern *funny bone*.

dove   It's not the dove of peace, but the *dove* of "Yesterday I dove into the lake." Although it is based on the pattern of *drive–drove*, it's something new for the verb *dive*; the older form is *dived*. In England, and in the South, the past tense of that verb is still that old-fashioned *dived*.

faucet   Water comes out of a *faucet* in the North and West, a *spigot* or *spicket* in the South. At least that used to be the case; now Southerners often say *faucet* too.

frosting (on the cake)   When you're in the North, from New England west across New York State, through northern Ohio and Illinois and Iowa and the Dakotas, and along the Pacific Rim, you can count on your cakes and pastries being *frosted*, not iced.

gesundheit!   It's a German word meaning "health." Northerners and Westerners are likely to say it when someone sneezes.

head cheese   Well known almost everywhere outside the South is the name *head cheese* for the boiled meat of a hog's head and feet, molded into a cheese shape or stuffed into a sausage.

jibe   When people, ideas, or pieces of wood don't match up, a Northerner or Westerner can say that they just don't *jibe*.

kitty-corner   In the North and West, something diagonal is likely to be *kitty-corner*, while in the South it's more likely *catercorner*. On the other hand, it could be *catawampus*, or *caliwampus*, *cankywampus*, *cattywampus* and the like, almost anywhere in the North or South except the Northeast and North North Central states.

potluck   In most parts of the North, you can bring food to share at a *potluck dinner*.

rapids   Where the water in a stream becomes swift and turbulent, you're in what the North knows as *rapids*. Outside of North Carolina and Virginia, that word isn't used much in the South, perhaps because the South doesn't have many swift and turbulent streams. Where they do, they tend to say *shoals* or *shallows*.

New England

In terms of dialect, New England is aptly named, just as the original namer might have wished. Captain John Smith, of Jamestown and Pocahontas fame, first used *New England* in print in 1616 as a way of advertising England's claim to that caped corner of the New World north of Virginia. A few years later the adventurers we call the Pilgrims arrived to take permanent residence in New England. Though they had differences of religion with the mother country — and from the first had to add words like *powwow*, *wampum*, and *rattlesnake* to their vocabulary — over the years the inhabitants of eastern New England were inclined to stay closer than those of any other part of the present-day United States to the speech and culture of old England.

Eastern New England, for example, along with New York City and the plantation South, in the eighteenth century learned old England's new fashion of dropping the "r" sound after vowels. Even when they espoused distinctively American ideas and ideals, the elite of New England espoused them in language attuned to norms across the sea. Boston-born and bred Ben Franklin, for example, took the English essayists Addison and Steele as the models for his own prose. In the next century, growing up in Salem, Massachusetts, and in Maine, Nathaniel Hawthorne looked to English novelists for style even as he wrote on American themes. Bostonian Ralph Waldo Emerson may have admired Walt Whitman's un-British *Leaves of Grass* but he hardly emulated it in his own work. And Emily Dickinson of Amherst, Massachusetts, followed the cadence and diction of English hymns in her striking poetry.

In the early twentieth century, perhaps the most egregious example of New England culchah was St. Louis-born T.S. Eliot, a bloke whose sojourn at Hahvahd only whetted his appetite to cross the sea to old England and become a famous British writah.

In the mid twentieth century when America, not England, became the dominant English-speaking culture, the norm for American English migrated from the shores of New England — moving inland to Ohio and points west. Indeed, at the start of the twenty-first century, New England seems peripheral to the American culture of Hollywood, Coca-Cola, and rock music spreading around the world. Silicon Valley is in California, not Massachusetts, and Disney World was built in Florida instead of Maine.

With the waning of national prestige for New England speech patterns and habits, the college-educated children of New Englanders are now less likely to sound like New England than their parents, and even their parents are susceptible to change. Massachusetts Senator Edward M. Kennedy, for example, once sounded much more Bostonian than he does nowadays, and in the younger generation of Kennedys there is little to be heard of the New England pronunciation so prominent in the speech of John and Robert Kennedy in the 1960s.

But though it has lost most of its influence on the rest of the nation, and not everyone uses it, the accent of eastern New England is far from vanquished. In New England, as elsewhere in the country, speakers have choices between the distinctive local variety and a more neutral way of speaking. Many still choose to sound native.

What is that native sound? It depends on where you ask that question. And that, in turn, depends on the Connecticut River, which separates New Hampshire on the east from Vermont on the west, cuts through Massachusetts, and bisects Connecticut. To the east of this river (and for a little distance to the west, in Vermont) can be heard what we think of as the most distinctively New England features of speech. To the west is language more like that of the rest of the North, and in fact western New England provided much of the original English-speaking population of upstate New York and the Great Lakes area.

New England Pronunciation

Eastern New England has three patterns of pronunciation that distinguish it from the rest of the country: the dropped "r," the "broad a," and the "New England short o." One is prominent, another is still well established, but the third is almost gone.

"r": Not here, but there it is   In the eastern New England way of speaking, the "r" sound follows the British pattern of disappearing after a vowel, sometimes to be replaced by an "uh" sound. So *fork* loses its "r" and becomes something like "fohk"; *hear* becomes "heah"; and *care* becomes "caeh" (or "kay-uh," to attempt a better phonetic spelling).

This is a feature of New York City speech and of many Southern dialects too, and for the same reason. In the eighteenth century, despite the movement for independence, the New England Yankees as well as the New York City traders and the Southern planters valued their cultural ties with the mother country. Some of them sent their children to England for a proper education. And England during the eighteenth century had been dropping its "r"s in distinctly un-Shakespearean fashion.

But England, New England, and New York put a twist on the "r" sound that Southerners didn't allow. The English, New English, and New York fashion became *not* to drop the "r" at the end of a word if the very next word begins with a vowel. So *hear* and *care*, for example, which usually lose their "r" sound, may be followed by words that start with a vowel, and in these instances, each keeps its "r" sound. That leads to differences like *hear me*, with "r"-less "heah" for *hear*, and *hear it*, with a strong "r" sound at the end of *hear*.

Keeping the "r" in those circumstances prevents a vowel sound at the end of the first word from being immediately followed by a vowel sound at the start of the second. New Englanders and New Yorkers go one step further, extending that rule to *all* words ending in a vowel. In these cases, they actually insert an "r" sound, even if the first word has no "r" to begin with. In other words, in eastern New England and New York City, the "r" sound becomes a mechanism to keep two vowels from touching — the vowel at the end of one word and the vowel at the start of the next. So in the second

---

The distinguished American writer, Henry James, very European in tastes and residence, visited his native country in the early twentieth century and wasn't happy with the American English he heard. His commencement address at Bryn Mawr College in June 1905 includes this lamentation about the inserted "r" sound:

> You will perfectly hear persons supposedly "cultivated," the very instructors of youth sometimes themselves, talk of vanilla-r-ice-cream, of California-r-oranges, of Cuba-r- and Porto Rico, of Atalanta-r- in Calydon, and (very resentfully) of "the idea-r-of" any intimation that their performance and example in these respects may not be immaculate. You will perfectly hear the sons and daughters of the most respectable families disfigure in this interest, and for this purpose, the pleasant old names of Papa and Mamma. "Is Popper-up stairs?" and "is Mommer-in the parlor?" pass for excellent household speech in millions of honest homes. . . . You will, again, perfectly hear a gentle hostess, solicitous for your comfort, tell you that if you wish to lie down there is a sofa-r-in your room. No one is "thought any the worse of" for saying these things. . . .

James is even less happy with the vast majority of Northerners west of the Atlantic coast who ignore English fashion and keep the "r" sound after vowels:

> It is not always a question of an r, however — though the letter, I grant, gets terribly little rest among those great masses of our population who strike us, in the boundless West perhaps especially, as, under some strange impulse received toward consonantal recovery of balance, making it present even in words from which it is absent, bringing it in everywhere as with the small vulgar effect of a sort of morose grinding of the back teeth. There are, you see, sounds of a mysterious intrinsic meanness, and there are sounds of a mysterious intrinsic frankness and sweetness; and I think the recurrent note I have indicated — fatherr and motherr and otherr, waterr and matterr and scatterr, harrd and barrd, parrt, starrt, and (dreadful to say) arrt (the repetition it is that drives home the ugliness), are signal specimens of what becomes of a custom of utterance out of which the principle of taste has dropped.

1960 debate between Presidential candidates, Bostonian John F. Kennedy said, "Today Cuba(r) is lost to freedom," putting an "r" between *Cuba* and *is;* but he also said, "I've never suggested that Cuba was lost except for the present," without "r" after *Cuba* because the next word begins with a consonant.

Sometimes it balances out. *Linda and I will take the car* loses the "r" sound at the end of *car* but inserts one between the first two words so that the full statement still has the same number of "r"s: "Linda-r-and I will take the cah."

The "New England broad a"   *Park the car in Harvard Yard.* That saying is a well-known test for New England pronunciation. If you say "Pahk the car in Hahvahd Yahd," you're saying the "r"s in true Bostonian, as described above. (Notice that the "r" sound remains in *car* because the next word begins with a vowel.) That sentence also contains four examples of the vowel called the "New England broad a." Those who use this "broad a" make a distinction between the

Havahd Yahd: No place to pahk the cah

vowels in *father* (which has the "broad a") and *bother;* speakers elsewhere in America rhyme those words. To anyone outside of New England the "broad a" is difficult to describe, because it's not in anyone else's repertoire of pronunciation. If it's not in yours, you can approximate it by saying the "o" of *bother* and the "a" of *hat* and then trying for a sound that is between the two.

The "broad a" is the norm in eastern New England. A recent survey by Naomi Nagy, coordinator of the linguistics program at the University of New Hampshire, and her students found the "broad a" pronounced by over 80 percent of those they interviewed in Boston and vicinity. It is also the norm in New Hampshire, which is east of the Connecticut River, but not in Vermont, which is west of that river.

New England is also where you're most likely to hear *aunt* pronounced with the vowel of *father.*

Linguist Steven Pinker teaches at the Massachusetts Institute of Technology near Boston. He is originally from Montreal and does not drop "r" after vowels or use the "broad a" himself, but he knows that pronunciation well enough to write about "the remembrance of things parsed" in his book *The Language Instinct.* This allusion to Proust's *Remembrance of Things Past* works only with pronunciation like that of eastern New England.

The "New England short o"   In words like *coat, road,* and *home,* eastern New England is noted for a pronunciation that to outsiders sounds like "cut," "rud," and "hum" respectively. This is the "New England short o." Those who use this "short o" still distinguish between *coat* and *cut* and *home* and *hum* like the rest of us, but their vowel is close enough to the vowel of *cut* that it can confuse others. Part of the distinctiveness of the "New England short o" is that it is usually very short, even in words like *home* and *stone* where English speakers generally have a "long o." Nowadays you may have to go far off the beaten track to hear the authentic "short o."

New England Vocabulary
The sea, ties with England, and nearly four hundred years of settlement history have given New England the opportunity to develop vocabulary as well as pronunciation different from the rest of the country. Some of New England's distinctive vocabulary, however, is

distinctively old-fashioned, reflecting an earlier rural way of life. Only in New England, for example, could you call cows with the exclamation *Coaf!* (To the west, and in some parts of New England, *Boss!* is the call.) *Hurrup!* is what you can say to a horse or cow to get it to move, or move faster. And an eastern New England horse makes a *whicker* instead of a whinny.

You *belly-bump* when you throw yourself face down on a sled and coast downhill. Two sleds joined together side by side are known in New England as *double runners*. If you have a stack of hay extending from the floor to the roof of your barn, you'd call it *ground mow*.

Most of the country is happy to call a small river a *creek*, but in New England a creek is an inlet of the ocean, and the small river is a *brook*. "I am no more lonely than the Mill Brook," wrote Henry David Thoreau in *Walden* a century and a half ago.

Along the brooks and rivers of New England, an *intervale* or *interval* is rich flat land. It's what the South and part of the Midwest call a *bottom*.

In the eighteenth and nineteenth centuries, *mooncussers* made their living on the shores of New England. On dark nights they would use false beacons to cause shipwrecks, then plunder crew and cargo. They would "cuss the moon" because it gave sailors enough light to steer away from their lures. Both the spelling and the pronunciation of *cuss* reflect the dropping of the "r" sound after the vowel in *curse*.

New Englanders and some upstate New Yorkers are famous for *ayuh*, their way of saying yes. And there are distinctive New England expressions for attitudes and states of mind, though many of them are rarely heard nowadays. *Gimp* is a word for courage. To *mump* is to be unhappy or grumpy and to *mux up* is to mess up. If you're tired, in New England you can be *beat out*.

And *Hannah Cook* isn't worth much in New England; "not worth a Hannah Cook" is said of both people and things. Why that name? Apparently it comes from "hand or cook," the job description of someone who signed on to work on a ship without specialized skills. He would help out on deck or in the galley, depending on the ship's needs. It was the lowest and least paid assignment, not worth a Hannah Cook.

Upstate New York, northern Pennsylvania, and even parts of New Jersey join New England in going *down cellar* — that is, into the basement.

In most of the country, office workers wrap maps or papers with a *rubber band*, but from Massachusetts south to northern New Jersey it's also known as an *elastic*. If you call it a *gumband*, you have distinctively located yourself in the Pittsburgh area of western Pennsylvania.

Food and Home

New England has distinctive foods going back to the early days. There is, for example, *hasty pudding*, a name for cornmeal mush immortalized in the words of "Yankee Doodle." There is *Indian bannock*, a thin bread or cake of cornmeal cooked in a frying pan. And there's a cold fruit pudding known as *flummery*. But you might prefer a deep-dish dessert called *apple slump*, *apple pandowdy*, *apple pot pie*, or *apple John*, made with the crust blended into the middle.

In New England, you're likely to put *jimmies* on your ice cream rather than *sprinkles*.

A well-known New England specialty is *brown bread* or *Boston brown bread*, soft bread made with molasses, corn meal, and rye or wheat flour. Even better known are *Boston baked beans*.

In New England, a *dropped egg* is not a slip by a careless chef but the deliberate result of cooking the egg by dropping its contents into hot water, elsewhere known as a *poached egg*.

In western and southern New England, the sandwich generally known as a *submarine* is called a *grinder*.

Chankings are the part of a fruit you chew but don't eat. In 1855 Thoreau wrote in his journal about "apples, sometimes three or four, carried to the mouth of a striped squirrel's hole . . . with the marks of his teeth in them, by which he carried them, and the chankings or else fragments of the skin of others there."

The *dooryard*, in New England and New York State, is the yard near a house. Walt Whitman, a New Yorker, made the word generally known with his eulogy for Abraham Lincoln that begins, "When lilacs last in the door-yard bloom'd."

Seaside houses in New England may have a *captain's walk*, a porch or platform at the highest point of the house to catch sight of arriving ships. It's more generally known as a *widow's walk*.

An *off-islander* is someone who lives on the mainland, from the point of view of someone who lives on an island off the coast, especially in Maine and on Nantucket Island, Massachusetts.

In northern New England, a *dish wiper* is sometimes not a person but a towel used for drying dishes.

The Common

Where municipalities in other parts of the country might have a *square*, a New England city or town may have a *common* in its center, like the well-known Boston Common. It's also called a *green*, though that term is used elsewhere along the Atlantic coast too.

New England was and still is known for its *township* system of government, with officials elected at annual *town meetings*. Among these officials was the *hog reeve*, a person responsible for rounding up stray hogs. There are still hog reeves in Dunbarton, New Hampshire, though their position nowadays must be largely honorary. Ac-

The Boston Common: Winslow Homer's view in 1858 for *Harper's Weekly*

cording to the town minutes, "On March 26, 1998, Somer and Bob Andrews were sworn in by Leslie Hammond, Chairman, Board of Selectmen, as Hog Reeves for the Town of Dunbarton for the 1998 year."

An office still widely held in New England is that of *fence viewer*, the official who regulates the building of fences and settles disputes between neighbors about the fences between them. "Good fences make good neighbors," mutters a character in Robert Frost's "Mending Wall," a poem that recognizes the subtleties of fencing in New England.

Old Home Day is an annual reunion and festival in many towns of New England. Despite its name, it is a relatively new invention, conceived in 1899 by Governor Frank Rollins of New Hampshire. In the twentieth century the celebration of Old Home Days spread throughout New England and as far west as Indiana.

Leaf peepers are tourists who invade in fall to watch the leaves turn color. This New England term is now used as far away as West Virginia and Missouri.

In the states of New England, the license number of a car is displayed on a *marker* or *number plate*. It's the same thing as the license plate in other parts of the country.

New England: State by State

MAINE: DOWN EAST

"I went down New Yahk a few weeks ago foah some meetins," declares a 35-year-old resident of Portland, Maine, in a fictitious news bulletin on "Yankonics." "It took me close to two days to figuah out what people weah tahlking about. Rest assuahed, I was wicked confused when I gawt bahck."

That's a rough representation of the famous "Down East" accent heard on the coast of Maine. "Down East" itself requires an explanation. Eastward from Maine are the St. Croix River and the Canadian province of New Brunswick, not the coast. The Maine seacoast mainly faces south. Why is it, then, that it's called "Down East"?

Blame it on Boston. Back in the days of sail, ships sailing eastward from Boston would head downwind. The prevailing winds took them "downwind to the east" along the southern coast of Maine. Eventually "downwind to the east" became shortened to the present-day Down

> **For the first time,** I heard the cadence of the Maine accent, the vowels broadened, the *r*'s dropped, the making of two syllables out of simple words like *there*. The words and sentences had a lilt and a rhythm that was appealing. The accent grows on you like an old tune.
>
> — Anita Shreve, *Strange Fits of Passion*

East. That coastal area, including Portland, Augusta, and Bangor, was the earliest and still is the most densely settled. Its language epitomizes the eastern New England pronunciations already mentioned.

But by no means do all the men and women of Maine speak with a Down East accent. In the north, far from the seacoast, Maine is surrounded on three sides by Canada and influenced by both of Canada's languages. Northern Maine reflects the French influence of neighboring Quebec, for example, in the name *loup-garou* for a creature elsewhere called a *werewolf* or *bigfoot*. Northern Maine also has the distinctive Canadian English pronunciation of *ou* in words like *out*, *about*, and *house*, a pronunciation that makes it sound like "uh-oo" rather than the usual American "ah-oo." (This Canadian *ou* also spills over the Canadian-U.S. border far to the west, in Minnesota. In between, the St. Lawrence River and the Great Lakes keep the two countries apart.)

And then there is the Maine vocabulary. With the editors of *Down East* magazine, John Gould was able to fill a whole book with "Maine Lingo." He titled it *Maine Lingo: Boiled Owls, Billdads, & Wazzats*, explaining that a *boiled owl* is a "last ditch meal than which, in Maine cookery, there is nothing tougher"; *billdads* are little mythical creatures of the Maine woods; and *wazzat* is the noise a billdad makes catching trout by slapping them with its tail. "Anybody scouting billdads is looking for a drink," Gould writes. "If he finds one, he's had one."

To *fub*, Gould explains, is to bungle something, and to *fub around* is to fool around without accomplishing much. The winter weather in Maine provides occasion for *dingle*, a covered walkway, storehouse or pantry. A *nubble* in coastal Maine is a small hill or island, used in names like the famous Nubble Lighthouse on a small hill near York, Maine.

A number of New England words are especially prominent in Maine. These include *dozy,* referring to rotten or decayed wood; *culch* for trash; and the approving term *finest kind.* Something that is *gaumy* or *gormy* is awkward or stupid. And *Italian sandwich* is the general Maine term for what elsewhere is called *submarine, hoagie,* or *grinder.*

MASSACHUSETTS

The oldest of the New England colonies has had nearly four centuries to develop its distinctive way of speaking. It has had such an effect on New England, however, not to mention the rest of the country, that there remain few locutions absolutely distinctive to Massachusetts. To *coast* downhill on a sled, for example, seems originally to have been a Boston term, but now it is known throughout the snowy parts of the United States.

Maine and Massachusetts have some words in common. One is *hosey,* which means "to claim or reserve something," as in "I hosey that seat." In coastal Massachusetts and Maine you can also get something to eat known as a *joe flogger.* Depending on the establishment, a joe flogger will be a distinctive kind of doughnut, a pancake, or a molasses cookie. And you can get a *lobster roll,* a lobster salad sandwich in a hotdog bun.

A *hole* in Massachusetts, as in Virginia, is a small harbor or channel. Many sailors spend their vacations *gunkholing,* sailing from one hole to another, where they can safely anchor the boat for the night. That term is used by sailors on both American coasts.

A *mountain day* is a beautiful fall day used as the occasion for an unscheduled holiday from classes — a tradition dating from 1877 at Smith and Mount Holyoke colleges along the Connecticut River in western Massachusetts.

There's also the phrase *so don't I,* what one observer calls the "Massachusetts negative positive." It's used to express agreement, not disagreement: "I love ice cream!" "Oh, so don't I!"

BOSTON

Boston is the focal point of New England. The basic pronunciations and vocabulary characteristic of Boston thus have already been described in the discussion of eastern New England. But the city also

has a variety of dialects within itself. Linguist Robert L. Parslow has identified three, which he calls types A, B, and C: A for the average middle-class speech, B for the upper-class Brahmins, and C for the speech of the central city.

Type A Boston speech is the most widespread, geographically and socially. It is essentially the same as heard elsewhere throughout eastern New England.

Type B is the consciously upper-class and nearly British speech of the social elite known as Brahmins, whose forebears in the nineteenth century included literary giants like Ralph Waldo Emerson. In the twentieth century the most significant Brahmin literary work was a satire by one of their own, Cleveland Amory's *The Proper Bostonians* (1947). Like the British, Brahmins say *glass* with the vowel of *father*. Their "long o" vowel in words like *ago* and *home* is like the "eh-oo" of southern England. They always have an "ee" sound before the "oo" sound in *new, suit,* and *due*. And Brahmins make *four* a two-syllable word, of course without the "r": "fow-uh."

Type C, on the other hand, the central Boston dialect, is associated with the working class. It's not so different from type A, the general eastern New England, but Parslow found a few particular pronunciations to be distinct. In the central city, for example, *washed* has more of an "o" vowel sound than in the other dialects, where it is more like the *a* in *father*. The *t*'s in *potatoes* sound more like *d*'s: "b'daydas" in Adam Gaffin's phonetic spelling. And central city speakers are more likely than those of the other two groups to insert an "r" sound when one word ends with a vowel and the next begins with one, as in *law and order*, though this is a trait heard throughout eastern New England.

The actor, Leo Carroll . . . found no less than thirteen recognized Boston Brahmin accents. The broad "a" and the stern omission of the "r," generally regarded as typically Bostonian, is not an invariable rule. Actually the Proper Bostonian is more inclined to speak with a clipped "a." He says not Haa-vaad for the college he loves so well, but Hah-vud. He may leave out the "r" in a word like marbles, but he doesn't say maa-bles; he says mabbles. In a word like idea, he has even been known to add an "r."

— Cleveland Amory, *The Proper Bostonians*

The Kennedy Accents

I have never heard a JFK accent on the street. It is a combination of upper class Bostonian and the traditional Boston Irish accent.

I don't think the young of the upper classes are permitted to have Boston accents anymore: we're all speaking mid-Atlantic now. There are still a lot of people of all ages who have Boston Irish accents, or variations thereof. But the ones I've heard on younger children are weaker, and tend to become very diluted by the time they leave for college, and lost once they get there. There are lots of people our age with such accents, but they're the cops and the firemen: a Harvard guard actually did tell me, once, "Ya cahn't pahk ye cah in Hahvahd yahd."

My friends from the Congregation of the Sisters of Saint Joseph, who are all Boston Irish of a certain age, and many of the older people at town meeting, who have lived here for all their 80 years, have wonderful examples of a Boston accent. But it is definitely working class, not patrician as JFK's was.

For that matter, if you listen to Teddy Kennedy today, his accent is much less Boston Irish patrician than his brothers' were. And by the time he died, Bobby's accent was becoming more dilute, too. The accent doesn't seem to survive well when exposed to the other accents of the country.

I suspect the Kennedys were in a unique position. Old Joe was rich enough to send his kids to the best prep schools and to Harvard, and to give them all the advantages associated with that. But if they sounded Boston Brahmin rather than Southie, they'd have a hard time winning Boston elections. Hence this prep school/Irish Boston mix.

— Rene S. Mandel on the American Dialect Society Internet discussion list

There are also a few matters of vocabulary that are unique to Boston and give pause to visitors. In particular, in the Boston area what others call a soft drink is a *tonic* and what others call a milk shake is a *frappe*. Visitors beware: if you order a milk shake, it will be just that — flavored milk, but without ice cream.

Scrod is a kind of fish, a name of unknown origin that emerged in the nineteenth century. It's the generic name for catch of the day: something that might be small cod, haddock, or pollock. Cod has been so important to the city that a gilded wooden memorial known as the "Sacred Cod" is displayed in the State House.

Spucky or *spuckie* is yet another name for a submarine sandwich, used in a few Italian neighborhoods of Boston.

Wicked seems to be a favorite Boston intensifier, as in "He's wicked nuts!" an example from Adam Gaffin's "Wicked Good Guide to Boston English" on the Internet.

Then there's the traffic situation known as the *gawker blocker* or "gahkablahka," in Gaffin's transcription. As he says, "Only in Boston could you get 'gawker' and 'blocker' to rhyme."

In Boston if someone asks you to go to the *spa*, you won't be anticipating a session in a whirlpool. A *spa* is a local convenience store. Originally the name referred to the soda fountains found in the stores, where customers could get refreshed. Gradually the soda fountains were replaced by glass-doored refrigerators with cold drinks, but the name remained.

And in eastern New England at the start of the twentieth century, dry cleaning establishments were known as *cleansers*. At the start of the twenty-first century, most called themselves *dry cleaners* like their counterparts in the rest of the country, but the Boston Yellow Pages still list Bonney Bros. Cleansers, Emerson Cleansers, and Rocket Cleansers & Launderers, among others.

Boston, by the way, is called the "Hub City" because in the nineteenth century Oliver Wendell Holmes (father of the Supreme Court justice) called it the hub of the universe. Actually, he just said, "Boston State-House is the Hub of the Solar System." In any case, Bostonians got the idea, especially newspaper headline writers who found "Hub" conveniently short. A plaque on the sidewalk in front of Filene's downtown store marks the precise hub of the Hub of the universe.

CAPE COD, MARTHA'S VINEYARD, AND NANTUCKET

On Cape Cod, a four-lane divided highway has been called a *double-barrel* and a pine needle has been called a *diddledee*.

On the island known as Martha's Vineyard (drop the "r"s, please), a pronunciation has developed that helps distinguish true islanders from interlopers. The "long i" in words like *right* and *wife* is "uh-ee" instead of the "ah-ee" on the mainland and throughout the North. This distinctive pronunciation was once most prominent among natives who were fishermen but now seems to have become a general sign of loyalty to the island's traditional ways.

Nantucket, once the center of New England's whaling industry, gave its name to the *Nantucket sleigh-ride*, the fast towing of a whaleboat by a harpooned whale.

NEW HAMPSHIRE

New Hampshire is a good illustration of the fact that dialect boundaries do not necessarily follow state lines. In pronunciation and vocabulary, New Hampshire shares the general characteristics of eastern New England with its neighbors. If you look hard, you can find a distinctive word or two in New Hampshire, like *larbo*, an old-fashioned candy once made by pouring hot maple syrup on snow. With Maine it shares the terms *minge* for midge, a little stinging fly, and *crom* or *crawm* for food waste or worthless junk.

But in one respect, New Hampshire is strengthening its linguistic boundaries against "Taxachusetts" next door. Linguist Naomi Nagy of the University of New Hampshire finds that younger residents of New Hampshire just across the line from Massachusetts make an effort to be different. Right next to Massachusetts, half of those she interviewed said they pronounced *merry* the same as *marry* compared with ten percent of those interviewed in Massachusetts. One of the few east-west differences in American pronunciation is the word *marry*. Along the Atlantic coast it has the vowel of *hat*; to the west, in most of the rest of the country, *marry* has the same "short e" sound as *merry*. The boundary between the two pronunciations is especially distinct at the Massachusetts-New Hampshire border.

VERMONT

West of the Connecticut River from New Hampshire, Vermont has had a divided linguistic personality. The part of western Vermont that is near the river shares eastern New England speech patterns with New Hampshire; farther to the west, Vermont sounds like neighboring upstate New York, both in pronunciation and vocabulary. You can hear the euphemistic exclamation *jeezum crow!* in both of the latter places, for example.

Nowadays the western pronunciations seem to be moving east, making it harder to find old-fashioned Yankee speech anywhere in the state.

> **When Dwaine Marshall,** a logger who sold the family dairy farm in the early 1960s, confides that he never did like "ka-ows" much, it's cows he's referring to. And when Marshall proclaims, "I be 80 in June," his manner of speaking seems to symbolize Vermont as much as the plaid wool cap that sits on his head.
>
> — Molly Walsh, *Burlington Free Press*

A few vocabulary items appear to be unique to Vermont. An *apron*, in Vermont, can be a coating of thick liquid on a spoon; jelly or maple syrup is said to be ready when it *aprons* or *aprons off*. The *frog run* of sap taken from maple trees is the last one, so late in the season that frogs are beginning to be heard. And *lunge* or *longe* is a Vermont name for the fish known elsewhere as *lake trout*.

In Vermont as well as some other places, a ski hat is a *toque*. From the Vermont Teddy Bear Co. you can buy a Skier Bear "geared up in green snow overalls, purple fleece toque hat, and awesome sunglasses."

Vermont's contribution to American cuisine consists of twenty scoops of ice cream, four bananas, three chocolate chip cookies, a fudgy brownie, ten scoops of chopped walnuts, four ladles of hot fudge, and two scoops each of four toppings of your choice, all embellished with whipped cream. That's a *Vermonster*, named after the home state of Ben & Jerry's ice cream and available at their stores everywhere. If you prefer something lighter, you can get a *Bride of Vermonster*, with low-fat yogurt substituting for ice cream.

RHODE ISLAND

The smallest of the states is the only place where you'd want to drink a *cabinet*. That's what is known elsewhere in the country as a milk shake. Supposedly the Rhode Island version was invented by a pharmacist who kept his ice cream in a cabinet. If you ask for a milk shake in Rhode Island, as in Massachusetts, you'll get flavored milk without ice cream.

A *New York system* is something you can't get in New York. In Rhode Island, it's the name for a hot dog with everything on it. For dessert you might have *cob pie*, a deep-dish apple pie referred to elsewhere as pandowdy or apple cobbler. The pantry where it cools might be called a *closet* or *kitchen closet*.

While children in the rest of the country would play on a seesaw or teeter-totter, in western Rhode Island they might call it a *dandle* or *dandling board*. And children in Rhode Island might speak of *bandudelums*, large pieces of ice in salt water.

In Rhode Island and nearby southeastern Massachusetts, a *cade* is a farm animal raised by hand and treated as a family pet. *Cade* is also therefore a name for a spoiled child.

And you might hear of an *eaceworm* instead of an earthworm in Rhode Island.

CONNECTICUT

Geographically Connecticut is part of New England, but it's far enough west so that only its eastern half partakes of the eastern New England pronunciations. Western Connecticut therefore has more in common with upstate (and downstate) New York; in fact, a good part of the state is far enough south to be a suburb of New York City.

But there are a few words that are apparently distinctive to the state. Low-lying waterlogged grasslands are known in Connecticut as *bog meadows*. The state used to ship *box oysters* to New York City, oysters of medium size packed in boxes rather than barrels. And Connecticut is the home of the *glawackus*, a doglike monster that terrified the town of Glastonbury in 1939 but whose existence remains to be verified.

New York City and the Mid-Atlantic

NEW YORK CITY

Just as New England is Northern — with a difference — so is New York City. Who does not know the "Noo Yawk tawk" or "Brooklynese" so familiar from radio, movies, and television? And who in New York doesn't talk like that? Well, as it turns out, many New Yorkers don't, and for just the same reason the rest of us know it so well: radio, movies, and television.

Ever since they came into being in the early and mid twentieth century, the spoken media have given New Yorkese a bad reputation. They have put New York speech in the mouths of people we might enjoy listening to, but wouldn't necessarily want to be associated with: music-hall entertainers, petty criminals, ne'er-do-wells, the uneducated and the uncultured — even such unlikely characters as Bugs Bunny. Let an actor ask for a cup of coffee (make that "cawfee" or more precisely "co-uh-fee") and talk about 33rd Street (make that "toity-toid" or more precisely "tuh-eety tuh-id"), and with a word or two you've identified a lowlife, a stumblebum. Maybe with a good heart, but not much upstairs.

That's how Hollywood, out there on the Left Coast, has taught us to react to the city's famous sounds. (Curiously enough, Hollywood is often enough run by Noo Yawkers.) The result has been that natives and visitors alike look down on New York accents as lower class. And whether it is cause or effect, that perception is accurate: in New York City, the higher you go in social status, the less likely you are to sound like you're from New York.

It's striking how different New York City is from other great American cities in this regard. Take Boston, whose speech is not so different from that of New York. Both cities drop the "r" sound after vowels, for example, but insert "r" between words when the first ends with a vowel and the second begins with a vowel. That is, in both cities *law and order* can be heard as "lore and ohdah." Bostonians are happy to point this out; New Yorkers try not to say it. Or at least they don't brag about it.

On the Internet you'll find guides advertising the colorful speechways of other cities: "How to Speak like a Baastonian"; "Talking the Talk in Rhode Island"; "The Guide to Buffalo English"; "An Adventure in Pittsburghese"; "Hillbonics: Learn to Speak Southern West Virginian"; "Hey HON! The Bawlamerese Lexicon"; "Say What? A Lesson in 'New Orleansese'"; "Texas Talk"; "Las Vegas Lingo"; and "'Extreme Hawaii Fun' Pidgin." Notably missing are sites inviting you to talk like a New Yorker. Who would want to?

Well, it turns out, some people do. Some natives of the city, that is, and for the very reason that outsiders aren't interested in picking it up: New York talk is a way of showing that the city is yours. Speaking New Yorkese, you sound like you belong, you're tough, you

For much of the twentieth century, New York talk was mislabeled "Brooklynese." The New York style of speaking is certainly heard in Brooklyn, but it's prevalent in the other boroughs of the city as well. Researcher David Shulman found that the misnomer "Brooklynese" had its beginning in the title of an anonymous poem published in *The New Yorker* in 1926, the magazine's first year:

Brooklynese Champion 1926

I thought the winner had been found
The day I heard a woman make
The butcher cut her off a pound
Of fine and juicy soylern steak

Imagine then the dizzy whirl
That through my head did swiftly surge
The day I heard the gifted girl
Who wished departing friends "Bon Verge."

Shulman traces the fame of distinctive New York City speech back to the Irish-accented "Bowery b'hoys" of the early nineteenth century, especially as portrayed in the role of Mose the Fireman by actor Francis S. Chanfrau.

won't be pushed around. Exuding that bravado, New York talk has even expanded eastward out into Long Island (say that with a hard "g") along with a lot of exurbanite New Yorkers.

Within the city, for those reasons, New York talk isn't quite ready to be put on the list of Endangered Dialects. But it has been losing adherents, as more and more natives find advantage in speaking like the rest of the country, and as new immigrants to the city find little incentive to adopt it. It also has been losing some of its more blatant features.

(There is a little book called *New York Fun-ics*. It's published in Pennsylvania.)

New York City Pronunciation
"r" City   The New York accent is pronounced. There are a few words and phrases distinctive to the city, but most of the effect of New

Yorkese is its vowels and consonants. They make it identifiable in just a few words.

The humorous spelling "Noo Yawk" exemplifies in two syllables three of the features of New York speech. "Noo" is nothing new; it's the usual Northern pronunciation, not the "nyoo" more typical of the Southern states. But "Yawk" describes both a vowel and a consonant, or rather the absence of the latter.

That consonant is the "r" after vowels, missing in prime New York speech as it is in eastern New England and much of the Deep South. In a word that ends with a consonant after the letter *r*, the "r" sound just disappears: "cahd" for *card* or "buhn" for *burn*. In words that end with *r* like *ear, care,* and *four,* the "r" sound is replaced with an "uh" sound in a separate syllable, to make "ee-uh," "cay-uh," and "fow-uh" respectively. As in eastern New England, this is true *unless* a word starting with a vowel follows. In that case, when a word ending in "r" is followed by another word starting with a vowel, the "r" sound is retained, as in *ea"r"* of *corn; ca"r"e about it;* and *fou"r" apples.*

And, as in eastern New England, there's one more complication, or perhaps simplification. It's not just that New Yorkers keep the "r" if the next word begins with a vowel. They extend the rule to insert an "r" sound between vowels even when the first word has no hint of an "r," as in *the idea"r" of it.* This happens in eastern New England, too, but there the inhabitants seem more proud of it. When New Yorkers think about it, when they're in formal situations or being careful of their speech, they tend to switch from their special pattern to the usual Northern norm, pronouncing "r" in words like *card* and *burn* and avoiding it in *the idea of it.*

Linguist William Labov conducted a famous and highly efficient study of New Yorkers' use of "r" by visiting three department stores: upscale Saks, midrange Macy's, and down-to-earth Klein's. He asked store personnel for directions that would call for the response *fourth floor,* a phrase with two "r"s. He found the most "r"s at Saks, the fewest at Klein's; more "r"s when people were asked to repeat what they had said, and presumably were being more careful in their speech; more "r"s from the managers than the sales clerks, and more "r"s from the salesclerks than the stockboys. That was almost forty years ago, but the pattern still remains.

coffee, please   A second distinguishing feature of New York speech is the vowel sound in *all, walk, talk, dog,* and *caught;* the second syllable of *because;* and the first syllable of *coffee.* Americans generally pronounce this vowel much like the "ah" a doctor asks for in order to inspect one's throat. But New Yorkers are more close-mouthed about it. They pronounce the vowel with pursed or rounded lips, like the vowel in *grow,* so that *drawl* in New Yorkese sounds like *droll.* And that's why the *York* of *New York,* is often rendered with the "phonetic" spelling "Yawk."

Cup of Cawfee

toity-toid street   You won't find much "erl" on "toity-toid street" these days. These famous pronunciations — "oi" where the rest of the country has "er" and vice versa — have largely been shamed out of existence. In this style of speaking, words like *girl* and *learn* are pronounced something like "guh-il" and "luh-een." To a lesser extent the reverse also happens: "erl" for *oil* and "berl" for *boil.* In the "Brooklynese" poem quoted above, *soylern* shows both reversals, *sir* to "soy" and *loin* to "lern."

The well-known substitution of "t" or "d" for "th" in words like *this* and *third* is also heard only among more extreme versions of New Yorkese. Both of these became elements of New York City speech a century or so ago, courtesy of the Irish.

shh   Another Irish-derived feature of New Yorkese is the "sh" sound where other Americans have plain "s", as in "shelf" for *self;* "offish" for *office;* and "sherioush" for *serious.* It too is becoming rare.

dropping "h"   In most of the United States, the words *huge* and *human* start with an "h" sound, as their spelling indicates. In New York City and on Long Island, however, they are generally "yuge" and "yuman" respectively.

New York City is also noted for pronouncing the *g*'s in words like *singer, finger,* and *Long Island.*

And in New York speech in words like *bottle* and *kettle* the "t" sound can be just a catch in the throat.

New York words

Throughout the country millions of people get *on line* and wait *on line* every day at their computers. In New York City and its environs, you don't need a computer. You wait *on line* just by joining a line at a bank or a restaurant or a theater, any place where a human waiting line forms. It's what the rest of the country calls standing or waiting *in line*.

The New Yorker might be waiting on line for an *egg cream*. That's a drink made with soda water, milk, and chocolate syrup — but no eggs. (The original recipe had both eggs and cream.) Or maybe the New Yorker is standing on line for a *hero*, or what elsewhere might be called a *submarine sandwich*.

While you're standing on line, you might just *bunk into* someone you haven't seen for a while. That translates as *bump into*. And then you might go home to your *elevator apartment*. It might be a *floor-through*, taking up the entire floor of the building.

Being *ditzy* is a New York City twist on *dizzy*, as in scatter-brained or disoriented.

Children in New York City, at least in the past, played street games with a pink ball known as a *spaldeen*, made from the inside of a tennis ball by the Spalding Co. They also played *potsy* with a *potsy*: a hopscotch game with a beanbag. Playgrounds were equipped with *sliding ponds* or *sliding pons*, known elsewhere in the country simply as *slides*. And *aikie* or *aikies* was a children's way of demanding half of something somebody else found.

For extensive samples of New York City speech, listen to Brenda Monte and Mikey Russo, two of the four characters playing themselves in Nicholas Barker's 1998 documentary-comedy movie *Unmade Beds*.

NEW JERSEY

Just to the south of New York City, but still in the North of the United States, lies New Jersey, bounded by the Atlantic Ocean and the Delaware River. Not surprisingly, the speech of New Jersey resembles that of its neighbors. Northernmost New Jersey takes part in the speech patterns of New York City, as exemplified by the talk of Frank Sinatra. He was from Hoboken, N.J., just across the Hudson River from New York City.

The southwestern part of the state shares some vocabulary with Philadelphia, its neighbor across the Delaware River. In both places, to play hookey is to *bag school*. And a remote or obscure place is *Jabib* or *Japip*. Sometimes the middle of nowhere is known as the intersection of *Fifth and Japip*.

In Philadelphia and throughout New Jersey, the night before Halloween is known as *Mischief Night*. Camden, New Jersey, is renowned for its arson fires on that night. In 1991 the city had 300 arson fires on Mischief Night, and in 1996 almost that many. In Philadelphia, the Family Resource Network is concerned enough to issue a warning about Mischief Night, urging parents to "Go to a movie or go bowling with your children. Make Mischief Night a 'family night' and choose an activity everyone can enjoy."

Across the river in New York City, David Letterman spread the word about Mischief Night with his October 30, 1998, Top Ten list: "'Top Ten Hilarious Mischief Night Pranks To Play In Space' (No. 1: 'Egg the moon.')."

That night in New Jersey is memorable enough to have other names. "In northern New Jersey where I grew up," recalls one woman on the Internet, "the night before Halloween was called 'Goosey Night.' All the hoods and greasers snuck out and ran around soaping windows, egging cars, and tp-ing [toilet-papering] trees." It's also called "Cabbage Night," not just in New Jersey but also in New England, Ohio, and Wisconsin. The explanation is that pranksters would leave ill-smelling skunk cabbages on porches.

An important word in New Jersey and Pennsylvania is *shore*. In the rest of the country, people go to the beach, but New Jerseyites and Pennsylvanians (or at least Philadelphians) go to the shore. Sometimes it rates a capital letter. the *Shore* is the New Jersey Atlantic beachfront, from Sandy Hook on the north to Cape May on the south. For example, Mary Amoroso, the "Pressured Parent" columnist for the northern New Jersey newspaper, the *Bergen Record*, writes: "Do you let your child go to the shore or the city for a whole weekend of unsupervised activity that may include drinking and sex?" And a 4-H Club from Somerset County, also in northern

New Jersey, explains on the Internet: "When people come here we go to the shore, New York City, Statue of Liberty, Philadelphia, and have parties."

New Jersey is a place where you'll find *jug handles* alongside the roads. These are not fragments of empty vessels tossed aside by tippling travelers in the days of jug liquor, but elements of modern highway design. Jug handles are lanes that curve out to the right, then turn sharply left to cross the road at right angles, enabling an easy left turn. They get their name from their shape.

An important road innovation also bears the name of the state: the *Jersey barrier.* This is a tapered concrete slab, 32 inches high, used to keep vehicles from crossing a median into oncoming traffic and at the edge of roadways to keep cars on the road. It saves lives and prevents accidents by bouncing the vehicle back into the lane. Developed by the state highway department in the 1950s, it became known as the Jersey barrier as it was being adopted throughout the country. In 1998, the Rhode Island Public Transit Authority found another use for it, commissioning artists Bonnie Lee Turner and Cliff Clear to paint that state's longest mural on 45 Jersey barriers in Kennedy Park in Providence. The mural depicts different modes of transportation.

DELAWARE

Mason's and Dixon's line separating North and South dips down to keep Delaware on the side of the North, in contrast to its neighbor Maryland, which has a more Southern orientation. The difference reflects Delaware's close ties to Pennsylvania in colonial days. Delaware was granted to William Penn, the proprietor of Pennsylvania, in 1682, and the Delaware colony reported to the governor of Pennsylvania until 1776.

DELMARVA

Southern Delaware, however, is associated with Maryland and Virginia on the peninsula east of Chesapeake Bay appropriately known as *Delmarva.* That region is noted for its distinctive pronunciation of certain words with vowels *i, a,* and *o* followed by *r. Fire, barn,* and *corn* all are pronounced with the same "ahr" or "awr" sound.

Delmarva has *guts.* These are miniature creeks or streams, very narrow waterways connected to larger bodies of water.

And Delmarva has a particular use for *neither*, to mean "not any," as in "There used to be a lot of crabs here, but now there's neither one" and "Don't owe any man neither penny."

In older Delmarva usage, a *battery* was a deep-bottomed small boat in which a hunter could be concealed while shooting at wild-fowl. And a *bullnose* was a hard-shell clam too old and tough to eat.

The most famous contribution of Delmarva to the American vocabulary, however, as well as to its palate, is *crab cakes*. They are now widely known and available, but the fried crabmeat patties had their origin in Delmarva.

PENNSYLVANIA

Pennsylvania is a Northern state, on the north side of the Mason-Dixon Line, and its speech is basically Northern. But it is close enough to the South — embraced by West Virginia in its southwest corner — that Southern influences are increasingly heard toward the southern side of the state. And no other state, North, South, East, or West, has two such distinct centers of speech as Pennsylvania. Philadelphia at the eastern end has much in common with New Jersey, as previously mentioned. Pittsburgh on the other side of the Appalachians has its own westward orientation. Add to that Pennsylvania Dutch, and you have three major speech patterns distinctive to the state.

Pennsylvania cities are likely to have at their center a *diamond* instead of a square. A *square*, in Pennsylvania, more often refers to a city block.

In Pennsylvania and southern New Jersey, the area separating the opposite lanes of a four-lane road is known as the *medial strip*, instead of the *median* widely used elsewhere. *Medial strip* also happens to be the term in Hawaii.

It is mainly in Pennsylvania that bacon is still referred to by the Old English term *flitch*.

Among older terminology, Pennsylvania has *barn burners* in common with western Maryland and southern New Jersey. These aren't arsonists but wooden matches. You can use a barn burner to light a *hisser*, a defective firecracker that makes only a hissing sound.

And northern Pennsylvania has in common with upstate New York the name *horning* for the noisy celebration after a wedding, known elsewhere as a *shivaree*.

PHILADELPHIA

Alone among the major cities on the Atlantic coast, North or South, Philadelphia shows no inclination to drop the "r" after vowels. In that way, it's like most of the rest of the country to the west.

Philadelphia does, however, have its own distinctive pronunciations, which have been carefully studied over the past quarter century by the distinguished linguist William Labov and his Project on Language Change at the University of Pennsylvania. Here are a few examples of the complex patterns of pronunciation that make up the Philadelphia sound.

In Philadelphia, the "short e" has an "uh" sound when followed by an "r." So Philadelphia *very* sounds like "vurry"; *ferry* sounds like *furry*; and *merry* sounds like *Murray*. In fact, Philadelphia *merry* sounds exactly the same as *Murray*, though Philadelphians don't think so. Labov's researchers would ask one Philadelphian to read aloud a list of random *merry*s and *Murray*s, and another to note which word was said. The results were completely random, meaning that speakers and listeners could not distinguish between the two words. That made speakers and listeners so angry at each other that the *merry/Murray* test was dropped.

The "long e," in Philadelphia speech, comes out as a "short i," so you will hear, for example, of the Philadelphia "Iggles" in the National Football "Lig."

Speaking in 1905 to the graduating class at Bryn Mawr College near Philadelphia, Anglophile writer Henry James denounced the Philadelphia "short e" in his strongest language:

Let me linger only long enough to add a mention of the deplorable effect of the almost total loss, among innumerable speakers, of any approach to purity in the sound of the e. It is converted, under this particularly ugly light, into a u which is itself unaccompanied with any dignity of intention, which makes for mere ignoble thickness and turbidity. For choice, perhaps, "vurry," "Amurrica," "Philadulphia," "tullegram," "twuddy" (what becomes of "twenty" here is an ineptitude truly beyond any alliteration), and the like, descend deepest into the abyss. It is enough to say of those things that they substitute limp, slack, passive tone for clear, clean, active, tidy tone. . . .

Philadelphia has its own twist on the "short a" vowel of *man,
bag, hat,* and the like. As in other Northern cities away from the
Atlantic coast, the "short a" before *n* has an "ih-uh" sound, so *Ann*
becomes the same as *Ian.* The same is true when the "short a" is followed by *m* as in *jam; th* as in *bath; s* as in *pass*; and the "f" sound as
in *laugh* but generally not before other consonants. Thus, it does not
sound like the vowel of *Ian* in words like *bag* and *hat.* The rules and
exceptions for this pronunciation are so complex that only a person
who grows up in Philadelphia can master them.

Philadelphia's "long o" sound is often prefaced by a "short e"
sound. A Philadelphian has transcribed one resulting expression
semi-phonetically as "Yeowuh Jeowuh, threowuh the ball."

Sure in Philadelphia sounds the same as *shore.*

And for some Philadelphians, the consonant *s* at the start of a syllable is pronounced "sh," so you can hear a discussion of "shity
shtreets" without any criticism intended.

Philadelphia Words

Philadelphia also has some distinctive vocabulary of its own. There
is, to begin with, the *cheesesteak,* a venerable Philadelphia delicacy
whose name and fame still have not spread much beyond the city.
Take thin strips of steak, cover them with white cheese (anything
from provolone to Cheez Whiz) and sometimes onions and peppers,
enclose them in a long Italian roll, and you have a cheesesteak. It
was invented in the 1930s at a South Philadelphia place called Pat's
Steaks, where the first topping was pizza sauce instead of cheese.
According to *The Guinness Book of World Records,* the world's
largest cheesesteak was also made in Philadelphia. Weighing 1,790
pounds and stretching 365 feet 7 inches across a parking lot, it was
served in December 1998 to entice fans to a Philadelphia Eagles
home football game.

There are songs celebrating the Philadelphia Cheesesteak.
"Through the years I've seen lots of ladies and they all seem the same;
I need a taste of something exciting made the South Philly way," sings
the group WaXaNiMaLs. "Onions, relish, mayonnaise and a big bun,
fresh meat, dijonaise; greasy, steamy, melted cheese, one more bite
and I'm on my knees," rhapsodizes Big Bad Tough Guy.

Submarine: In Philadelphia, it's a hoagie.

Philadelphia is also the home of the *hoagie*, the sandwich that is elsewhere called a *submarine*. *Hoagie* is well known throughout the state, and southern New Jersey also uses the term.

In Philadelphia and parts of New Jersey, pedestrians walk on the *pavement*. That's the same as the sidewalks of New York and most of the rest of the country.

Philadelphians and some New Jerseyites push their infants around in a *baby coach* instead of the *baby buggy* or *baby carriage* spoken of elsewhere in the country.

With New Jersey, as mentioned before, Philadelphia shares the name and custom of *Mischief Night* on the night before Halloween, to *bag school*, and *Japip*. "All Mary's cookies are called biscotti," writes Ellen Diller, a baker and restaurant reviewer in nearby Lancaster, Pennsylvania. "These are not the hard, dunkable, crescent-shaped cookies available from here to Japip."

In boxing, even if you're not the best, you can hope for a *Philadelphia decision*, in which the judges vote for the home-town favorite, regardless of merit. During much of the twentieth century, despite or perhaps because of Philadelphia decisions, the city was a major venue for boxing. On the Internet, *Philadelphia decision* acquired another meaning in June 1996, when a three-judge panel in Philadelphia struck down the federal Communications Decency Act, allowing unlimited freedom of expression to continue. Internet postings refer to that action as the *Philadelphia decision*.

Philadelphia is in northern *you guys* territory, but for some Philadelphians "yous" is the singular and "yiz" the plural of the pronoun *you*.

PITTSBURGH

Far to the west in Pennsylvania, Pittsburgh is closer to the rest of the North than Philadelphia and in some ways shows it. Most notably, in Pittsburgh, and then in most of the country west of the Mississippi, the vowels of *caught* and *cot* sound alike. To the east, north, and south of Pittsburgh, most speakers use different vowels in *caught* and *cot*, or *Dawn* and *Don*. But Pittsburgh is where they begin to sound the same. If Dawn and Don are in the room, in Pittsburgh you won't be able to tell which one will respond when you call to one or the other.

Pittsburgh also has a language of its own. The sound that is spelled *ou* or *ow* is pronounced "ah" in Pittsburgh, as in "dahntahn" for *downtown*, "rahnd" for *round*, and "aht" for *out*. And the Pittsburgh plural for *you* is not *y'all* or *you guys*; it's *yinz*, derived from *you ones* but spoken as a single syllable.

Then there's the Pittsburgh term spelled *n'at* or *en at*, derived from *and that* and used simply for emphasis at the end of a statement. The example "What yinz doin en at?" on the Pittsburghese website is translated as "Tell me everything that you two are doing!"

Pittsburgh speakers, as well as those in many places to the west (but not east, south, or north) sometimes don't use *to be* with *need* or *want*: "This car needs washed" or, once again from the Pittsburghese website: "If yinz wants served, raise your hans."

Then there is the *jumbo sandwich*, filled with *jumbo*, which is just baloney elsewhere. A *jagger* is a thorn, and to *jag* is to jab. It's also just to fool around. Hence another possible sentence in Pittsburghese: "Quit jaggin around with dat jumbo." Other features indicated in Pittsburghese website transcriptions are more general in Northern urban vernacular and not limited to Pittsburgh, as *-in* rather than *-ing* and *dat* for *that*.

Pittsburgh and western Pennsylvania are noted for using *gumband* where most Americans would say *rubber band* or *elastic*. To *redd up* is to clean up or straighten up a table, room, or house. In that part of Pennsylvania, also, to be nosey is sometimes to be *nebby*, and a nosey person is a *neb-nose*. "Dawn is rilly nebby" in Pittsburghese translates to "Don is a really nosy fellow."

And the informal term *doc* can refer not only to a medical doctor but also to a dentist.

Pennsylvania German

Aside from William Penn's Quakers, one of the most important groups to arrive in Pennsylvania centuries ago seeking religious freedom was the Amish from Germany and Switzerland. Their language was German, and even today among the Amish there are those who speak German as a first language. Their German isn't the

Amish Children: When vacation is all, it's time to go to school.

same as the official language of present-day Germany, though; it's a distinctive variety known as "Pennsylvania German" or "Pennsylvania Dutch." That name has nothing to do with Holland; the German word for *German* (*Deutsch*) sounds like *Dutch* and because of anti-German sentiment during the world wars in the twentieth century, the pacifist Pennsylvania speakers of German preferred to be referred to as "Dutch."

Their German language has influenced the English language they and others speak in central Pennsylvania. The Pennsylvania German influence is heard in words such as *all* or *all anymore* meaning "all gone" or "dead," as in "The coffee is all" or "John is all." It is also heard in *for* meaning "to our disadvantage," as in "The horse died for us." Instead of waking up or falling asleep, in central Pennsylvania you can *get awake* and *get asleep*. And to rain or snow is to *make down*.

What others call gravy is *dressing* in Pennsylvania German territory.

Pennsylvania Germans have made famous the dish known as *scrapple*. It's made of ground pork and cornmeal, molded, sliced, and fried.

Dutch salad is dandelion greens with a hot dressing featuring bacon.

There is also the *funnel cake*, a Pennsylvania German specialty made by pouring dough through a funnel onto hot fat, moving the funnel so the dough spirals outward as it falls.

The Inland North

Northern Cities Shift

Northern speech has the advantage of being "normal" American English. But it also has the disadvantage. If you're "normal," how can you as an individual express your individuality? How can you let it be known that you're not just a face in the crowd? Or more precisely, how can you let it be known that your crowd is different from everyone else's?

The South doesn't have that problem. It distinguishes its speech from the American norm by being Southern.

Parts of the North also have no problem distinguishing their language. Maine, Boston, New York, Philadelphia, and Pittsburgh all have no trouble sounding different from "General American." A little Southern flavoring seeps into the southern and central parts of Ohio, Indiana, and Illinois. Wisconsin, Minnesota, and the Dakotas have their own Scandinavian and German-flavored styles of speech. But what about the heart of the North, clustered around the southern shores of the Great Lakes? Is there anything distinctive about this "true Northern" area?

Yes, there is. It's the "Northern Cities Shift."

That's the name given by linguist William Labov and fellow researchers at the University of Pennsylvania to the distinctive vowel sounds heard in this northern Great Lakes region. "The Northern Cities Shift is found throughout the industrial inland North and most strongly advanced in the largest cities: Syracuse, Rochester, Buffalo, Cleveland, Toledo, Detroit, Flint, Gary, Chicago, Rockford," Labov writes. It is called a shift because half a dozen vowels are shifted from their "normal" positions, beginning with the "short a" of *bad* or *family*.

Before venturing into particulars, it is important to recognize that not everyone there goes along with the Northern Cities Shift. In the eastern Great Lakes region, as in other parts of the country, there are many who opt for more neutral American English. It is a choice, often made subconsciously, between sounding local and sounding national. You can sound like you're from down home, or not. Some people are able to speak local to local pals and national to business associates; others have one style for all. But to the extent that you sound local, in upstate New York, lower Michigan, and northern Ohio, Indiana, and Illinois, you are likely to follow the Northern Cities Shift.

It begins with the "short a." In the Northern Cities Shift, the tongue goes up and to the front of its "normal" position, so that it becomes the "short i" vowel of *kid* or *bit*. At least, the shifted vowel starts out that way, but then it adds a twist back toward its "normal" sound. So *bad* is pronounced something like "biy-udd"; *cat* sounds like "kiy-utt"; *family* sounds like "fiy-umily"; and *man* sounds like "miy-un."

Here's an example. When British phonetician Ian Catford arrived on the campus of the University of Michigan, in the heart of Northern Cities Shift territory, some time ago, he was startled to hear a young woman call out his name. "Ian, Ian," she seemed to say as she hurried not to him but to another female student. The visiting linguist realized he hadn't been addressed at all. The young woman was calling her friend *Ann*, and the linguist had experienced the Northern Cities Shift.

Ian for *Ann* has been noted already as a characteristic of Philadelphia speech too. What makes Philadelphia different is that its shifted vowel occurs only before *n*, *m*, *th*, *s*, and *f*, while in the eastern Great Lakes area the shift takes place for every "short a."

When the "short a" has moved away from its usual position, it leaves an empty space in the pattern of vowels. That allows a short vowel usually pronounced with the tongue farther back to move forward. So, in the Northern Cities Shift, *cot* has the "normal" pronunciation of *cat*; *cod* sounds like *cad*; and *pop* is pronounced the way most people pronounce *pap*.

Larry Horn, a linguist at Yale University, tells of his encounter with this stage of the Northern Cities Shift as a student at the University of Rochester in upstate New York in the 1960s, when he talked for an hour "with a young woman from the area who seemed to be talking about *salads* and couldn't figure out what I was saying, since she meant *solids* as opposed to liquids."

What else? Well, the "short i" of *bit* and *kid,* displaced by the raised "short a," moves toward a "short u," making those words sound something like *but* and *kud* respectively. And the "short u" of *bud* moves to sound like the vowel of *bought,* so *busses* sounds like *bosses* to those who haven't made the shift.

Some people shift all these vowels, others just some. One person may say *Ann* as if it were *Ian* but use the "normal" pronunciation for *busses,* while another may say *bosses* for *busses* but keep the "normal" pronunciation of *Ann.* But these shifted vowels, in various combinations and to various extremes, are common in the eastern Great Lakes area.

The Inland North: "General American" States

Heading west from the Atlantic coast, and keeping not too far south of the Great Lakes, we begin to encounter the territory that makes up the heart of the North and that now serves as a model for "General American." It's not all McDonald's and KMart, though; in addition to the widespread Northern Cities Shift of vowels, different localities have individual ways of expressing themselves, and while some are unconscious of their distinctive speech, others proclaim and celebrate the sounds and words that set them apart from others.

NEW YORK STATE

To the north of Pennsylvania, and keeping away from the unique speech island of New York City, we find the vast area of New York State known as Upstate. The primary influence on its language came from New England — western New England, that is, the part that does not drop its "r"s or shuffle its vowels. Upstate New York is fundamentally Northern in its speech.

There are just a few words whose domain is limited to parts of New York State. Dutch settlement along the Hudson has left its trace in *clove,* a word for a mountain pass or gap. A *kill,* also from the Dutch, is a stream or channel. It's found in placenames like Catskill and Wynantskill. In central New York State, *gulf* is sometimes used for a gulch.

The Upstate menu includes *beef on weck*, beef sprinkled with coarse salt and caraway seed in a hard roll. The roll, called a *kimmelweck*, is a staple in Buffalo. That city on Lake Erie at the western edge of the state also has given its name to a delicacy of modern American cuisine: *Buffalo wings*. These are not pinions of flying bison but spicy chicken wings, said to have first been served at Frank and Teresa's Anchor Bar in Buffalo. As their fame spread, they took on the name of the city that gave them birth.

The Polish pastry spelled *chrusicki* or *chrusciki* is also well known in Buffalo, thanks in part to the EM Chrusicki Bakery downtown. Dough made with sour cream is shaped like a bow tie — not an easy task — and baked or fried, then sprinkled with powdered sugar. Chrusciki aren't limited to Buffalo, however, but are familiar in Polish-American communities elsewhere: Philadelphia, Milwaukee, and Williamstown, New Jersey, just to mention a few. Martha Stewart, whose mother is Polish, has a chrusciki recipe on her website. She stacks the finished chrusciki so they resemble a Christmas tree.

Buffalo partakes fully in the Northern Cities Shift. The "short a" in words like *family* can be heard as "fiy-umily"; *pot* and *box* can be shifted to sound like "pat" and "backs"; and *bed* and *rest* can become "bud" and "rust." The "long i" as in *I*, *night*, and *fine* can also change to a sound more like the "long a" of *fate* or *pain*. There are differences within Buffalo too, what linguist Wolfgang Wolck calls "ethnolects" for neighborhoods with different ethnic backgrounds, notably Polish and Italian. Polish ethnolects substitute the "t" sound for "d" at the end of words like *cold*, for example; the Italian is marked by heavy stress on words or word groups and a lower pitch of the voice.

OHIO

Moving west along the southern shore of Lake Erie, across the neck of Pennsylvania that includes the city of Erie, we come to Ohio. Like its neighbors to the east and west, Ohio has varieties of speech that are layered from north to south, with Northern the norm at the north and an outpost of Southern at the south. Northern Ohio was the home of John Samuel Kenyon, earlier mentioned as the author of definitive books on American pronunciation who took his own way of speaking as the norm.

The westward tide of American English can be heard in old recordings of American presidents from Ohio. Shortly before he died, William McKinley (1843–1901; president, 1897–1901) recorded a campaign speech demonstrating his decidedly British or at least eastern New England accent, declaiming about "govenment" and "mahkets" and "the Civil Wah." But the next Ohioan to be president, William Howard Taft (1857–1930; president, 1909–13) had a strong "r" pronunciation in *war, world, forward*, and all other such words.

Ohio is known as the "Buckeye State" in tribute to the *buckeye* trees that once abounded in the Ohio River valley in the southern part of the state. That tree, in turn, got its name from the resemblance of its fruit to the eye of a buck deer. Then in the 1820s settlers in the Ohio valley — in Kentucky, Indiana, and Illinois as well as Ohio — began to be referred to as *buckeyes*. Eventually Ohio got the *buckeye* distinction all for itself.

A number of words are distinctive to Ohio. A person others would call a *hillbilly* is in parts of Ohio a *hilliken*, and a railroad of small significance can be called a *hoodlebug*. In northern and eastern Ohio, the large short-lived insect others call a *mayfly* is known as a *Canadian soldier*. And only in Ohio is the syrup you put on ice cream sometimes called *dope*.

Akron and Cleveland in northeastern Ohio speak of the *devil's strip*. This is not a hellish part of town but simply the grass area between sidewalk and curb. The name apparently resulted from a legal dispute when a property owner and the city both disclaimed responsibility for maintaining the strip. The judge declared that it must belong to the devil, and the name stuck.

For some reason the city of Cleveland lent its name to a men's fashion in vogue several decades ago: the *Full Cleveland*. According to a 1982 *Washington Post* article on the subject, "The 'Full Cleveland' is a celebration of bad — no rotten — taste in clothing: a powder blue double knit leisure suit, bright blue and yellow flower patterned shirt with cuffs turned back over the jacket sleeves, white vinyl belt and matching loafers."

Marzetti's, an Italian restaurant in downtown Columbus, was the originator of a delicacy called *Johnny Marzetti* that appears on school menus in Ohio and surrounding states. At home you can make Johnny Marzetti with canned soup, noodles, and ground beef.

> **Goetta season,** if there is such a thing, seems to begin at back-to-school time in late August and continue through the fall. Goetta is an obvious hit as a breakfast food, served alongside bacon, eggs, fried apples or apple sauce, or with an egg on top. But it isn't just for breakfast anymore. Some people make goetta, lettuce, and tomato sandwiches, goetta turkey stuffing and goetta-and-cheese hors d'oeuvres.
>
> — *Insiders' Guide to Cincinnati*

The restaurant has long since closed, but the Marzetti Company is still in Columbus, famous for salad dressing.

Cincinnati enjoys *goetta*, pronounced "get a," a delicacy consisting of ground sausage meat mixed with oatmeal. It is first boiled, then cooled in a mold, sliced, and fried.

And then there is *Cincinnati chili*, often made with cinnamon and cocoa or chocolate as well as the usual spices. It's an acquired taste, not always appreciated by visitors; Bette Midler is said to have called it "Satan's own baby food."

Cincinnati chili is more watery than conventional chili because it functions as a sauce for spaghetti rather than as a dish in itself. But a true meal of Cincinnati chili doesn't stop with the spaghetti and the chili topping. Cincinnati restaurants serve it three-way, four-way, and five-way. "Three-way" adds a layer of American cheese; "four-way" adds onions under the cheese; and "five-way" adds red kidney beans above the onions and under the cheese. It's traditionally served with oyster crackers and two *Coney Islands* or *cheese coneys*, small hot dogs in buns topped with shredded cheese. (The term *Coney Island* or *Coney* for a hot dog is widely known. It derives from the marketing appeal of the name of New York's famous beach and amusement park. Cincinnati's coneys usually are miniature and are spelled without capital letters).

Credit for inventing Cincinnati chili in the 1920s goes to Athanas Kiradjieff, who founded Empress Chili. Empress eateries are still around today, but the current leading contenders for the best chili in Cincinnati are the Skyline Chili chain, founded by Nicholas Lambrinides in 1949, and the Camp Washington Chili Parlor, founded about 1940 by Steve Andon and Fred Zannbus. "Camp's chili just tastes better," writes columnist Emily Landers of the University of

Cincinnati's *News Record*. "It is smoother, sweeter, and has a meat taste Skyline misses. One can tell Johnny [the owner] makes that chili from scratch everyday."

INDIANA

One hardscrabble down-on-its-luck word has found a welcome in Indiana. The word is *Hoosier*, so beloved in Indiana that its official nickname is the "Hoosier State."

Hoosier, spelled in a variety of ways, was just another uncomplimentary label for someone from the backwoods when it arrived in Indiana not long after the first English-speaking settlers. No one knows its origin, but there has been no lack of proposals. Some say *Hoosier* derives from an English dialect word meaning "high hills." Others find the origin in a prominent early settler named Hoosier whose employees were known as "Hoosier's men." Still others speculate that visitors to an Indiana cabin would announce their presence by calling "Who's 'ere?" James Whitcomb Riley, the great "Hoosier Poet" (1849–1916), said with tongue in cheek that its derivation was "Whose ear?" — uttered in a tavern the morning after a fight by patrons who saw a bitten-off ear lying on the floor.

In any case, on the first of January, 1833, the Indiana meaning of *Hoosier* was established for once and for all by a humorous poem in the *Indianapolis Journal* that was reprinted throughout the country and around the world. It describes a traveler's visit to a "Hoosher's Nest," that is, a cabin inhabited by a crude but hospitable Hoosier couple and their children, "half a dozen Hoosheroons." This poem by John Finley made Indianans proud, and they have called themselves *Hoosiers* ever since.

Outside Indiana, however, *hoosier* takes on a different meaning. In St. Louis, two states away, *hoosier* is a great insult. "What is a hoosier?" asked *St. Louis Post-Dispatch* columnist Elaine Viets in 1990, and gave this answer: "A mean, nasty degenerate who infests city neighborhoods. Hoosiers often come from the country, and go back there every weekend and during hunting season. Do not confuse hoosiers with rednecks, who are simply ill-bred louts."

Even within Indiana, there are differences of opinion about *Hoosier*. The chair of the Folklore Institute at Indiana University

> **In its original** acceptation it was equivalent to "Ripstaver," "Scrouger," "Screamer," "Bulger," "Ring-tailroarer," and a hundred others, equally expressive, but which have never attained to such a respectable standing as itself. By some caprice which can never be explained, the appellation Hoosier became confined solely to such boatsmen as had their homes upon the Indiana shore, and from them it was gradually applied to all Indianians, who acknowledge it as good naturedly as the appellation of Yankee. Whatever may have been the original acceptation of Hoosier, this we know, that the people to whom it is now applied, are amongst the bravest, most intelligent, most enterprising, most magnanimous, and most democratic of the Great West, and should we ever feel disposed to quit the state in which we are now sojourning, our own noble Ohio, it will be to enroll ourselves as adopted citizens in the land of the "HOOSHIER."
>
> *— Cincinnati Republican,* 1833

noted that students from southern Indiana were proud of calling themselves Hoosiers, while those from the north found the name embarrassing.

One of the staunchest defenders of the proud definition of *Hoosier* was Dan Quayle, Vice President of the United States from 1988 to 1992. In 1987, while still a U.S. Senator, Quayle took umbrage at New York senator Alfonse D'Amato's remark that Indiana University's basketball team would lose to Syracuse because, according to one dictionary's definition, Hoosiers were "awkward, unskilled, ignorant," and inclined "to loaf on or botch a job." When his protest to the dictionary publisher failed to get the derogatory definition erased, and after Indiana won the game, Quayle introduced a non-binding resolution to define a Hoosier as "someone who is quick, smart, resourceful, skillful, a winner, unique, and brilliant." But even a U.S. Senate resolution wasn't enough to change the dictionary.

Indiana is at the center of a three-state area (including western Ohio and southern Illinois) where a potluck meal is sometimes called a *carry-in.* But Indiana's distinctive name for that kind of meal is a *pitch-in dinner.* The N.K. Hurst Company of Indianapolis (motto: "We Know Beans"), for example, promotes the use of its HamBeens Great Northerns in a recipe for Rosalie's Baked Beans: "an outstanding dish at picnics, family reunions, and pitch-in dinners."

Indiana is also the westernmost of the four states where the shoulder of a road is known as a *berm*.

ILLINOIS

For most residents of the state, there is no "noise" in Illinois. That is, the *s* at the end of the state's name is silent, more often when spoken of by residents than when discussed by outsiders.

For some residents, also, there is nothing "ill" in their state. Those who don't speak "ill" of Illinois say "ell-annoy" instead. They are the ones who drink "melk" instead of *milk* and lay their heads on a "pellow" at night. That pronunciation — with "short e" before an "l" sound — isn't used by everyone in Illinois, nor is it limited to that state; it's also heard in Arkansas, Iowa, Minnesota, Long Island, and Baltimore, among other places, and is said to be characteristic of Down East Maine as well. But Illinois can claim to be in the center of "melk" production. Curiously enough, this "short e" pronunciation is limited to those few words mentioned above. "Ell-annoy" speakers of their ilk pronounce *ilk* and *silk* and other *il* words with the usual "short i."

Although Illinois officially calls itself the "Prairie State," it has been called by some the "Sucker State" and its residents *Suckers*. This is reminiscent of its eastern neighbor, the Hoosier State, except that Illinois residents don't care much for their nickname and few use it anymore. One theory of the origin of this label is that thirsty early settlers actually used straws to suck up water from waterholes; another is that the men who first worked the lead mines in Galena, Illinois, went up the Mississippi to Galena in the spring and down to their Missouri homes in the fall, like migrating sucker fish.

For distinctive vocabulary Illinois has *hard road*, meaning a paved road, a term confined mainly to central and southern Illinois. Also distinctive to central Illinois is the *horseshoe*, a culinary contribution from Springfield, the state capital. A central Illinois horseshoe consists of melted cheese on top of shaved meat on top of french fries on top of a slice of white bread. If you can't stomach a whole horseshoe, you can order a smaller portion known as a *pony*.

Chicago, Illinois, is the adopted home of *clout* — not a knockdown punch, but a specific form of political influence perfected in the Windy City. The term seems to have originated in New York City; the earliest known appearance of *clout* in its political sense is in a

Elanoy

Way down upon the Wabash, such land was never known;
If Adam had passed over it, the soil he'd surely own.
He'd think it was the garden he'd played in as a boy,
And straight pronounce it Eden in the State of Elanoy.

Chorus:
Then move your fam'ly westward,
Good health you will enjoy,
And rise to wealth and honor in
The state of Elanoy.

'Twas here the queen of Sheba came, with Solomon of old.
With bullock's load of spices, pomegranates and fine gold;
And when she saw this lovely land her heart was filled with joy
Straightway she said "I'd like to be a queen in Elanoy."

She's bounded by the Wabash, the Ohio and the Lakes.
She's crawfish in the swampy lands, the milk-sick and the shakes.
But these are slight diversions and take not from the joy
Of living in this garden land, the state of Elanoy.

Away up in the northward, right on the borderline
A great commercial city, Chicago, you will find.
Her men are all like Abelard, her women like Heloise
All honest virtuous people, for they live in Elanoy.

Last chorus:
Then move your family westward,
Bring all your girls and boys
And cross at Shawnee Ferry to
The State of Elanoy.

— Mid-nineteenth-century song

[Note: milk-sick was a sickness that affected milk cows; shakes is fever or ague.]

letter Walt Whitman wrote there in 1868. But in the twentieth century, Chicago took it over. In the rest of the country *clout* conveys the simple sense of political power, but in Chicago it has the nuance of power derived from connections with a higher-up.

In 1967 Chicago newspaperman Mike Royko devoted a whole column to the Chicago definition of *clout*, illustrating its proper use with a sample of what a bailiff might say: "Somebody beefed that I was kinky and I almost got viced, but I saw my Chinaman and he clouted for me at the hall." He translated that as: "A citizen complained that I did something dishonest and I was almost fired, but I contacted my political sponsor and he interceded in my behalf with my department head."

It has also been claimed that Chicago's Greektown was, in 1968, the first place in the United States to offer *gyros*, the sandwich of lamb roasted on a spit and wrapped in pita bread with onions, tomatoes, and sour cream.

Chicagoans speak of the *hawk*, the cold wind of winter. Its name is said to have been inspired by an African-American trumpet player, Erskine Hawkins (1904–69), "The 20th Century Gabriel" who was known for his "cold blast." Since 1886, incidentally, Chicago has been known as the Windy City, an appellation spread by the editor of the Louisville (Kentucky) Courier-Journal in response to Chicago's promotion of itself as the "Garden City."

MICHIGAN

While Pennsylvania, Ohio, Indiana, and Illinois are fully Northern only at their northern ends, Michigan is Northern in its language through and through. The lower peninsula also partakes of the Northern Cities Shift mentioned earlier.

And what about the Michigan vocabulary? Sometimes it takes just one person to make a difference. Only one person seems to know about the *Michigan handshake*, but that person is advice columnist Ann Landers. Her use of the term in a 1996 column prompted more than 5,000 letters asking about it. "It's a firm, nononsense grasp that means 'goodbye' and lets the recipient know you really mean it," she explained to her national audience. Two years later a letter from a puzzled Michigan reader prompted her to explain again: "A Michigan handshake is a firm grasp that means

'Goodbye, adios, it's all over.' I first heard this phrase applied to the losing candidate when G. Mennen 'Soapy' Williams was elected governor of Michigan."

That would have been in 1948. Researchers at the Michigan Electronic Library were unable to trace it. Nowadays you won't find Michiganders, or anyone else, using the term. But the Iowan Ann Landers keeps the Michigan handshake alive in her column.

There's a little more currency in *Michigan Bankroll*, a wallet stuffed with one-dollar bills or a roll with a big bill on the outside and one-dollar bills inside. Why it should be "Michigan," nobody knows.

Detroit has *Devil's Night* as its distinctive term. That's the night before Halloween, the same as *Cabbage Night*, *Goosey Night*, and *Mischief Night* in New Jersey and elsewhere. And like those nights in New Jersey, Devil's Night in Detroit has been noted for arson. In 1984, Detroit had 810 reported fires on the three nights October 29 through 31. Detroiter Eunice Park wrote in *Asian Week* in December 1999: "Oct. 30 still remains Devil's Night — the phenomenon described by author Ze'ev Chavets in the early 1990s as the ultimate manifestation of urban rage and African-American rage against an unresponsive Caucasian government. The weary, wary remains of Devil's Night stand on every street corner, reminders of the city's incontrovertible decay."

In 1995 the city began a campaign to change the name to "Angel's Night," with billboards declaring "Help Stop Arson in Detroit." Gangs were enlisted to help, and volunteers patrolled the streets to discourage fires. By 1999, the number of fires between October 29 and 31 had been reduced to 182.

Elsewhere in Michigan, a *fish tug* is a boat used for commercial fishing. The term is also known in Wisconsin. You can see a restored fish tug of the 1930s, the 48-foot *Bob S*, at the historical society of Beaver Island, Michigan. Or you can dive down 20 feet by Silver Island near Traverse City and see the well-preserved wreck of the 35-foot fish tug *Victory*.

Michigan is also the home of the once-common *Mackinaw boat*, made of wood, pointed at both ends, and often with a mast or two for sails.

If you ask for a *lunch roll* in Michigan, you may get an oblong doughnut or sweet roll, sometimes with filling.

Fish Tug: The *Bob S,* Beaver Island Historical Society, Michigan

Southwest Michigan has a Dutch flavor, centering on a city appropriately named Holland. There at the Queen's Inn, for example, you can find a Dutch pea soup known as *erwten soup,* pronounced to rhyme with *certain.* Some call it *snert* instead, pronounced just as it looks. Erwten soup is also available at other Dutch places like Caramel Cookie Waffles, a Dutch cafe in Billings, Montana.

Another Dutch dish of southwest Michigan, which you can also get at the Queen's Inn, is *hutspot,* a vegetable stew featuring potatoes, often made with meat.

With Upstate New York, Michigan shares the term *brush* or *brush cut* for a crew cut haircut.

Wilderness campers all over the country know to dig a *cathole* to contain human waste without disturbing the environment. In Michigan, however, a *cathole* can be something cleaner, a small deep place in a pond or river.

Michigan shares some features with the other states of the northern Great Lakes. In Michigan, Wisconsin, and Minnesota you can hear *baga* for rutabaga, and what is elsewhere a serviceberry is called in the northern parts of those states a *Juneberry.* The fish commonly called *burbot* has a different name in northern Michigan,

Wisconsin, and Minnesota. There it is known as a *lawyer*, with a nineteenth-century explanation that "he ain't of much use, and is the slipriest fish that swims."

Michigan, Wisconsin, and Minnesota territory is also where crowds gather for *booya*, a stew of meat and vegetables and sometimes the name for a festival featuring that dish. In 1999, for example, the volunteer fire department of Apple Valley, Minnesota, held a fund-raising "booya bingo," and Finland, Minnesota, held a "Harvest Booya & Finn Fest."

The northernmost part of Michigan, separated from the rest of the state by Lake Michigan, is called the Upper Peninsula. Some denizens of that chilly, demanding land enjoy calling themselves *Yoopers*, from the initials *U.P.* A band called Da Yoopers has such memorable songs as "Second Week of Deer Camp" and "Da Fishing Trip (One Can Short of a Six Pack)." Near Ishpeming they operate Da Tourist Trap, "one of the seven wonders of Yooperland," with displays like the world's largest working chainsaw.

The Inland North: North North Central States

Detective Sibert? Yah, this is Marge Gunderson from up Brainerd, we spoke. Yah. Well, actually I'm in town here. I had to do a few things in the Twin Cities, so I thought I'd check in with ya about that USIF search on Shep Proudfoot . . . Oh, yah? . . . Well, maybe I'll go visit with him if I have the . . . No, I can find that . . . Well, thanks a bunch. Say, d'ya happen to know a good place for lunch in the downtown area? . . . Yah, the Radisson . . . Oh, yah? Is it reasonable?

— Fargo (1996)

O yah, you betcha! Far from the East and West Coasts, and as far as you can go north in the United States, is the language characterized and caricatured in the 1996 movie *Fargo*. This style of speech has some distinctive turns of phrase, as illustrated above. It also retains a bit of the Scandinavian and German accents of the immigrants from northern Europe who looked for comfortably cold places to settle in the United States. The North North Central accent especially affects the long vowels. Take the expression *OK*, for example. If you say it slowly in most dialects of English, it sounds like "owe-kay," with a "w" sound at the end of the "long o" and a "y" at the end of the "long a." In the North North Central accent, however, the long vowels are unwavering, and *OK* is more like "ohh-keh."

To put it more generally, in most dialects of English, long vowels usually "glide" up or down at the end rather than staying the same. But in Wisconsin, the Upper Peninsula of Michigan, Minnesota, and the Dakotas, where the North North Central accent is heard, such vowels follow the pattern of other European languages and do not glide. So the names of the states can be a giveaway: The third syllable of *Minnesota* and the second of *Dakota* are "owe" when visitors say these names but "ohh" in the mouths of natives.

There's also some Canadian influence this far north in the United States. As is the case in northern New England, so here in the northern Midwest the *ou* in words like *out*, *about*, and *house* has the sound "uh-oo" rather than the usual American "ah-oo."

As in other parts of the country, not everyone puts on the local accent. Ethan and Joel Coen are from Minnesota and enshrined its distinctive ways of speech in their Academy Award-winning script for *Fargo*, but they themselves talk a more neutral Northern. Likewise, tales of fictional Lake Wobegon are told with just a hint of a Minnesota accent by "Prairie Home Companion" radio host Garrison Keillor. His accent, and that of others in the far north, sometimes changes the sounds made by ending letters *b*, *d*, or *g* to the "p," "t," or "k" sounds, respectively, so *tab* sounds like "tap"; *head* sounds like "het"; and *dog* sounds like "dok."

WISCONSIN

Wisconsinites say they can tell "foreigners" just by their pronunciation of the name of the state. Visitors are likely to say "Wis-CON-sin," but natives put the first "s" sound at the start of the second syllable: "Wi-SCON-sin."

In addition to sharing in the North North Central pronunciations, Wisconsin has some distinctive words of its own. Because it is the home state of the great *Dictionary of American Regional English*, for which the editors conducted a preliminary "Wisconsin English Language Survey," the vocabulary of Wisconsin has had expert scrutiny. The experts confirm that:

In Wisconsin a drinking fountain is a *bubbler*, especially if it is outdoors and has a continuous flow. An on-line newspaper for the state of Wisconsin is called the *Bubbler*, with its address thebubbler.com. This name is also heard in nearby northern Illinois, and in some places along the northern Atlantic coast.

In Wisconsin, people who don't wait their turn for a bubbler or anything else are said to *budge in line.*

Flowage in Wisconsin refers not only to water that overflows the banks of a river but also to a lake created with overflow water.

In the east central part of Wisconsin, you can add *inso* to a statement to mean "Isn't that right?"

Wisconsin seems to have originated the idea of the "golden birthday," the once-in-a-lifetime day when your age in years is the same as the day of the month on which you were born. It calls for special celebration.

The ethnic heritage of Wisconsin is reflected in its distinctive foods. Among the culinary treats of Wisconsin is the *Berliner,* a jelly-filled sweet roll more widely known in the upper Midwest as a *bismarck,* and also sometimes (but not in Chicago) called a *Chicago.* There are *kolaches,* Czech pastries filled with fruit or cheese, also known beyond the boundaries of the state. And there is the Danish *kringle,* a ring-shaped pastry that bakeries in Racine, Wisconsin, now ship all over the country. *Lefse,* common in Minnesota as well as Wisconsin, is a flat Norwegian bread made with potatoes by bakers like the Countryside Lefse Company of Blair, Wisconsin. Other Wisconsin delicacies are cold *cherry soup,* a dish of Hungarian ancestry, and hot *German potato salad.*

The highlight of "A Taste Of The North Coast" will, of course, be the food. Students from the Culinary Management program, under the direction of Instructors David Knutson and David Cifrese, have prepared a menu of cold and hot hors d'oeuvres which run the gamut from "good ol' Packer Sunday" fare — such as bratwurst and cheddar fondue — to elegant delicacies using regional foods — such as venison and blue cheese logs with beer bread, lake perch casino, and smoked lake trout puffs.

— Website announcement from Wisconsin Indianhead Technical College-Ashland, on Lake Superior

The *brat*, more formally the *bratwurst*, also from Germany, is a pork sausage that takes the place of hot dogs in the buns of Wisconsin. Increasingly it is also available elsewhere as an upscale alternative to the hot dog. *Brat* is pronounced to rhyme with *hot* rather than *hat*. Traditionally the brat in its bun is covered with sauerkraut, but now it takes whatever the hot dog can. In Wisconsin the brat is so venerated that you can buy a facsimile of a brat to be worn as a hat. Its maker, the Celebrat Corporation of Plymouth, Wisconsin, describes the "Brat Topper" as "A panorama of six brilliant colors depicting a double brat, with-the-works, on a semmel-style hard roll."

Much better known than the Brat Topper is the *cheesehead*, a lightweight sculpture of a large piece of cheese worn as a hat. This is in tribute to the state's leadership in the dairy industry and also to show support for the state's athletic teams, especially the Green Bay Packers. Thanks to this headgear, Wisconsinites are now widely known instate and out as *cheeseheads*. The appellation is too recent to have made the 1985 first volume of the *Dictionary of American Regional English*, whose only definition for *cheesehead* is "a stupid, awkward person." Like *Hoosier* in Indiana, Wisconsin has transformed a derogatory epithet into a term of pride.

Green Bay, Wisconsin has given its name not only to the Packers football team but to a big bug that comes out of its shell for a day or two early in the summer and flies around in great swarms, not biting anybody but still causing a nuisance. It generally goes by the name *mayfly*, because it makes its first appearance in May, but in Wisconsin and across the lake in Michigan it's also known as a *Green Bay fly*.

In both Wisconsin and Minnesota, *ish* is an expression of disgust, and something that is *ishy* is something disgusting.

A *jackpine savage* in those states is an ignorant person from back in the woods. Spooner, Wisconsin celebrates its Jackpine Savage Days every summer with a carnival and entertainment.

In Wisconsin, as well as in Indiana and a few other places, the light that controls traffic is sometimes called a *stop and go light*. One traveler in Ashland, Wisconsin described a shopping experience like this: "I asked if there was a NAPA store in town and he said, 'Ya, sure there's one just around the corner. You just take a right out of the parking lot, take a right at the stop and go light, go two blocks and you can't miss it.' So I went down to the stop and go light, took a right and sure enough, after a couple of blocks there's the NAPA store. I told the fella I needed a new fan belt and some other stuff, and what do ya know but it wrecked a twenty dollar bill."

You get the full flavor of Wisconsin speech in the song "Com'ere Once" written by J. Krueger for the Happy Schnapps Combo of Manitowoc, Wisconsin. The song tells of a stranger who is baffled by a Wisconsinite's invitation:

> Com'ere once . . . com'ere once . . . for cry I come by here
> We'll have a brat and kraut and den a couple two tree beers
> Or you can go dere by dat bubbler, but don't you budge in line
> She's a nice day out, ain' so

MINNESOTA

If you travel far enough north in Michigan or Wisconsin, you'll reach the Great Lakes. If you travel far enough north in Minnesota, you'll reach Canada. So as mentioned earlier, in addition to the *Fargo* accent, and like northern Maine, northern Minnesota has some Canadian characteristics as well.

In most of the United States, the sound made by the letters *ou* (as in *out* or *house*) and also the "long i" sound (as in *I* or *right*) begin with an "ah." Many Canadians begin both with an "uh" instead, so *out* is pronounced "uh-oot" and *right* is "ruh-eet." Linguists call this "Canadian raising" because the tongue is raised from the "ah" position to make "uh." You'll hear more and more "Canadian raising" as you get close to the northern border of Minnesota.

Canadians are sometimes called the "eh team" because of the Canadian propensity to end statements with a little question, eh? That's also heard in the United States near the Canadian border. Makes sense, eh?

Northern Minnesota also shares with Canada and Alaska the kind of swamp known as *muskeg*. It consists of a top layer of peat moss, which absorbs large amounts of water, with other slowly decaying plants underneath. Trees find it hard to gain footing in muskeg, but other plants thrive in the wet acid soil, and flowers bloom in muskeg in the brief summers. Watch your step, though; even where it looks dry, muskeg is wet. The U.S. Forest Service warns that "stepping on muskeg is like stepping on a sponge."

The Norwegian heritage of Minnesota and nearby states is heard in the common expression *uff da*. Literally it means something like

"Well, then!" Figuratively, Minnesotans and Wisconsinites use it in place of *oops*, *ouch*, *good grief*, or stronger expressions of surprise and disgust. Humorists explain that *uff da* is "eating a delicious sandwich and then discovering the spread is cat food" or "waking yourself up in church with your own snoring."

Minnesota is one of the few places outside of Sweden where you can get *ostkaka*, a Swedish curd cake or cheesecake. Ingredients include rennet and almonds as well as milk, cream, flour, and sugar.

When Nat King Cole sang about "Those Lazy Hazy Crazy Days of Summer," he wasn't thinking of the upper Midwest. In the far northern United States, summers are too short for lazy. But they do provide an opportunity for retailers to go crazy. Downtown merchants in towns in the far northern United States, from Michigan west to Idaho, use the term "Crazy Days" for sidewalk sales that are also community celebrations. In Minnesota, for example, there are Crazy Days far to the northeast in Grand Marais on Lake Superior, to the west in Battle Lake, and in Hutchinson and North St. Paul in the south. Northern winters are too cold for loitering on sidewalks, but that doesn't stop the craziness. In February, towns like Henning and Park Rapids, Minnesota, simply have indoor Crazy Days.

Minnesota seems to be the eastern limit of the Pacific Northwest word *spendy* meaning "expensive." Here are some examples of its Minnesota use:

New Hope, Minnesota: "Great automatic car wash. . . . Kind of spendy but worth it."

Faribault County, Minnesota: "I voted for Arne Carlson because he is a good businessman and reined in our spendy legislature for two terms and turned up a surplus."

NORTH DAKOTA

Where's Fargo? Not in Minnesota, as the Minnesota-based movie *Fargo* might make you think, but just across the border in North Dakota. You don't have to go far from Minnesota to get to Fargo, and the language of eastern North Dakota isn't far from that of northern Minnesota either. Farther west in the state the North North Central begins to fade into the Western pattern.

Northern North Dakota, like northern Minnesota, picks up the "Canadian raising." Winnipeg, Manitoba, is just fifty miles north of the state's northeastern corner.

In North Dakota and Wisconsin, as well as Canada, a *bluff* can be a clump of trees instead of a steep hillside. That is perhaps because in flat unforested lands, a clump of trees can look like a hillside.

Among the creatures of North Dakota is the *flickertail*. Despite its name, it is not a bird but a squirrel, known elsewhere as *Richardson's ground squirrel*. This squirrel is suited to the plains of North Dakota, burrowing underground rather than jumping around in trees. It's like a prairie dog, but smaller. North Dakotans call it a flickertail because its little tail flicks quickly back and forth. The state itself is generally known as the "Flickertail State," although a bill to adopt the flickertail as the official state emblem failed in the legislature in 1953.

"You must be from North Dakota," Tom Isern wrote in his "Plains Folk" newspaper column in 1997, "if you pronounce it Nor'Dakoda" and "if you hear 'yah, sure,' not 'yes, sir.'" Other North Dakotaisms, according to Isern, are *snow-stayed* to mean "detained by snow" and the expression "Outside, zero is below" for "it's below zero."

The Inland North: States of the Heartland

SOUTH DAKOTA

Except in the east, near Minnesota, South Dakota does not show the distinctive qualities of the *Fargo* accent. It is more typical of the West, the Mountain West in particular.

There are *badlands* throughout the West — barren, arid, and eroded — but South Dakota has badlands pride of place. Along with western Nebraska, western South Dakota is home of the Badlands with a capital *B*, and within those Badlands, South Dakota is host to Badlands National Monument. The official state song proclaims South Dakota as

Home of the Badlands, and Rushmore's ageless shrine,
Black Hills and prairies, Farmland and Sunshine.

Badlands: A park in South Dakota

To the southeast of South Dakota is Iowa, and one of the distinctive features of the language of South Dakota is its name for its neighbor. A linguistic survey of the Upper Midwest, published in 1976, found that South Dakotans were more likely than residents of Iowa to call it "Ioway." Perhaps in Iowa the famous song written in 1912 now sounds old fashioned:

We're from Ioway, Ioway;
State of all the land,
Joy on every hand;
We're from Ioway, Ioway.
That's where the tall corn grows.

NEBRASKA

Nebraskans love *pickles* so much that they pay hundreds of millions of dollars for them each year. You wouldn't want to eat these pickles, but you do peel them. That's because the Nebraska *pickle* or *pickle card* is a printed card used in a lottery. You peel the tabs from the pickle to look for winning symbols.

A Pickle, Nebraska style

The pickle gets its name from the former practice of selling the cards from pickle jars at bars. Pickles still raise more funds for charity in Nebraska than bingo and all other forms of gambling combined.

Why pickle jars? Because they're portable. In the days when such gambling was illegal, at the approach of a state revenue agent a jar could be quickly removed from the bar and hidden. Furthermore, there might be some hazard in asking for a gambling card, but nobody could object to someone wanting to buy a pickle. By the time this type of game became legal, the name had established itself.

In other parts of the country, the Nebraska pickle goes by ordinary descriptive names like *pulltab* and *charity game ticket*.

Pickles may not always be for eating in Nebraska, but *Runzas* are. Probably related to the German word *Ranzen* meaning "bag or pouch," *Runza* is a brand name for a Nebraska sandwich of ground beef, onions, and spices baked inside a roll of fresh bread. Runza became a proprietary name in 1949 when Sally Everett and her brother Alex Brening opened the first Runza Drive-Inn, using a recipe brought from Russia by their mother, a recipe said to have eighteenth-century German-Russian roots. They omitted one traditional ingredient, cabbage, from their commercial version. At a Runza Restaurant nowadays you can get "Original," "Cheese," "Italian," and "Swiss Cheese Mushroom" Runzas. There are now more than fifty Runza Restaurants in Nebraska, including a Rock 'N Roll Runza with roller-skating waitresses.

When Runzas are carried out-of-state, they still retain a Nebraska flavor. The Runza Society of the Greater Twin Cities Metropolitan Area (a.k.a. "Minnesotans for Nebraska," a University of Nebraska alumni group) offers a Runza recipe on its website and this cheer:

Runzas to the Left, Runzas to the Right.
Stand Up, Sit Down, Bite, Bite, Bite.

> **On October 25, 1997,** Darren, my wife and native of Lincoln, and I were married at The Top of The Rock. This is the second floor reception hall of Rock 'N Roll Runza in Lincoln, Nebraska. . . . Always the wise one, Darren was adamant that party size runzas would be included in the buffet! . . . Heheh, we also flew the leftover Runzas back with us to Arlington, Virginia. Yeah, we're talking hardcore Husker tradition!
>
> — Internet posting

In Iowa, *corn husker* has been noted as a term for a rustic. In Nebraska, "Cornhusker" or "Husker" is the nickname for University of Nebraska athletic teams. *Husk*, by the way, is what Northerners do to corn when they remove its leaves and expose the ear; Southerners *shuck* it.

Lincoln, Nebraska, is the home of yet another culinary favorite, the *frenchee*. To make a frenchee, you take an ordinary cheese or tuna-and-cheese sandwich, bread it, and french-fry it.

In the nineteenth century, Nebraska originated the term *blowout* for a bare hollow place on the side of a hill or in the ground where the wind has blown out the sand or dirt. Nebraska also has *chop hills*, otherwise known as *chops* or *choppies*. These are bare low hills that get their name because they look chopped up.

In the late nineteenth century and early twentieth, some of the first settlers of Nebraska, Kansas, and Oklahoma did their own digging in hills or the prairie to make humble homes called *dugouts*. They would frame the entrances with wood and use some of the excavated dirt to make a roof for the front part. A door and a stovepipe would then make a hole a home.

In more recent times, central and eastern Nebraskans have used *oil mat* to refer to what is known in other places in the North and West as an *oiled road* or *blacktop* — that is, a gravel road topped with oil or asphalt.

Paul Fell's illustrated primer, *Nebraskaspeak*, says that the Nebraska vocabulary includes *sack* (for groceries), *pop* (for soda), *wiener* (for hot dog). He also explains that in Nebraska "you show plays in a 'theatre' . . . you show movies in a 'thee-A-ter.'"

IOWA

Iowa is comfortably Middle American in its speech as well as its location. Sandwiched between Minnesota on the north and Missouri on the south, Iowa is Northern enough to avoid the Southern rhyming of *pen* with *pin* you'll hear in Missouri but Southern enough to avoid the *Fargo* accent.

At least two vocabulary items are distinctive to the state. *Grinnie* is an Iowa name for a ground squirrel. (In other places, especially western Pennsylvania, a *grinnie* is the striped ground creature otherwise called a chipmunk.) And an Iowa culinary favorite, the *loose-meat sandwich*, attained national prominence when it was the center of attention on two Iowa episodes of the "Roseanne" television series.

The loose-meat sandwich is indeed made of loose meat: ground or shredded beef on a bun. It is a specialty of Iowa's Maid-Rite restaurants, where the loose meat is always steamed, not fried. When you buy a Maid-Rite sandwich, you get a spoon to scoop up the meat that falls out of the bun. Taylor's Maid-Rite in Marshalltown, Iowa, will ship frozen loose-meat sandwiches anywhere in the country, with pickles and onions on the side.

Davenport, one of the "Quad Cities" on the Mississippi River at the state's eastern border, apparently has no connection with the type of furniture bearing the same name. *Davenport* as a synonym for sofa or couch is widely used in the North and West, but not so much in Iowa.

"You know you're an Iowan if you know what 'Hawks' and 'Clones' are," says a website. They aren't the particulars of a biological experiment, just athletic teams. Hawks are the University of Iowa "Hawkeyes." Clones are the Iowa State University "Cyclones," named for the windstorms we now call tornadoes. "Hawkeye" is by no means confined to athletics; Iowa calls itself the "Hawkeye State," supposedly after the name of an Indian chief of the Iowa tribe early in the nineteenth century, and residents of Iowa sometimes are referred to as Hawkeyes. For some reason, they aren't called Clones.

KANSAS

Kansas almost made it into the South rather than the North. In the decade before the Civil War, Kansas was settled in a hurry by both Northerners and Southerners after the Kansas-Nebraska Act of

You know you're an Iowan if:
Down south to you means south of I-80; in southern Iowa, it means Missouri.
Stores don't have *bags*, they have *sacks*.
You know what a Maid-Rite is and know they cannot be served with ketchup.
People from other states love to hear you say *Iowa* and other words with Os in
  them.
You drink *pop*, do the *warsh*, fish in the *crick* and shingle the *ruff*.

— Internet posting

1854 authorized the inhabitants to vote on whether they would allow slavery. A thousand Missourians crossed over to swell the numbers for slavery; the anti-slavery societies of New England rushed in abolitionist settlers. Both sides engaged in raids and skirmishes. The abolitionist John Brown fought his first battles in "bleeding Kansas," an epithet the state earned because of the fighting. After more than 50 violent clashes in four years, Kansas finally voted against slavery.

Linguistically, both sides left their mark on Kansas. Kansan English has Northern "ah-ee" rather than Southern "ah" for "long i," but the southern and eastern parts of the state show Southern influence in that *pen* sounds like *pin* and *men* sounds like the first syllable of *minute*.

The fighting before and during the Civil War also left Kansas with the nickname "Jayhawk." There's no such bird, but someone must have thought that the combined attributes of the jay and the hawk would be an appropriate label for those who fought skirmishes over slavery in what became known as the "Jayhawker war." After the Civil War, *jay-hawker* or *jayhawk* was used as an uncomplimen-

Kansas Jayhawk:
From marauder
to mascot

tary epithet for an outlaw, and in states other than Kansas *jayhawk* became an insulting term for an ignorant rural person, much like *hoosier* in states other than Indiana. But like Indiana, Kansas embraced its potentially shameful label and now displays it with pride. The University of Kansas mascot is the Jayhawk, and Kansans are officially Jayhawkers.

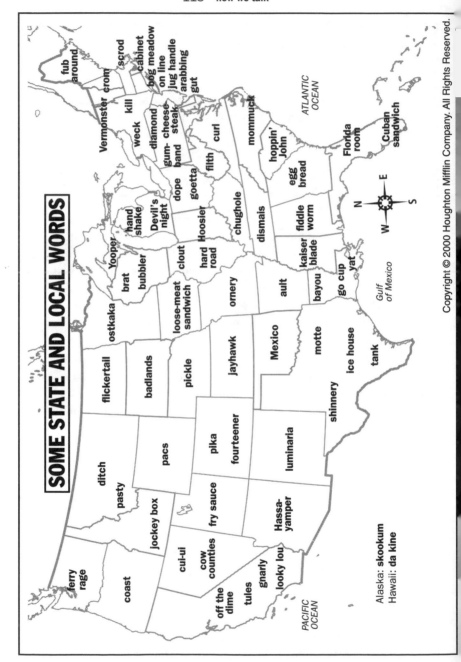

SOME STATE AND LOCAL WORDS

THE WEST

Where the mountains rise out of the plains and the time zone changes from Central to Mountain, the North-South layering of American dialects comes to an end. The English accents that had established themselves on the Atlantic shores of North America in the 1600s and then flowed gently westward with the course of settlement, maintaining North-South distinctions, eventually bumped into the Rocky Mountains and spilled every which way, leaving the West to pick up the pieces and put them together in its own way.

The turbulence of the mountains was evidently too great to preserve Eastern regional distinctions. From the mountains westward to the Pacific coast, and beyond to Hawaii, our language cannot easily be distinguished by place. Not everyone in the vast American West talks alike, but Western settlement developed in such a way that the language varies more by group, gender, and occupation than by place of residence. Therefore, though we recognize local and regional accents in the eastern half of the country, we rarely do in the West. We can't help but notice a Maine accent, a New York City accent, or a Southern accent — but not a Denver accent or a Seattle one. And it's not easy to distinguish the speech of Denver or Seattle from that of San Francisco or Los Angeles.

The basic speech of the West is like the Northern back east, but with a hint or two of the Southern. It came about, of course, because the majority of early English-speaking settlers of the West came from the Northern states. But there were Southerners too, including considerable numbers who sought a new start after the end of the Civil War. Still, instead of adding spice, the slight Southern flavoring makes the speech of the West more bland. In the desert Southwest and Pacific Northwest, for example, some speakers soften the "r" after vowels in words like *horse* and *charm*: they wind up sounding a little like Southerners who drop the "r" entirely, but because they keep some of the "r," they sound like Northerners too. Likewise, northwest from Texas all the way through the mountains to Idaho, you can hear an echo of the Southern "ah" in words like *ride* and *fire*, though it still has some of the "ah-ee" of the North. And in California some people pronounce *pen* like *pin*, as Southerners do. But the Southerners' vowel in *pen* is obviously drawn out — a prominent "pih-un" — while the Californians say the vowel so quickly you can barely notice it.

The Southern influence was apparently stronger in the Wild West days of the nineteenth century, as evidenced by the stereotyped "r"-less pronunciations of cowboy stories: *hoss*, *cuss*, and *podnuh* for *horse*, *curse*, and *partner* respectively. After the defeat of the Confederacy, many Southerners were attracted to the opportunities of the West. But by the twentieth century they were outnumbered by immigrants from the Northern part of the eastern United States, and the Southern influence virtually disappeared.

In the present day, two matters of pronunciation distinguish West from East in the United States, although for both the West-East boundary begins way to the east of the Rockies. In the far eastern United States, *marry* has the vowel of *hat* rather than that of *merry*, while to the west of those Atlantic states, *marry* and *merry* sound alike. This West-East difference holds for other words spelled with *a* followed by *rr* and a vowel. For example, in the far East, *carry*, *Harry*, *barrel*, and *wheelbarrow* all have the vowel of *hat*, while in the West they all have the vowel of *merry*.

The second East-West distinction is between those (in the East) who say *caught* and *cot* differently and those (in the West) who say those words alike. The dividing line in this case is roughly the Mississippi River, but the Western *caught-cot* equalizers are also joined by the inhabitants of Pittsburgh. Those in the East who say *caught* with a different vowel than that of *cot* often also have different vowels in the first syllable of *daughter* and *dot*, for example, and in *law* and *lot*; in the West they're all the same.

The coyote also helps mark the boundary between East and West. Its habitat is historically to the west of the Mississippi River,

The children and parents who helped name Coyote Creek Elementary [in Highlands Ranch, 12 miles south of Denver] pronounce the word in three syllables, putting a long "e" on the end. . . .

Many recent Colorado transplants are content. They brought the three-syllable pronunciation with them. But some in the Douglas County school district —especially those like [school secretary Annette] Westphal who grew up in rural areas of Colorado or the Midwest — are struggling. Will a brand-new Highlands Ranch school ever have a united front when it comes to the name affixed above its front door?

Westphal was raised in Iowa, where "coyote" has always and forever more will be a two-syllable word. She doesn't know why three syllables are so hard, except that only city folks ever said it that way. School district planner Denny Hill, raised in Nebraska, also stops short of the third syllable. "I would have to think before I said it that way," he said. "It's just (a two-syllable) coyote to me." Only people from New Jersey, like his boss, Superintendent Rick O'Connell, pronounce the "e."

— *Denver Post*

so not surprisingly *coyote* is more of a Western word. But the recent movement of this canine into wooded areas of the East, along with the cartoon character Wile E. Coyote, has made the coyote familiar to Easterners too. The difference is that in the West the coyote's name generally takes just two syllables, with emphasis on the first: "CUY-oat." In the East, and for cartoon lovers, it's three syllables with emphasis on the second: "cuy-OAT-tee."

There are also some matters of vocabulary that separate Americans who live *out West* from those who live *back East*. Whichever of those terms you use, you're from the opposite side of the country. An Easterner will speak of a place *out West*, and a Westerner will refer to *back East*, the exact meaning depending on where the speaker lives. To a Californian, Colorado is east enough to be back East, and to a New Englander, Ohio is west enough to be out West. Why *out* and *back?* That reflects the historical direction of American migration — out to the West, looking back at the East.

Mountains provide some of the most distinctive vocabulary as well as distinctive features of the West. The *mountain lion,* for example, roams the Western states. And in the West, a *butte* is a hill or ridge that stands out from its surroundings. In Appalachia, a similarly prominent ridge is called a *butt.*

West of a line from the Dakotas through Texas, cattle or horses are kept in a *corral.* East of that line, they would be in a *barnyard, barn lot, lot,* or *pen.*

Dried beef serves as a snack and portable food in much of the West, going by the name *jerky.*

The Interstate Highway system has given a vocabulary distinction to the West too. Where the eastern part of the country generally calls its limited-access divided highways *expressways* or *Interstates,* the West refers to them as *freeways.* That's partly because many of the roads back East are *tollways* or *turnpikes,* so they can hardly be called free.

When practical Westerners get together and no one wants to pay for anyone else, they call it a *no-host* event: reception, meal, or bar. The Millennium New Year's Eve celebration at Ocean Shores Convention Center in Washington state, for example, began with a *no-host bar.* In such cases, Easterners would be more likely to speak of a *cash bar.* The term lends itself to use in other situations where payment is not involved. "50th Emmys Will Be a No-Host Affair," headlined the *Los Angeles Times* in 1998.

The Mountain West

Linguistically the least noticed part of the United States, as well as the least populated, is the Mountain West. It comprises the double tier of states in the wide open spaces between the Great Plains and the Pacific coast. If a butterfly flaps its wings in California, chaos theory tells us, it becomes a storm on the East Coast; to stretch the analogy perhaps beyond the breaking point, if a teenager makes a remark in Beverly Hills, television and movie microphones pick it up, and it just might take the rest of the country by storm. But the national media aren't tracking the latest locutions from Montana or New Mexico. Nor do the business barons, fashion trendsetters, and urban hipsters of New York City or the political pundits of Washington, D.C., pay much attention to what happens off in the western mountains. The Mountain West, consequently, is on the receiving more than the giving end of developments in American English.

As noted for the West as a whole, the language of the Mountain West is basically Northern with a little Southern flavoring. But the geography of the region gives it a few vocabulary items of its own.

We've observed that hills and mountains that rise abruptly from the Western plains are known as *buttes*. The city of Butte, Montana, home of the famed copper mines, is named after a notable butte just outside of town. To the south, in Colorado and the desert Southwest, are the buttes with flat tops known as *mesas*.

In the Mountain West, if you "borrow" dirt from the side of a road to create a drainage ditch, you've made a *borrow pit*. Originally it was called a *barrow pit*, because of the barrow or mound that is created when the ditch is dug. But few people nowadays have heard of a barrow, and everyone knows "borrow," so *borrow pit* it became.

Outside of the mountains, *borrow pit* has a different meaning: a pit from which dirt or gravel has been dug for use elsewhere. This kind of borrow pit has been a concern for environmentalists. For example, when one contractor proposed to remove topsoil for fill elsewhere, a county council member worried that the resultant "borrow pit" could become a landfill or dump.

The Mountain West: State by State

COLORADO

The boundary between Midwest and Mountain West is most clearly marked in Colorado, where the tallest of the Rocky Mountains rise abruptly out of the flat plains. In recognition of its elevated state, Colorado labels newcomers and tourists *flatlanders*, regardless of how mountainous their places of origin might be. Coloradans, likewise, are exalted enough by the presence of the mountains to be exempt from being called *flatlanders*, even if they live in the shadow of the mountains on the flatlands of Denver or Boulder.

The elevated topography of Colorado breeds its own terminology. *Fourteeners* in Colorado are mountain peaks of 14,000 feet and higher. The state has fifty-four of them, plus four near-fourteeners. Many are concentrated southwest of Denver in "Fourteener Country." The nineteen-mile stretch of U.S. Highway 24 west from Trout

Fourteener: At 14,015 feet, Wetterhorn Peak is 49th of 54 in Colorado.

Creek Pass through the town of Buena Vista is called the "Highway of Fourteeners" because it passes ten of these mountains. It continues north in the shadow of fourteeners to Leadville, the highest city in the United States at 10,430 feet.

If you go to a *park* in Colorado, you may be surrounded by mountains. Nineteenth-century adventurers and settlers in Colorado, following the usage of French trappers, called a mountain valley a *park*. This legacy remains in present-day Colorado names, including the great valleys known as North Park, Middle Park, and South Park between the ridges of the Rocky Mountains. On the eastern slope of the Rockies, the name Estes Park has a similar derivation. The national and state parks of Colorado, however, use *park* in the conventional sense of land set aside for public use in its natural state.

In the mountains of Colorado and neighboring states, another term for a mountain valley is *hole*. A *hole* is smaller than a park and usually carries a person's name. Brown's Hole is an example from northwest Colorado. Others include Jones Hole near Dinosaur National Monument in Utah and Jackson Hole in Wyoming. Holes like these served as meeting places and hideouts in the old West. Between robberies Butch Cassidy and the Sundance Kid hid in Brown's Hole and in the so-called "Hole in the Wall" in Wyoming.

In a Colorado park or hole, you might see an animal unique to the state: a little mammal of the mountains known as a *pika* or *cony*. A close relative of the rabbit, the pika stretches to about eight inches long but weighs only half a pound. It is good at hiding but reveals itself in loud squeaks of warning. It lives high up in the mountains in piles of rocks, storing hay in burrows for food so that it can keep active during the winter.

Colorado miners spoke of *blossom rock*, quartz that was rich with oxides indicating the likelihood of gold or silver nearby. The place where a vein of ore ended was called a *cap*. And in Colorado a round stone good for throwing might be called a *doney*.

WYOMING

"You know you're in Wyoming," writes Jim Nichols on the Internet, "if you put on a pair of Pacs to get the morning paper." *Pacs* are boots with thick felt liners, also known as *shoepacs*. Shoepacs themselves aren't unique to Wyoming. They are standard military issue for cold weather. But their abbreviated name — *pacs* — seems especially at home in Wyoming. Nichols also says you know you're in Wyoming if you own more than four pair of gloves, if *chill factor* is part of your daily vocabulary, and if you hear *stream* or *brook* pronounced *crick* (a widespread Northern and Western pronunciation).

MONTANA

A course in "How to Speak Montanan" wouldn't take very long, but there are a few distinctive terms in Montana vocabulary. One is *ditch* meaning "water" when used in a drink, as in "a shot and ditch" or even "Jack Daniels ditch." The word *ditch* also refers to an irrigation ditch, of which there are many in the state.

If you were hungry as well as thirsty in Montana, you might ask for a *pasty*. (Be sure to pronounce it right: "pass-tee.") It's a dish brought to Butte, Montana, by miners from Cornwall, England: a meat pie made with cubes of beef, potato, turnip, and onion, covered with gravy. The gravy is a Montana addition to the original Cornish recipe.

And if you think your meal (or anything else) is expensive, in Montana as in neighboring states you'd say it's *spendy*, according to the *MontanaCyberzine* website. *Bitterroot*, a daisy with an edible root that is bitter indeed, is known throughout the Mountain West but especially celebrated in Montana, where it is the state flower. *Bear grass*, with leaves long and strong enough to weave baskets, is also known in the northern Mountain West. It is honored in "Montana Melody," the Montana state ballad: "Where the bear-grass blooms In the spring-time of the year."

IDAHO

In the midst of the Mountain West, Idaho is not strikingly different from its neighbors in pronunciation or vocabulary.

Two noteworthy Idaho usages found by Sonja Launspach's students at Idaho State University are *cube* instead of *stick* of butter and *fry sauce*, the name coined in Utah for a combination of ketchup and mayonnaise to put on french fries.

Cars in most parts of the United States have a glove box or glove compartment, but in southern Idaho and some parts of neighboring states, the place for storing maps, warranties, a few tools, a first aid kit, and candy wrappers is called a *jockey box*. It reflects the pioneer spirit. Before automobiles, the term was used for a covered box serving a similar purpose on the front of a wagon.

In common with Utah, Idaho is said to be one place where alfalfa is referred to by its French and British name, *lucerne*.

UTAH

If Jane says Dick was *born in a barn*, don't take it as a statement of fact or as a tribute to Dick's humble beginnings. In most parts of the United States, it's an insult to Dick's manners and upbringing, implying that Dick is no better behaved than a barnyard animal. The phrase is widely used in most parts of the United States, except for New England, which apparently has its own stock of epithets.

But if Jane says Dick was *barn in a born*, reversing the vowels of the first and last words, it gives us some insight into Jane, the speaker, as well as Dick. Chances are that Jane was born in Utah, or at least grew up there.

It's not a complete reversal of *a* and *o* before *r*, but it's pretty close. Close enough that celebrators of "Utahnics" like Salt Lake City radio hosts Kerry Jackson and Bill Alread are able to construct a whole sentence with *a* for *o*, like this one complimenting a woman on her dress: "Lard, Darthy, that's a garjus arnge farmel."

Utah is the only Western state whose inhabitants are conscious of a distinctive way of speaking that involves pervasive patterns of pronunciation. But then, Utah is the only Western state with such a distinctive cultural heritage. Brigham Young chose Utah for his Latter-day Saints because it was so removed from the rest of the developing American nation, and Utahns have been able to maintain a distinctive Mormon-influenced culture to the present day. Not that everyone in present-day Utah is a Mormon, and certainly not that every Utahn speaks "Utahnics." But the opportunity is there both to hear Utah pronunciations and to participate in them.

At Sullivan's Cafe in Cedar City, those who use and promote the Utah pronunciations hold meetings of what they call the Overhomer's Society of Southern Utah. *Overhome* means "back home," as in "The hay is ready to mow overhome" or "We don't got one of these overhome."

Salt Lake Tribune writer Christopher Smith describes Utahnics this way: "It's also a twang you will detect in the more populous corners of Zion, when an alfalfa 'former' wearing 'overhauls' is buying a new 'Fard' pickup in 'St. Jarge' or when someone threw out their back as they 'bant over to pick up my begs at the Salt Lake airpart.'"

In addition to changes in *a* and *o* before *r*, things can happen in Utah English before *l* as well. *Sale* is pronounced *sell*; *jail* is *jell*; and *feel* becomes *fill*. And Utahns tend to shorten words even more than other Americans, so that two-syllable *crayon* becomes one-syllable "cran" and *corral* is spoken "cral." A benchmark is the city named Hurricane, which in Overhome or Utahnics is pronounced "Hairikin."

Mormon influence is felt in the softening of epithets in Utah English. The *f*-word, Alread says, in Utah used to be replaced by *flip*, as in "Oh, flip" or "That flippin' guy." More recently it has become *freakin'*: "This freakin' this and this freakin' that." Other softened terms of exasperation in Utah include *Oh my heck* and *Oh for heck*, *scrud, fetch*, and *Gol*, as in "Gol — He was being so ignernt to me!" On a happier note, things in Utah can be *for cute* ("Fer cuuuute!" for emphasis), *for cool*, or *for fun*. And the Mormon vocabulary includes *gentile* to refer to all who do not share their faith.

Mormons aren't supposed to drink alcohol or caffeine, and eating meat is not encouraged by the Mormon church, but that hasn't stopped Utah from making its own distinctive contribution to American cuisine: *fry sauce*. The basic ingredients of fry sauce are ketchup and mayonnaise, but it gets its name because it reaches its highest calling as a sauce or dip for french fries. Don Carlos Edwards, founder of Utah's Arctic Circle fast food chain, is credited with the inspiration for the sauce. Ketchup alone, he thought, was not sufficient sauce for hamburgers, so he added mayonnaise and then decided to offer his customers the convenience of a combined condiment: a blend of both ketchup and mayonnaise with flavorings like garlic, onion, mustard, spices, and maybe some pickle juice. At first he simply called it *pink sauce*. But since french fries proved to be the greatest beneficiary of his concoction, he renamed it *fry sauce* in their honor.

Fry sauce is now sold and made everywhere within the state. It is still mainly a Utah delicacy, but it has oozed across the border to Idaho, Oregon, and other nearby states. If you go to the Spud Drive-In Theatre, two miles south of Driggs, Idaho, for example, you can chow down on Idaho-style Spud Buds with fry sauce.

NEW MEXICO

Like Texas on the east and California on the west, the mountain and desert states of New Mexico and Arizona were once part of Mexico. More than urbanized Texas and California, they reflect their Mexican

Farolitos: The original luminaria

heritage and closeness to present-day Mexico in their culture and language. One notable contribution of Hispanic New Mexico to American English is a custom known as *luminaria*. Originally the luminarias were small bonfires on the roofs or in front of houses to light the
way for the passage of the Christ Child on Christmas Eve. Also on
Christmas Eve, candles were set into paper sacks and placed in a row
along a walkway or rooftop; these were called *farolitos*, meaning "little lanterns." As Anglo-Americans began to copy the custom, they

applied the name *luminaria* to the candles. In Santa Fe, the distinction between farolitos and luminarias still is carefully preserved, but the rest of the country now enjoys the lights as luminarias.

In New Mexico, a *colcha* is a bedspread. But the word can also refer to an embroidery stitch in wool yarn used to make designs on a wool bedspread, a tradition dating back to the earliest Spanish colonial days. One scholar says, "Colcha means softness, warmth, a gentle gaiety, richness and intimacy."

The American Indian influence in the Southwest also remains strong, with a significant population, especially of Navajos. The Navajo term of respect *Hosteen,* meaning "old man," is one that has been popularized by Tony Hillerman's novels.

The general English spoken in the Desert Southwest has picked up a few names of plants from the Spanish: *inmortal* (with the Spanish *nm* instead of *mm*) as the name for a plant elsewhere called *spider milkweed,* for example. And what is elsewhere a *prickly pear* is sometimes called *cholla* or *cane cholla* in these states (the plant was originally used to make canes for walking). A *datil* or *datil yucca* is a plant with fruit that resembles a date, so it takes the Spanish name for date.

Overall, however, the English language has not been strongly affected by Spanish or American Indian influences, aside from the numerous Spanish place names like Santa Fe, Los Alamos, and Alamogordo.

ARIZONA

A number of plant names seem distinctive to Arizona: the *desert saltbush,* for example, and a flowering perennial with tuberous roots known as *covena.*

In Spanish, *hediondo* means "stinker," and the creosote bush ("a resinous, ill-smelling, yellow-flowered shrub," in the words of the *Dictionary of American Regional English*) has earned the name *hediondilla* in this region. Arizonans also call it *greasewood.*

There's a river northwest of Phoenix, the Hassayampa, that has the unusual property of flowing underground for most of its 100 or so miles. It makes a contribution to Arizona wildlife by flowing to the surface and watering a nature preserve near Wickenburg, and it also made a singular contribution to American English. In the nineteenth century, those who came to a gold rush on the river were called *Hassayampers*. After suitable passage of time, *Hassayamper* came to mean an "old timer," someone who had come out for the gold rush and was staying on. Then, perhaps through the old-timers' story-telling, a legend arose that anyone who crossed the Hassayampa would be unable to tell the truth, and *Hassayamper* came to mean "liar." Regrettably, that meaning seems to have become almost as invisible as the river itself. Without blushing, the Wickenburg Chamber of Commerce now calls its monthly newsletter *The Hassayamper*.

The Far West and Beyond

WASHINGTON

The young people of Washington, or at least Seattleites, seem to be *yeah*-sayers. They'll agree with what you're saying with an emphatic *YEAH* at the start of a sentence. Linguist Allen Maberry of the University of Washington gives two examples and explanation of Seattle dialogue:

"She's a total fox." "YEAH-she-is."

"Man, that's a long commute!" "YEAH-it-is."

By which I mean a very quick response with a hard stress on *Yeah* and then a sharp decrease in emphasis on the rest of the phrase.

Roving language inquirer Jim "the Mad Monk" Crotty goes so far as to declare that this *yeah* is "the most important and tricky piece of Seattle vernacular. It's almost *Fargo*-esque but different (not as dorky, almost surfer-like)."

Even before Boeing, Microsoft, Starbucks, and the grunge scene, Washington State had made a name for itself with seafood. Washington State, and Puget Sound in particular, is the home of the largest burrowing clam in the world, the *geoduck*, pronounced "gooey-duck." A good-sized geoduck has a six-inch shell from which it can extend its two-inch-thick neck (or "foot") eighteen inches or more. It inspired Ron Konzak and Judy and Jerry Elfendahl to compose and record "The Gooey Duck Song," with these lines:

Oh it takes a lotta of luck, and a certain kinda pluck
For to dig around the muck, for to get a gooey duck.
For he doesn't have a front and he doesn't have a back,
And he doesn't know Donald, and he doesn't go quack!

Washington State is also known for knowing its salmon. "You might be from Seattle," says one columnist, "if you know the difference between Chinook, Coho, and Sockeye Salmon." *Chinook, coho,* and even *sockeye* (originally *sukkegh*) are all names that English-speaking settlers learned from local American Indians. The name *coho* is now well known in the Great Lakes, because coho were imported there starting in the 1960s to control the nuisance fish, alewives. *Chinook* has multiple meanings in the Pacific Northwest. In addition to naming a type of salmon, it is the name of an American Indian nation. *Chinook Jargon* is a trade language consisting of American Indian and English words that was used as far north as Alaska in the nineteenth and early twentieth centuries. And the *Chinook wind* is a dry winter wind from the southwest that warms up the whole northwest territory, from Oregon to the Dakotas, and north to British Columbia and Alaska.

Seattleites are as sophisticated about types of coffee as they are about types of salmon. But thanks to the Seattle company Starbucks and its rivals, the whole United States now knows coffee variations like *latte* (with milk); *mocha* (with chocolate); *macchiato* (with foamed milk); *skinny* (with skim milk); and *doppio* (double espresso).

Washingtonians also love the ferries that carry them and their cars from mainland to island to island in Puget Sound, and they don't like cars that cut ahead of them in the line for the ferry. That provokes what the Washington State Patrol calls *ferry rage*, and in 1999 it provoked a proposal for legislation that would carry a double penalty for those who tried it: a fine and a trip to the back of the line. Road rage runs rampant around the United States, but only in Washington will anyone speak of ferry rage.

OREGON

Oregon is not a satellite of Washington State, but Oregonians are happy to leave the spotlight to Seattleites. There's nothing striking about the way people in Oregon speak that distinguishes them from their neighbors up and down the Pacific coast. Well, there is that word: *coast.* In Oregon, that's the name for the water's edge. "Port-

---

Spendy is the Oregon word for "expensive," as it is elsewhere in the north-western United States and as far east as Minnesota. Here are some comments and headlines:

Boise, Idaho: "Kempthorne Plan May Be Too Spendy, Some Critics Say"

Anchorage, Alaska: "Getting season hockey tickets is a spendy plight wherever you go."

Seattle: "Ferry Ramp Proves Spendy Folly"

Harbour Pointe Golf Club, Mukilteo, Washington: "[The back nine is] a spacious track that tumbles up and down a steep hillside amidst spendy homes with spendier views."

Southeastern Washington: "Spendy Mulberries Returned to Hanford"

Portland, Oregon: "Parking Overtime in Portland Gets Spendy"

---

landers *go to the coast* for a weekend or buy *a place at the coast*," says Peter McGraw, a professor at Linfield College in McMinnville, Oregon. "Though once they are there, of course, they may go for a walk on the beach." *Coast* can be found elsewhere, but in other places different names are typically used. Peripatetic researcher Jim Crotty observes that in Oregon you *go to the coast* "to see the big waves . . . . You do not go to *the beach* (that's California) or *the ocean* (that's Washington) or *the shore* (that's 'Joisey')."

CALIFORNIA

It's the end of the line, the grand finale, the culmination of American English: California!

Other Western dialects could make that claim too, of course. The basic accent of Los Angeles is hard to distinguish from that of Seattle, Phoenix, or for that matter Denver, to take a few urban examples. The high school students of Littleton, Colorado, in the suburbs of Denver speak with the same accent as their counterparts in Los Angeles or San Francisco.

But California has place of pride among dialects of the West because it has the microphone. California language is amplified across the whole country, including the rest of the West, thanks to the nerve center of American entertainment in southern California. On television, in the movies, and in popular music we hear the real and simulated accents of California kids, cops, cranks, comics, crusaders, and just plain citizens. From the heights of Beverly Hills to the depths of the San Fernando Valley, from Malibu Beach to the San Gabriel Mountains, from Santa Barbara to San Diego, the California word is broadcast to America and the world.

Maybe it is no accident that California sets the tone for American media and Western American English, because California captured the world's attention almost from the moment it became part of the United States in the mid-nineteenth century. Long before modern electronic media were invented, newspapers and magazines the world over marveled at the discovery of gold at Sutter's Fort in 1848 and avidly reported on the gold rush that followed. Accounts of the mining activities and communities established by the Forty-niners introduced *pay dirt, placer,* and *square meal* to American English, along with other mining terms that have since faded away, such as *color* referring to visible gold. "If the prospector finds one or more particles of gold in his search," explained a writer on "Californianisms" in 1859, "he says he has found the *color.*" Appropriately, California also has a wildflower known as *gold fields*, which grows in masses of small plants with yellow flowers.

Placerville, in gold rush territory, was once known as *Hangtown.* In 1849, shortly after the town was founded, a miner who had struck it rich supposedly went to the town's best establishment and asked for their most expensive meal. The cook responded by making an omelet with fried eggs, breaded oysters, and a side dish of bacon, the most expensive ingredients on hand. You can still get *Hangtown fry* in modern Placerville and a few other places in California.

In the early twentieth century, strangely enough, California also apparently was the birthplace of one of the most famous of twentieth-century words: *jazz.* It first appeared on the sports page of the *San Francisco Bulletin* in 1913. Reporting on spring training of the San Francisco Seals baseball team, E.T. "Scoop" Gleeson wrote that a certain player was "very much to the 'jazz.'" Evidently that provoked some curiosity, because he subsequently had to explain:

Boontling

In an obscure corner of Mendocino County in northern California is a town which once had a form of English that was incomprehensible to strangers. The town is Boonville, with about 1000 inhabitants, and its special vocabulary of about 1000 words is known as *Boontling*. Between about 1880 and 1920, Boontling was developed from people's names and new combinations or abbreviations of old words. To *charlie* means "to embarrass," for example, because one Charlie Ball was known for being easily embarrassed. *Zeese* means "coffee," because Zeese Blevens drank a lot of it. A cup of coffee is a *horn of zeese,* and *ball* means "good," so for example you might inquire in Boonville for a *ball horn of zeese.* Abbreviations included *ale* for *a letter,* *abe* for *a bitch.*

Apparently the first words of Boontling were invented in order to gossip without embarrassment about an unmarried pregnant woman who had just come to town. (A pregnant woman was a *keishbook,* supposedly a word from an Indian language.) Much of the Boontling jargon was concerned with matters of that sort, talk about objectionable subjects known as *nonch harpin's.* As it developed, the Boontling jargon was also useful to make sure outsiders from places like neighboring Ukiah wouldn't understand.

A whole book was published about Boontling in 1971, but by then it was largely obsolete. At the turn of the twenty-first century only five old-timers were said to remember anything of the Boontling vocabulary.

Here is part of a story in Boontling, told by Mrs. Austin Rawles to two investigators from Humboldt State College in the 1960s:

The hob [dance] started with the apple-heads [women] all nettied [fancy-dressed], and the seekers [ladies' men] active. But the high-heeler [man in charge] got teetlipped [angry] when he deked [noticed] that raggin' [indecent dancing] was going on and harped [spoke] to the raggers to either shy [quit] or pike [leave].

What is the "jazz"? Why, It's a little of that "old life," the "gin-i-ker," the "pep," otherwise known as the enthusiasalum. A grain of "jazz" and you feel like going out and eating your way through Twin Peaks. It's that spirit which makes ordinary ball players step around like Lajoies and Cobbs. The Seals have it. . . .

A month later, prompted by Gleeson's articles, columnist Ernest J. Hopkins wrote a long commentary on *jazz* in the same newspaper, calling it a "futurist" word of "utter usefulness and power." And so it proved. Within four years musicians had carried it from San Francisco to Chicago to New Orleans. Soon it was adopted as the name for that city's new style of music and then for a whole era in American history.

For the most part, nowadays as in the past, California English sounds unaccented to most Americans. It is the neutral common denominator, the average of American English, based on the speech of the North back east but also including touches of the South — as manifest, for instance, in the equivalence of *pen* and *pin* in the speech of some Californians. President Richard Nixon, a Southern Californian, drew attention to himself in many ways, including unrepentant pursuit of his enemies, real and imagined, but no one questioned or even noticed his accent. Also unremarkable was the accent of California-based President Ronald Reagan. He was not a California native, but the northern Illinois pronunciations of his youth needed little adjustment to California, and whatever training he had as an actor simply reinforced his neutral American accent.

The influence of the California accent on the rest of American English therefore is largely unnoticed. California media simply reinforce our sense that the state's language is "normal." But there is one notable exception where the language of California impinges on the consciousness of the rest of us: the language of the young. *Dude*, for example, was just an old-fashioned term for a fashionably dressed man, and an item of African-American slang, when young Californians made it their form of address: "Yo Dude! Dude? Dude!! Totally, dude. No way, dude! Way, dude! Check it out, dude!" Young Californians also gave the rest of us lessons in pronouncing the venerable slang term *cool*. When it means approbation rather than temperature, California *cool* can sound almost like *cull*.

Surfers and beach bums in particular, and then Valley Girls, caught the attention of the media and thereby of young Americans throughout the country, attuning them to the fashions of young California's language as well as its clothing and culture. The California hippies of the 1960s and the Californian-speaking Teenage Mutant Ninja Turtles of the 1980s also helped focus attention of the young on California language.

The surfers were first. Hawaii is the native land of surfing, of course, but California brought it to the attention of American youth.

Tubular: Catching a wave in La Jolla, California

That was especially due to the 1959 beach and surfing movie *Gidget*, starring Sandra Dee, and the two sequels and television series that followed in the 1960s. They were reinforced beginning in 1963 by the *Beach Party* and *Beach Blanket Bingo* movies starring Frankie Avalon and Annette Funicello.

From such sources young Americans learned surfing words like *gnarly*, for example, which began as a slang term for waves that were difficult or dangerous and was eventually applied to anything unpleasant or disgusting. It was further extended, or turned on its head, when it began to be used to mean just the opposite: splendid, wonderful, awesome. Either the dudes who used it in this way didn't have much experience in the surf, or the word was just too cool not to develop a positive use. *Tubular*, to take another example, refers to the perfect wave, one whose crest falls over to make a tube of air for surfing inside. It was extended as another all-purpose synonym for excellent. To *bail* means to jump off your surfboard to escape a dangerous wave. Now you can bail from almost any activity. *Hot-dogging* is showing off, and it too has moved beyond the reach of the waves.

Two decades later, the focus of California teen slang moved up from the beach, over the Santa Monica Mountains, and down into the San Fernando Valley north of Los Angeles. The young teen Valley Girls had picked up surfer slang and added vocabulary adapted to their pastime of hanging out at shopping malls. In 1982, the song "Valley Girl" by Frank Zappa and his daughter Moon Unit, proclaimed this new phenomenon to the world. The song introduces the Valley Girl as obsessed with shopping and grooming, and includes expressions like *fer sure, bitchen, totally, awesome,* and *tubular,* but above all *like.* The song ends with the Valley Girl's complaint about doing dishes:

> *Like my mother like makes me do the dishes*
> *It's like so gross . . .*
> *It's like grody . . .*
> *Grody to the max*
> *I'm sure*
> *It's like really nauseating*
> *Like barf out*
> *Gag me with a spoon*
> *Gross*
> *I am sure*
> *Totally . . .*

Cameron Crowe's 1981 book *Fast Times at Ridgemont High,* an inside story of life in a Redondo Beach high school, also brought national attention to the world of Southern California teens. It incidentally introduced the word *wussy,* a combination of *wimp* and *pussy* that is still with us. The 1982 movie, *Fast Times at Ridgemont High,* featuring Valley Girls at the Sherman Oaks Galleria shopping mall, and a year later the movie *Valley Girl* (starring Nicholas Cage as the Hollywood Hills punker who has a romance with a girl from the Valley), brought the image as well as the talk of the Valley Girl to the rest of the country. Twenty years later, many of the Valley Girl expressions like *like* are still widely used among young Americans.

Like is, like, totally awesome in the conversations of young Americans today. Not only can it serve as a kind of punctuation mark at the end of every phrase, but it can even take the place of saying or thinking, and this *like* has, like, worked its way into the heads of

Americans of all ages. Instead of saying "I said" or "I thought," many Americans now say "I'm like." Here is a teen example:

> And she's, like, "Omigod where are you going in that sweater?" and I'm, like, "Duh! to my grandma's, you don't think I'd wear this, like, gross Shetland thing to school ever?"

Californians also have the option of saying "I'm all" instead of "I thought" or "I said." Both expressions are exemplified in this line from the movie *Clueless*, the "Bronson Alcott High School" updating of Jane Austen's *Emma*:

> This weekend he called me up, and he's all, "Where were you today?" and I'm like, "I'm at my Grandmother's house."

The poem "Surfer Dude" by Camper English, a San Francisco socialite and critic, encompasses the whole development of California

---

Surfer Dude

i'm a hella good surfer
and i hardly behave
cause man i'm just searching
for the most perfect wave

without my surfboard
i feel hella nude
i may know your first name
but i still call you "dude"

the surfer chicks love me
cause i got the best moves
on the board or in bed
its a fact i can prove

i listen to stoner music
like phish or bob marley
and if i smoke much before surfing
the waves seem more gnarly

i totally dig riding
those 30 foot swells
and looking good doing it
wearing my pooka shells

a day job i cant take it
it's just out of reach
i spend each waking second
out here on the beach

often people make hella fun of me
they just cant understand
like, i'm bonding with the ocean
and the crabs in the sand

— Camper English

(Reprinted by permission of the author)

youth slang from the surfing era to the present day, including the drug scene for good measure.

Recently, as Camper English's verse reflects, California youth have pioneered *hella* and *hecka* as terms of emphasis. Those words also hint of slight dialect differences between Northern California, centered on the San Francisco Bay area, and Southern California, centered on Los Angeles. *Hella* seems to be more Northern, and *hecka* more Southern. According to Peter Hong, a writer for the *New University* newspaper at the University of California, Irvine, in Southern California:

> I once broke into a conversation about dialect. "What's with the word 'hella'?" asked the Southerner. "You use 'hella' for every single adjective: 'She's hella fine, that was hella good, that was hella hard.'" The Northern Californian complained, "Then stop starting and ending a sentence with 'dude.' 'Dude, that was a killer exam' or 'Let's get out of here, dude.'"
>
> I voiced my solution, "Why don't you utilize both 'hella' and 'dude.' You could say, 'Wow dude, I'm hella bored.'"

A few other differences between north and south in California are not limited to youth. For example, in referring to highways, Southern Californians use *the* with numbers, as in *the 101* for U.S. 101, the main coastal route, while Northern Californians (and Oregonians and Washingtonians, for that matter) just call it *101*. So a Southern Californian giving directions might say, "Take the 210 to the 5" (at the north end of the San Fernando Valley), while a Northern Californian might say, "Take 24 to 13" (in Berkeley). Southern Californians don't use *the*, however, if some other term comes before the number, like *I-10* (for Interstate 10) or *state 60* (for California state highway 60).

Northern California used to think of itself as more cultivated than the south. Perhaps that is why San Franciscans so vigorously reject the nickname *Frisco* for their city. It's taken as an insult worse than any four-letter word, an instant revelation that the speaker is a hapless visitor from "back East" (that is, anywhere east of the Rockies). Even Southern Californians know to avoid it unless they want to start a fight.

Northern California also used to call a large couch a *chesterfield*, as Canadians do, but that part of California, like the rest of the state, has mostly couches and sofas nowadays.

Southern Californians speak of the *Santa Ana wind*, a term that is regionally restricted because it gets its name from the Santa Ana River, whose canyon (and others) it blows through. Southern Californians are also more likely than northerners to pronounce *rodeo* in the Spanish style, with emphasis on the second syllable: there is upscale "Ro-day-o" Drive in Hollywood, as opposed to the emphasis elsewhere in the United States on the first syllable, "Row-dyo." But though Southern California abuts Mexico, and all of California has a Spanish history, there are few traces of Spanish in the English of California, except for place names and the Spanish-flavored English of Mexican-Americans, which will be discussed in a later chapter.

Southern California also is the home of the *looky lou*. That is a person who looks without buying: at houses, merchandise, or advertising. In recent years the term has spread from real estate to describe other kinds of onlookers, as in Paula L. Woods' 1999 novel *Inner City Blues*, set in Los Angeles:

> A camera was slung over his shoulder. A news photographer? Or maybe just a Looky Lou, one of a score we'd seen since the riots started, capturing the fiery moments on everything from video cameras to disposable thirty-five-millimeter Kodaks and Fujis.

Looky lou is an example of a California term that remains largely limited to the state, despite media attention. So is the use of *ditching school* rather than *skipping school* or *playing hooky*. Californians also speak of *earthquake weather*, hot humid still days that supposedly portend an earthquake. A 1995 episode of the television show "Beverly Hills 90210" was titled "Earthquake Weather," as was a 1997 novel set in California by science-fiction writer Tim Powers.

The *Dictionary of American Regional English* gives evidence that busy Californians *get off the dime* more than residents of other states. "If this government of ours doesn't hurry up and get off the dime soon, we're going to miss the chance to make one hell of a man a U.S. citizen," declared the *Los Angeles Daily News* in January 1998. Originally, in the early twentieth century, the phrase apparently referred to people in a dance hall who weren't moving from where they stood. It was never limited to California but seems especially prevalent there.

If you get out into the countryside, California has a considerable amount of distinctive vocabulary for naming its distinctive climate, geography, flora, and fauna. For example, hard clay soil is known as *adobe* in California. Marshy or swampy land in northern and central California is known as the *tules*, derived from a Spanish word (derived in turn from a Nahuatl Indian word) for the bulrushes that grow there. Fog in such places is *tule fog*. The *California Central Coast Dictionary* defines it as "Fog occurring in dense patches with little or no warning, usually in valley areas," but also lists it as archaic. In the San Francisco Bay area, when the sky is overcast it's not cloudy, just a *high fog*.

Californians cultivate a ground cover known as *ice plant*, named for water-filled finger-shaped leaves that glisten as if covered with ice. Ice plant has to stay close to the temperate coast, however, because temperatures low enough to make ice of the water would burst the leaves.

Among other examples, there is in California and further north on the Pacific coast a tree with large evergreen leaves and bright purple branches known as *madrone*. There is a purple bean known in northern California as *bayo*, a flower known as *meadow foam*, and a flowering plant known as *mariposa lily* or *beavertail grass*. There is a plant known as *burr clover* with its seed in a prickly pod. There is an evergreen shrub known as *chamise*, which grows in groves known as *chamisal*. There is a medicinal plant known as *canchalagua*. The eucalyptus tree, imported long ago from Australia, is known in California also as a *gum tree* or *blue gum*. A Western plant generally called *owl's clover* goes in California also by the names *johnny-nip* and *johnny-tuck*, and the fish generally called *rock bass* has the California name *Johnny verde*. St. John's Wort, in vogue nowadays for treating depression, has the California name *Klamath weed*.

A dart-shaped flower that others call a *shooting star* in California is called a *mosquito bill*. And a tree elsewhere known as a *groundsel* has the California name *mule fat*. The flower known as *fritillary* is called *mission bells* in California.

Some of these California names come from Spanish. California not only has *fiestas*, but deep-purple *fiesta flowers*. There is a fish called *medialuna*, the half-moon. And the owl's clover, mentioned above, is also known in California as *escobita*, "little broom" in Spanish — and it does look like a little broom or duster.

The cuisine of California has generated little in the way of regional vocabulary, but San Francisco cooking includes the Italian fish and shellfish stew called *cioppino*. And California, with its orange groves, seems to be the place of origin (around 1950) of the *screwdriver*, the drink that is a healthy mix of orange juice and vodka.

California Sounds

Do Californians speak with an accent? They don't think so, and neither does the rest of the country. And they're basically right: the California style of pronunciation, like that of the rest of the West, is a rather neutral blend of Eastern dialects, with the Northern predominating.

But if you listen carefully, you can hear some slightly distinctive California sounds. One person who *has* listened carefully is Hollywood dialect and accent specialist Allyn Partin Hernandez.

One of the most unusual sounds she has noticed among Californians under age 25 is the pronunciation of the second syllable of *garden* the way it is spelled: that is, with the same vowel as the separate word *den*. This is a violation of the normal rules of pronunciation in the English language, which reduce vowels in unstressed syllables to the "schwa" sound, a short unstressed "uh," regardless of spelling. In *garden*, the first syllable ("GAR") carries the stress, leaving the second without stress or emphasis. So in most other varieties of English, the pronunciation is "GAR-dun" or even a vowelless "GARD-'n." But some Californians now articulate *garden* as "GAR-den."

It's not just a matter of spelling. These same young Californians say *shouldn't*, which has no *e* in the spelling, as if the second syllable were *dent*: "SHOULD-dent." And they use the same sound in other words ending in *n* or *nt*, like *warden*, *Jordan*, and *didn't*. Partin notes that the pronunciation seems to be spreading beyond California.

Another pronunciation even more widely heard among older teens and adults in California and throughout the West is "een" for *-ing*, as in "I'm think-een of go-een camp-een." It contrasts with the two usual pronunciations of *-ing* back East: the formal one that rhymes with *sing* and the informal one that rhymes with *sin* and is often spelled *in'*, as in "I'm thinkin' of goin' campin'." Like the California pronunciation of *garden*, the "een" for *-ing* gives more prominence to the vowel of an unstressed syllable at the end of a word.

One other sound characteristic of younger Californians is harder to describe: the momentary stopping of the voice in the back of the throat while pronouncing emphatic syllables, which lengthens the sound of vowels and gives them what Partin calls a "crackle" or "creaky voice." The same stop at the back of the throat also can take the place of the "t" sound between vowels, so *about a* comes out as "abou' a" with a pause where the "t" should be. Likewise, *I've met a lot of others* comes out as "I've me' a lo' of others," and the familiar expression *whatever!* comes out as "wha'ever."

And high-school and younger Californians seem to be turning the "s" sound to "sh" before "t" in words like *restaurant* ("reshtaurant"); *lobster* ("lobshter"); and *Nordstrom* ("Nordshtrom"). Likewise, the "z" sound can become "zh," as in *dollars*, which ordinarily ends with a "z" sound but becomes "dollarzh." This, at least, hasn't yet caught on with the rest of the country.

NEVADA

Nevada, the Silver State, is closely related to the Golden State of California. Even their histories are alike: both boomed in the nineteenth century from mining in the north, and both boomed in the twentieth century from mass marketing of popular culture in the south. Today Northern Californians go to Reno and Carson City for recreation, while Southern Californians go to Las Vegas. And as the whole world lends an ear to Hollywood, so the world lends an eye to the spectacles of Vegas. The analogy could be extended further. Television didn't put Hollywood out of business but gave it a new means of influencing the world. The legalization of gambling in other states didn't put Las Vegas out of business but stimulated it to diversify into "family entertainment" and conventions, and into building the world's biggest and flashiest hotels.

Not surprisingly, then, the English language of Nevada corresponds closely to that of California. Even when you get away from the cities, the states have much in common. Since the middle of the nineteenth century, both have called their rural areas *cow counties*. In fact, in the nineteenth century, Los Angeles was called the "Queen of Cow Counties." Nowadays it is Nevada that makes everyday use of this term, since geographically the state still consists largely of cow counties. The three political divisions of Nevada are North (Reno and Carson City), South (Las Vegas), and the cow counties. Often enough, they are at odds with the cities in matters like water rights. The online publication *Electric Nevada* provides an example: "Just as an important new study suggests urban Nevadans care greatly about what is happening to their cow-county compatriots, the federal destruction of the Silver State's cow counties is gaining powerful new momentum."

Californians and Nevadans also share the name *French frog* to refer, simply, to a frog. Sometimes it means a large frog, or one suitable for eating. As a website for the Blue Sky Ecological Reserve near San Diego, California, explains, "No foreign species of frog is established in the United States. Terms such as *French frog, jumbo frog*, and *Louisiana frog* are often applied to the American bullfrog. Edible frogs are often called *French frogs*."

The frogs of California and Nevada are most plentiful in the Sierra Nevada mountain ranges of California's north and Nevada's northwest. Much more restricted in range is another water creature known in Nevada alone, the *cui-ui*. An endangered species, this fish is found only in Pyramid Lake, 50 miles north of Reno in the cow counties of northern Nevada. It's a sucker, that is, a fish that sucks plankton for food. It has something of a prehistoric look, as well it might; it goes back at least ten thousand years to a much larger prehistoric lake on the same spot. A cui-ui will live forty years or more, a trait that recently allowed the species to survive twenty years of being cut off from its spawning grounds at the Truckee River. The Paiute Indians who live on a reservation surrounding the lake place such importance in the cui-ui that they call themselves *Kuyui-odokado* or "cui-ui eating people."

ALASKA

At the top of America's Pacific coast, inhabited by sourdoughs and cheechakos, is the skookum state of Alaska. What's that? Well, *sourdoughs* are old-timers, that is, residents who have spent at least one winter there. The original sourdoughs, gold prospectors a century ago, got their name because they had no yeast to make bread and used sourdough instead. *Cheechakos,* on the other hand, are newcomers. The term comes from Chinook Jargon, a trade language that used a mixture of Indian and English words; *cheechako* came to Chinook Jargon from the Lower Chinook and Nootka Indian languages. Nowadays being a cheechako is not too much of a handicap, as long as you're respectful of the sourdoughs.

But *skookum* is the best of all. That's what it means. "*Skookum* is an adjective that makes anything it describes really cool or very useful," explains Marjy Wood, a travel agent and fourth-generation Alaskan from Wrangell. A skookum house, for example, is well built; a skookum night might have "a gorgeous display of northern lights against a field of stars"; and a skookum lay "could be a good place for fisherman to lay out their nets . . . (we won't go into what other things this term is used for)."

The famous discoverer of gold in the Klondike in 1897 was Skookum Jim Mason, a Tagish Indian. That's where the word came from. In the Tagish language, *skookum* means "strong," a nickname given to Jim because of his strength. His fame may have helped spread the word about skookum.

Skookum, a thoughtful dog, also happens to be the lead character in Doug Urquhart's "Paws," the only comic strip set in Alaska and the Yukon.

If you're from *Outside,* or more specifically the *Lower 48,* you'll need to add those words to your Alaskan vocabulary. But if you're *Inside,* you'll find that Alaska English is not much different from that of the other Western states, especially those of the Pacific Northwest. That's not too surprising, since the majority of English speakers who populated Alaska came by way of the West Coast, especially Seattle.

Still, they have picked up techniques and terminology for dealing with Alaska's extreme climate and terrain. Alaska has cities, but most of the state is what Alaskans call the *bush:* "anyplace not connected to the rest of Alaska by road or state ferry," according to *Anchorage Daily News* columnist Mike Doogan, author of *How to Speak Alaskan.*

In the Alaska bush, ten percent of the surface is *muskeg.* As mentioned in the discussion of Minnesota, *muskeg* is a special kind of northern swamp covered with sphagnum moss and dotted with pools ready to suck a traveler under. Muskeg can look like solid ground until you step on it.

Alaska's distinctive weather includes several names for winds. There is the *taku* of the southeast, sweeping down from a glacier to whisk at speeds of up to 100 miles an hour through Juneau, the state capital. Even worse is the *williwaw* of the Aleutians, a sudden blast from the mountains to the sea. Doogan says it makes the taku "seem like a breeze."

In most parts of Alaska except the southeast coast, *freeze-up* is a season, the time when lakes, rivers, and seaports freeze, preventing travel by water. Freeze-up generally lasts from October to May. It's a winter counterpart to *ice-out*, a New England term for the time in spring when the ice on lakes and rivers melts.

When Alaskans travel by dogsled, they *mush* (a corruption of the French *marche* or *marchons*).

An all-purpose material in Alaska is *babiche*, strips of rawhide from caribou or moose used, in Doogan's words, "to keep body and soul together when nails won't work. Good for making lean-tos, snowshoes, even fishing nets." In case of necessity, he adds, babiche can be boiled for soup.

Knee-high rubber boots, so useful in the bush, are sometimes called *Sitka slippers* or *Alaska tennis shoes*.

Women and children in Alaska wear the decorative garment known as a *kuspuk*. It's a parka, or sometimes a parka cover, with a short fringe or skirt. Companies like Kozy Kuspuks have adapted the traditional Inuit women's garment to modern fashion. In Dana Stabenow's mystery *A Cold Blooded Business*, set in Alaska's far north, detective Kate Shugak observes "the most beautiful kuspuk [she] had ever seen. The knee-length parka was made of cinnamon-colored corduroy with gold cord and red fox fur edging hem, wrists and hood. The wearer was a redhead with pale redhead skin and the combination was enough to cause a momentary pause in the din."

Kuspuk: By Kozy Kuspuks Inc. of Dillingham, Alaska

A *cache*, in Alaska as elsewhere, is a place to store supplies. But an Alaska cache goes to unusual heights to escape scavenging animals. It is a log cabin raised on poles eight or ten feet off the ground. To get in, you climb a ladder, which otherwise is set aside so animals can't do the same.

One of the stranger animals of Alaska is the *ice worm*. It's about an inch long and lives just below the surface of glaciers, eating pollen and spores that come its way. Long before this ice worm was discovered, however, in gold rush days, sourdoughs made up stories of mythical ice worms to impress cheechakos. Robert W. Service offered such a story in his "Ballad of the Ice-Worm Cocktail" about an Englishman, Major Brown, who reluctantly accepts a dare and downs the ice-worm drink:

> *And ere next night his story was the talk of Dawson Town,*
> *But gone and reft of glory was the wrathful Major Brown;*
> *For that ice-worm (so they told him) of such formidable size*
> *Was — a stick of stained spaghetti with two red ink spots for eyes.*

Not fictional at all is the beverage known as *hoochinoo*. The word is from the Tlingit Indian language, where it was first used to refer to an alcoholic drink the Tlingit made in the late nineteenth century from a mixture of rum and molasses. At the turn of that century, much hoochinoo also was brewed and consumed by those who came for the Alaska gold rush. Shortened to *hooch*, the word has since spread throughout American English as a name for home brew or liquor of low quality.

The distinctive foods of Alaska include *Eskimo ice cream*, made with whipped berries and seal oil. Sometimes it uses the bitter soopolallie or soapberry, which foams like soapsuds when whipped. Here is a recipe from an *Eskimo Cook Book* compiled by students at Shishmaref Day School in 1952:

> Grate reindeer tallow into small pieces. Add seal oil slowly while beating with hand. After some seal oil has been used, add a little water while whipping. Continue adding seal oil and water until white and fluffy. Any berries may be added to it.

Other Alaskan words, also from Indian languages, include *oogruk*, a bearded seal; *mukluk*, a sealskin boot; and *muktuk*, whale blubber used as food. One of the most respected Alaskan creatures is the *Kodiak bear*, a brown grizzly named after its favored habitat of Kodiak Island on the west side of the Gulf of Alaska.

For the first two-thirds of the nineteenth century, Alaska was under at least nominal Russian control. A few traces of that Russian heritage linger in the Alaskan English vocabulary, especially terminology used in the Aleutian Islands. There is the *baidarka* or *bidar*, a name the Russians gave to a type of kayak made by the Aleut Indians of wood or bone covered with sealskin. The Aleut home, half underground and covered with stones, driftwood, and earth, was given the Russian name *barabara*. Aleuts also would have a community steambath, called *banya* by the Russians, a name now sometimes used in Alaska for a sauna.

HAWAII

Even a haole tourist quickly recognizes that the American English spoken in Hawaii is a little different from the talk of the mainland. Sometimes it's as radical as this:

If I come stay go, an you no stay come, wat foa I go?

Eh, when you go'n get da poki from Nohea's house? Aaah, bumbai!

We wen spock dem at da mall.

These are translated by the Extreme Hawaii Fun website:

If I come and you're not there, why should I go?

Excuse me. When do you think it will be possible to pick up the fish salad from Lovely's house? When I get around to it!

We saw our friends enjoying themselves at the mall.

That's the extreme, the Hawaii Pidgin English that outsiders find practically incomprehensible. It's still basically English, though.

True Hawaiian is quite different: a Polynesian language, unrelated to English, that is famous for having few consonants, many vowels, and duplicated syllables. Only about 1000 people still speak Hawaiian as a native language, though it is taught as a second language in the schools. But about 600,000 people, half the population of Hawaii, use Hawaii Pidgin English, including some 100,000 or so who speak little else.

Pidgin developed late in the nineteenth century by combining English with a Hawaiian accent and some Hawaiian vocabulary. The very melody or intonation of Pidgin is different from the standard Western American English otherwise spoken on the islands. Where the voice rises at the end of a question in English, in Pidgin the voice goes up in the middle of the sentence and then down again. Pidgin also whittles away some of the sounds and word endings of English and simplifies the vocabulary and grammar.

Of all the Pidgin vocabulary, the most versatile item is the phrase *da kine*. It has so many meanings it's hard to define, but you know when it's da kine, it's good — or skookum, as an Alaskan might say. It derives from *this kind* or *those kind* in English, and sometimes it means just that, as in "You saw da kine car he wen' get?" Other times it signals approval, as in "I jus caught da kine wave, brah," or enthusiasm, as in "Man, he da kine 'bout her!" A column of coming events in the *Honolulu Star-Bulletin* is called "Da Kine." A Hawaiian teenager helpfully explains that it is like *smurf* or *smurfy* in meaning whatever you want it to mean: "Feel free to make up your own meaning, i.e., 'Did you hear about Frank? He had to go to the hospital to get his da kine (smurf) fixed.'"

Another important Pidgin word is *bumbye*, from *by and by*. In his short story "Da Word," Lee A. Tonouchi's character offers a definition:

> Bumbye gotta be one word, I heard my Grandma use 'em sooo many times. "Grandma, wen you going take me Disneyland?" "Bumbye." So bumbye can mean later on, indefinite kine, possibly nevah. Or "Grandma, hakum you no always flush da toilet aftah you pau shi shi?" "Cuz bumbye poho water." So bumbye is also like consequently or as one result of. See, so das two definitions already.

There is also *hana hou*, a Pidgin term from the Hawaiian language, which literally means "one more time." It's a way of asking a performer for an encore. It's also the name of the Hawaiian Airlines inflight magazine and of broadcasts recognizing outstanding community volunteers on Honolulu's KITV4. The famous "Don Ho Show" has its home in the Hana Hou Lounge of the Waikiki Beachcomber Hotel.

If you *go holoholo*, you're going out for a good time. Literally, *holoholo* means walking or running. It gets used like this, in a story by Izabel Ramos: "Anyway dis one time, when I waz one teenagah (waznt too long ago), we nevah have nothing bettah fodo on one Saturday nite, so my three friends wen pick me up fo go holoholo town sai [in town]."

Hoomalimali is flattery or nonsense. It figures in a song by Leonard and Ruth Hawk that begins: "'Twas the night before Christmas and all through the hale [house]/ Was singing and dancing and hoomalimali." Another seasonal song, by Johnny Kamano, ends, "Here comes Santa in a red canoe/ Paddling on a magic sea blue/ With a ho'omalimali Merry Christmas to you."

A website called Da Kine Language, named in honor of that versatile term *da kine*, explains three other important Pidgin terms:

> *One:* Instead of using *a* as an article, *one* is used. For example, "I get one headache!" Or also, "I want one beer."
>
> *brah* [a form of *brother*]: Pronounced like the undergarment, this term is like saying *you*, but in a friendly, not accusatory manner. Locals often call one another *brah*.
>
> *try* [meaning something like "please"]: For example, *Try come* means "Please come over here." Also, *Try wait* means "Please wait for me."

But despite the prominence of Pidgin, the majority of English spoken in Hawaii is much like what you will hear in other Western states. Even the standard English of Hawaii, however, is flavored with words from the Hawaiian language. Everyone knows *haole*, originally meaning "foreigner," now referring to a person of European rather than Hawaiian ancestry. A *hapa haole* (*hapa* meaning "half") is one who is part haole, that is, part native Hawaiian ancestry and part something else. A *coast haole* is one from the "coast," that is, anywhere on the American mainland, and thus little acquainted with Hawaiian ways. But even a haole can be a *kamaaina*, one who is native born or at least fully assimilated. Many Hawaiian businesses make *kamaaina* part of their names, including Kama'aina Computers, Kama'aina Careers (an employment agency), Kama'aina Creations (hand made cards), and Kamaaina Loan and Cash for Gold (a pawn shop).

Hawaiian English also has a word for visitors, strangers, or beginners. The Honolulu official "Lifeguards' Guide to Popular Oahu Beaches" warns that "Newcomers, or as we say in Hawaiian *malihini*, should take extra special care in choosing where they will recreate or otherwise enjoy Oahu's beaches and surrounding ocean waters."

Da Kine Hula

There are terms for native customs that have survived Americanization — or that sometimes are Americanized into tourist attractions: the *luau*, for example, and the *hula*. *Luau* gets its name from the edible leaves of the taro plant, used in cooking food for the feast. There is the *hukilau*, a community fishing expedition, celebrated in the "Hukilau" song ("Oh, we're going to a hukilau") by a haole written in 1948. There is the colorful coverall Hawaiian dress, the *muumuu*, and the garland of flowers, the *lei*. In Hawaii, May Day is *Lei Day*.

Hawaii's culinary distinction is *poi*, made from the tuberous underground stem of the taro plant. Before the coming of the Europeans, it was the staple of the Hawaiian diet, providing carbohydrates, vitamin B, calcium, and phosphorus in easily digestible form. Poi is prepared by cooking, peeling, and mashing the taro tubers. It can be eaten fresh or allowed to ferment, which gives it a sour but supposedly pleasant taste. The consistency of poi is measured by the number of fingers required to eat it, *one finger* being the firmest and *three finger* the most watery, with *two finger* said to be the ideal. Visitors might prefer the appropriately named *malihini poi*, pudding made of banana bread instead of poi.

If you don't care for poi, you can always get your taro in a pudding called *kulolo*. For this, to the taro you add coconut milk, brown sugar, melted butter, and vanilla, and then steam the mixture in a pan, tightly covered with ti leaves or foil, for four to six hours.

Meat or fish steamed in ti or taro leaves is called *laulau*. Salted salmon mashed with the fingers, seasoned, and served chilled is known as *lomilomi*, (*lomi* is Hawaiian for "mash" or "crush"). Or you can have pork in a steamed bun, originally the Chinese dish called *char siu bao*, but renamed in Hawaiian *manapua*. It is said to mean "mountain of pig," deriving from *mauna* "mountain" and *pua* "pig."

Directions in Hawaii are often not points of the compass but *mauka*, meaning "toward the mountains or inland," and *makai*, "toward the sea."

The Hawaiian contribution to architecture is the porch known as a *lanai*, roofed but open sided, often screened in. You can even get a poly-nylon lanai from Walrus Gear to make a vestibule for your tent.

And then there's Hawaii's contribution to the world of music, the *ukulele*. The instrument itself actually came from Portugal, in the hands of immigrant João Gomes da Silva, on a ship that docked in Honolulu in 1879. Da Silva couldn't play it, so he loaned it to someone who could, João Fernandes from Madeira. Fernandes entertained crowds on shore, and later the Hawaiian king and queen and many others. In Portuguese the instrument was called a braguinho, but to Hawaiian listeners its music sounded like a dancing (*lele*) flea (*uku*), so *ukulele* became its name when other Hawaiians adopted it.

Another Hawaiian musical innovation, though given an English name, is the style of guitar playing known as *slack-key guitar*. This style features fingerpicking a guitar tuned to an open chord.

Three Hawaiian words figure in Margarita Lane's song, "That's the Hawaiian in Me":

> *No pilikia, no huhu*
> *That is my philosophy*
> *If the sun is bright and the trade winds blow*
> *The world is maikai to me*

Pilikia is "worry"; *huhu* is "angry"; and *maikai* is "good" or "fine."

Hundreds of Hawaiian words are also used to name the natural features and creatures of the island: *aa*, for example, which means rough jagged volcanic lava (as distinct from *pahoehoe*, a smooth rock formed from lava), and *oo*, an extinct bird, both beloved of Scrabble players; *ahi*, *aku*, and *kawakawa*, kinds of tuna; *au*, a marlin or swordfish; *oio*, a bonefish; *mahimahi*, a fish now well known on the mainland too; *hau*, a hibiscus; *hinahina*, a broadleaf grass or

Spanish moss; *honohono,* a kind of grass or a dayflower; and *lilikoi,* the passion fruit.

Birds of Hawaii, some of them endangered, include *apapane* and *iiwi,* honeycreeper birds; *io,* a hawk; *alala,* a crow; and *nene,* a goose, the state bird.

The weather includes the *kona,* a strong southwest wind, often with heavy rain.

Another Scrabble favorite taken into English from the Hawaiian language is *ae,* meaning "yes" and pronounced like *aye* (encouraged also by Japanese *hai*). There's also the short word *e,* pronounced like *hey* and meaning the same thing.

And of course there's the biggest Hawaiian word of all, the one that is the state's motto and greets friends and visitors coming and going, *aloha.* It means not only "welcome," "hello," and "goodbye," but a whole spirit of friendliness, fun, and love.

AMERICAN ETHNIC

Our American ways of speaking depend on where we are and who we listen to. In the South we listen to *y'all* and in the North to *you guys*, and unless we choose to be different, we speak that way too. In Rhode Island, when we want an ice cream treat, we learn to ask for a *cabinet*; in Louisiana, we're grateful for *lagniappe*; in Oregon, we're careful not to be too *spendy*. We learn to stand *on line* in New York City. That's the way we make ourselves understood to those who live around us. It's the way we show we're not strangers.

But it's not just a matter of geographic place. We have professional and social places too. We talk like lawyers or laundry workers, revivalists or rappers, farmers or financiers; we live in the city, country, or suburbs; we are toddler, teenager, senior citizen, or something in between. We talk like — or sometimes we avoid talking like — the people around us. Our way of speaking depends both on who we associate with and on who we want to be associated with.

In the United States, our sense of place also depends significantly on the ethnic group we belong to. We are not just Southerners, Bostonians, or Californians, but also various kinds of hyphenated Americans: Anglo , German-, Italian-, Irish-, Jewish-, Hispanic-, and African- Americans, to name some of the long-established groups; Philippine-, Chinese-, Vietnamese-, and Indian-(from India) Americans, to name some of the more recent. Or of course we may be American Indians, or Native Americans, who got here ahead of all the other Americans by thousands of years. Lest we forget, we are constantly asked by surveys, application forms, and the U.S. census to label ourselves *Black, White, Hispanic, Asian, American*

Indian, or as a last resort *Other*. It is a rare American who tries to step out of the conventional categories like golfer Tiger Woods with his self-designation *Cablinasian* (combining Caucasian, Black, American Indian, and Asian).

So a proper understanding of American English requires that we look at racial and ethnic spaces as well as geographic ones. Of course, the kind of English we speak is not a matter of heredity but of environment: who we grow up with, not who our parents happen to have been. Someone born in Virginia or Vietnam who grows up in Minneapolis will sound Minnesotan; someone born of white parents who grows up in an African-American community will sound African American, and vice versa.

Our speech is also determined by how closely and exclusively we identify with the community we find ourselves in, regardless of whether the community is geographic or ethnic. Often we can make choices. If we grow up in New York, do we always want to talk in the New York style? If we are born into an African-American community, are there times when we want to emphasize or de-emphasize the "soul" in our speech? For one reason or another, many of us choose to speak one way within the community and another way among outsiders.

African American

Historically the most important of the ethnic varieties of American speech is *African American* — also known as *Black English, Ebonics*, or *Spoken Soul*, to use a phrase coined by Claude Brown, author of *Manchild in the Promised Land*. African American English, as we will call it here in parallel with other designations like Latino English, has some distinguishing features that are the same South and North, East and West. It could be said, in fact, to be the variety of American English with the greatest uniformity throughout the nation; every other variety is more influenced by differences of place.

But that would be to overlook the great differences within the African-American community in the use of African American English. It ranges from a highly cultivated formal style to earthy street

"I Have a Dream": Martin Luther King, Jr., at the March on Washington

slang. The range of styles may in fact be greater than for any other variety of American English, because most other varieties have lost the highly formal manner still admired and used in oratory by African Americans. Consider the famous "I Have a Dream" address by Martin Luther King, Jr. at the 1963 March on Washington. It has no hint of slang and follows the most careful grammatical patterns of Standard English, but it also uses the repetitive phrasing central to the African-American preaching style:

> . . . There are those who are asking the devotees of civil rights, "When will you be satisfied?" We can never be satisfied as long as our bodies, heavy with the fatigue of travel, cannot gain lodging in the motels of the highways and the hotels of the cities. We cannot be satisfied as long as the Negro's basic mobility is from a smaller ghetto to a larger one. We can never be satisfied as long as a Negro in Mississippi cannot vote and a Negro in New York believes he has nothing for which to vote. No, no, we are not satisfied, and we will not be satisfied until justice rolls down like waters and righteousness like a mighty stream. . . .

This was spoken also with King's cultivated African-American accent, and with dramatic pauses and changes of pitch also characteristic of African-American preaching.

That tradition continues today. It comes to the attention of the nation in the speeches of the Rev. Jesse Jackson, as in this excerpt of his address to the Detroit Economic Club on October 30, 1995:

> We must change direction.
>
> We all know that it is wrong that urban African-American babies die at rates that surpass many of the poorer nations in the world. We must change direction.
>
> We all know that it is wrong that black children risk mean streets to attend schools in mean straits, often so rundown as to threaten their health rather than lift their minds.
>
> And even those who do graduate face a world of unemployment and insecurity, of low-wage jobs and low-gauge hopes.
>
> We must change direction.
>
> We all know that the common threads that tie our democracy together are fraying.
>
> That Dr. King's dream is turning into Newt's nightmare.
>
> That the hopes of a generation are dying on the streets of our cities, every single day. For African-American youth, it is not Generation X; it is a generation in exile, cast aside from the American dream. We must change direction.

("Newt's nightmare" refers to cutbacks in government spending for welfare proposed by Newt Gingrich, then Speaker of the House of Representatives.)

In making his points, Jackson repeats the phrase, "We all know," so that it is not simply a statement but an insistent reminder. Again and again, the response to "We all know" is the refrain: "We must change direction."

Of course, Americans don't have to go far to hear other types of African American English as well. It is spoken on city streets and is spread far and wide in rap and hip-hop music, on television and in the movies.

African Americans make up more than one-eighth of the entire U.S. population. African American English is significant among American dialects not only because it is spoken by such a substantial and long-established population, but because it is the model for certain aspects of American popular culture. Just as young Americans of all races imitate the clothing styles of streetwise African Americans, so they have learned both vocabulary and pronunciation styles of African-American vernacular. *Dude, jazz, groovy, cool, chill out,* and *you go, girl* — not all of these words originated in African American, but African Americans gave them their slang meanings before they were picked up by hip youth of all races.

American music has long had a strong African-American element, from spirituals to ragtime to jazz, rhythm and blues, rap, and hip-hop. White or black, when you write or perform such music, the dominant standard for language is African American. It is also highly influential in the vast category known as rock 'n' roll, a black-and-white amalgam of African American and Southern white. Where the Northern and Western accent gives *I* the "ah-ee" pronunciation and pronounces the "r" sound after vowels, as in *more*, "general rock 'n' roll" uses the African American and Southern "ah" for *I* and "mo'" for *more*. The very spelling *gangsta rap* shows African-American influence, omitting the *r* at the end of *gangster.*

And so rock musician Bob Dylan, for example, from Minnesota in the far North, becomes African American or Southern, saying *ambassador* with a "duh" instead of "dor" in the final syllable, and "You maht lahk to dance," in his song "Gotta Serve Somebody" (1979).

African-American culture also was the subject and inspiration for the first original style of American theater, the minstrel show, which began with the Virginia Minstrels in New York City in 1843. In minstrel shows, white performers wearing blackface sang songs and told jokes in imitation of the speechways of African Americans. Needless to say, this was the opposite of high culture, and the representations of African Americans were caricatures, but minstrel shows were also the beginning of influence of African-American style on all America.

For many reasons, therefore, African American deserves first place in any discussion of ethnic American speech. Fortunately, others have reached this conclusion too, so African American English has been carefully studied from both within and outside the group. Much is known about what African American has in common with other American dialects and what makes it unique.

Two facts are clear about African American English: It is Southern, and it is not. That is, African-American speech has much in common with Southern white speech, but also much that is different.

The Southernness of African American English is hardly surprising. After all, for nearly three hundred years more than 90 percent of African Americans lived in the South, hearing and speaking the language of that region. In the twentieth century, substantial numbers of African Americans left for the North and West to find better jobs in industry. But in the cities of the North and West, outside of the workplace, African Americans generally remained apart from whites, partly by choice but also because of housing policies that kept them confined to their own neighborhoods. Rather than adopting the speech patterns of the Northern and Western white communities, therefore, they kept their Southern culture and language.

Until that mass migration, African Americans outside the South had been so few that they had generally adopted local speech patterns. But migration and housing segregation spread the Southern style of African-American speech to African-American communities across the nation.

How Southern, then, is African American English? It has many of the same sounds and words discussed in the chapter on the South, particularly the "ah" for *I* and the dropping of the "r" after vowels (as in "mo'" for *more*). *Pen* is pronounced as *pin*. *Y'all* is the plural of *you*. People say "It's a good reason why African American is Southern" instead of "There's a good reason". . . . You *might could* find good reasons for the similarity.

But there also are notable differences between African American English and Southern, or any other variety spoken by whites. The first is the use of *be* under certain circumstances where other dialects would use *is* or *are*. Those circumstances are limited to a permanent or ongoing condition or activity: "She be nice" (but not "She be looking at me"); "The kitchen be big" (but not "The kitchen door be open"); "Sometimes the jokes don't even be funny, but they still tell them."

There is another rule of African American English that involves *is* or *are* in a different way. Where other dialects allow a contraction of *is* or *are*, African American English can omit it altogether. In all varieties of English, "She is hungry" can be expressed informally as "She's hungry." In African American, it can also be "She hungry."

Likewise, "They are waiting for me" can be contracted in all varieties of English to "They're waiting for me" and in African American also to "They waiting for me." But where other dialects do not allow a contraction, as in the emphasized *is* of "Yes, it is!" African American also always keeps the full form of the verb.

The pronunciation of African American also has certain distinctive features. When there is more than one consonant at the end of a syllable, African American English can reduce the number of consonants to one. So *stand* can be *stan'*, *just* can *jus'*, and *disk* can be *dis'*.

Something similar happens in all varieties of English in normal conversation. "She lifts it," for example, becomes "She lifs it" in the speech of almost all Americans, unless they are being unnaturally careful. But African American English carries the reduction one step further, to a single consonant sound, so that *lifts* becomes *lis'*. Similarly, *desk* becomes *des'*, and the plural therefore is *desses*, along the pattern of other words ending in *s* like *messes*.

The rule is more complicated than this; you can't get rid of a *p*, *t*, or *k* after *m* or *n*, for example, so *junk* keeps both *n* and *k*, and *lump* keeps both *m* and *p*. Actually, it gets even more complicated, but the point is clear: consonant clusters are simplified according to specific rules. It's just as hard to master the pronunciations of African American English as it is to master those of a Philadelphia dialect, or Pittsburghese, or Utahnics.

Of course, African-American speakers do not need to carry rule books around with them in order to speak their language properly. Nor are they likely to be able to explain the grammar and pronunciation rules they follow, any more than speakers of other varieties of English can explain theirs, unless they happen to be trained in technical grammar and phonetics. In the same way, most people can't explain what muscles they move in order to walk, but they manage anyhow to do so. Every variety of every language has its complexities, which children learn as naturally as they learn to walk, and African American English is no exception.

To get back to specific African-American pronunciations: They also include the consonant sounds "d," "t," "v," and "f" for the sounds we spell *th*. So *this* can be *dis*, *thin* can be *tin*, *both* can be *bove*, and *tooth* can be *toof*. Which sound takes the place of "th" is again a matter of strict rules. "D" and "t" for example, substitute for "th" at the beginning of words and syllables, while "v" and "f" substitute at the ends. And "d" or "v" is used if the "th" is a "voiced" sound (that is, if the vocal cords are vibrating), while "t" or "f" is used if the "th" is "voiceless."

Another pronunciation difference between black and white speech involves the contraction of *going to*. White dialects often reduce that to *gonna*. African American English sometimes uses that *gonna*, but often it keeps the long "o" sound of *going* while dropping the second syllable: "He gon' be here." In constructions with the pronoun *I*, the "g" sound sometimes is lost, resulting in sentences like "I'm 'o' do it" or "I'm 'a' do it." Similarly, the sentence "I don't know" can lose the "d" and become "I 'on' know" in African American English, contrasting with "I dunno" of white dialects. All these pronunciations differ from formal English usage, but each according to its own rules.

One thing that is not heard much in African-American speech is the "Northern Cities Shift" of vowels. In Chicago or Cleveland, whites may pronounce *Ann* as *Ian*, but blacks generally will not. This is again because of the segregation of African Americans during and after their migration to the urban North. Perhaps even more important, it is because of the association of African American with Southern dialects, which do not make the Northern Cities Shift.

As with other dialects, there's also a considerable amount of vocabulary that distinguishes African American English from any other kind. Since the rest of America has long been attracted to the inventiveness of African-American speech, many African-American terms have crossed over into the general vocabulary, from *banjo* in the eighteenth century to *bad-mouth* in the twentieth. But there are also some words used mainly within the African-American community, little understood by whites. There is *kitchen*, for example, for the hair at the nape of the neck, which is especially *nappy* or kinky. There is *ashy*, the dry whitish look of skin exposed to cold weather. *Salty* means angry, and to *jump salty* is to get mad.

An older African-American woman may be referred to respectfully as *auntie*. That word, and its relative *aunt*, are likely to be pronounced with the "ah" vowel sound of *father* rather than the short "a" sound of *ant*, using the pronunciation associated with the cultivated speech of eastern New England and eastern Virginia.

Some words have multiple meanings in African American English. Take *stay*, for example. It can have the Southern meaning of living in a place, so that "Where you stay?" means the same as "Where do you live?" As African-American linguist Arthur K. Spears points out, it can also have a meaning of embarrassment or losing face: "You gon' stay from hit him?" meaning "Are you going to allow him to hit you and get away with it?" Finally, *stay* can act like African-American *be* in expressing something frequent or habitual. "He stay flossing" means "He's always dressed well."

Even words that are familiar to speakers of all varieties of English can be used in special ways within African American English. Take *come*, for example. It can express a speaker's annoyance with what someone else did, as in "He come walkin' in here like he owned the place" and even "She come goin' in my room — didn't knock or nothin'."

And along with the verb *be*, there is the related form *been*, which can be put to special use in African American English. In most other dialects, *been* refers to something that is over and gone, as in "They've been happy," implying that they may not be happy now. In African American English, "They been happy" means that they were once and still are. This can cause misunderstanding between dialects. Linguist John Rickford asked twenty-five African Americans and twenty-five whites about the meaning of "She been married." All but two of the African Americans said she was still married, while seventeen of the whites thought she was not.

In 1972 Robert L. Williams, the psychologist who also coined the word *Ebonics*, came up with *BITCH*, or *Black Intelligence Test of Cultural Homogeneity*, a survey of 100 items that tested knowledge of African-American vocabulary. Not surprisingly, Williams found that young African Americans did much better on the test than young whites.

The *Dictionary of American Regional English* has found hundreds of words used mainly by African Americans, even though the dictionary's focus is on regional rather than ethnic distinctions. African-American words

> **Blood** is
>
> a) a vampire
> b) a dependent individual
> c) an injured person
> d) a brother of color
>
> *Correct answer:* d.
>
> —Black Intelligence Test
> of Cultural Homogeneity

reported there include *ace* meaning "a close friend," *bad* meaning "excellent," *bro* for "brother," *chump change* for "a small amount of money," *dicty* or *hincty* for "high-class or snobbish," and *game* meaning "a deceptive or manipulative act or pattern of behavior."

Even though African American English is remarkably uniform around the country, there are some regional differences. *Airish*, for example, seems to be a Southern African-American term for chilly weather, while the *hawk* is Chicago's African-American name for a cold wind, a name now used by white Chicagoans as well. Among black speakers in the South, a toddler who is no longer the baby of a family can be referred to as a *knee baby*. Also in the South, African Americans may speak of a *dead cat on the line*, meaning something suspicious (probably referring to a dead catfish on a fishing line). Slang especially is variable; according to the recent book *Spoken Soul* by African-American scholars John Russell Rickford and Russell John Rickford, to agree with someone in Washington, D.C., you say, "I'm with it"; in New Orleans, "I'm 'bout it"; and in Philadelphia, "That's whassup."

So African American is a major and complex variety of American English. But is "African American" what we should call it? Even determining the proper name for this variety of American English is not a simple matter. It has been known as *Negro Dialect, Black English, African American English* or *African American Vernacular English, Ebonics,* and *Spoken Soul*. Behind each of those names is not only a linguistic but a political decision, reflecting the names given to or used by the people who belong to this ethnic group. The terms Negro, Black or black, and African American have been favored one after the other as designations for American slave descendants (to use a neutral term proposed by African-American linguist John Baugh). But Ebonics and Spoken Soul are something else, ways of characterizing the language itself.

When Robert L. Williams coined *Ebonics* in 1973 (from *ebony* meaning "black" and *phonics* meaning "sounds"), he did it "to define black language from a black perspective." Using names like *Black English*, he said, reflected a "white bias" toward African-American language and encouraged viewing African-American language as "nonstandard," "broken," or "bad English." *Ebonics*, in contrast, suggests that African-American speech has standards of its own. As we have seen, it does.

Ebonics was used by only a few Afrocentric scholars until December 1996, when it was widely publicized by a resolution of the school board in Oakland, California, identifying the speech of its African-American students not as a dialect of English but as a separate language — and asking for state aid to teach Standard English as a second language to those students, who made up 53 percent of the public school population.

In that case, the term *Ebonics* was used to support the view that African Americans speak a separate language — and an African one, at that — rather than a variety of American English.

The fact that only part of African American English is the same as Southern supports that view. Still, at least on the surface, it would seem a difficult case to make. African American English, after all, can be understood by speakers of other varieties of English, just as African-American speakers can readily understand those other speakers. Where mutual comprehension is possible, the varieties are usually considered to be dialects of the same language. Furthermore, someone who speaks African American English in Africa will be understood only by those Africans who have learned English.

Nevertheless, it can be argued that African American English has the same African ancestry as African Americans themselves. The people who were brought to North America centuries ago as slaves spoke a variety of West African languages. And certain distinctive qualities of those African languages are like certain distinctive qualities of African American English mentioned earlier: using *be* for permanent or regular situations; omitting *is* or *are* under certain conditions; omitting consonants at the end of syllables; and not using a "th" sound, for example. Those matters of grammar and pronunciation have been interpreted as evidence that when African slaves learned English, they molded it according to the languages they knew.

On the other hand, it can also be argued that just about every distinctive feature of African American English has a parallel in some dialect of English spoken in England. There are dialects in England that use *be* somewhat like African American English, and so on.

Since the English speakers who first arrived in North America came from a variety of places in England, the argument goes, that could explain the origin of the distinctive qualities of African American English.

There are experts on both sides of the debate. It hasn't been resolved, and the most likely conclusion remains that both Africa and England had something to do with making African American English distinctive. Whatever the ultimate outcome, the debate has had the good effect of making the existence and facts of African American English well known.

Latino English

The other major category of ethnic American English is what may be called *Latino English*, though as with African American English the name itself is a problem. Both *Latino* and *Hispanic* refer to Americans with present or past ties to Spanish-speaking cultures, and although the words are often used interchangeably, they have a slight difference in meaning. *Latino* is a shortening of *Latinoamericano* and thus refers to Latin America and its cultures, while *Hispanic* has a broader application in that it can also refer to Spain and Spanish culture. Thus a person from Spain living in the United States can be termed *Hispanic* but not *Latino*. When used to refer to residents of the United States, however, the terms are practically synonymous, since almost all Hispanic Americans have associations with Latin America. *Hispanic* is currently the official designation used by U.S. government agencies and also seems to be the preferred term among Spanish-heritage communities in Florida and Texas. *Latino* is more likely to be used to convey ethnic pride and seems to be preferred in California. There is no absolutely "right" term for all occasions. This chapter uses *Latino* except when referring to ancestry and the population as defined by the Census, where *Hispanic* seems more appropriate.

There are many local and regional varieties of Latino English. And although not all speakers of Latino English are also speakers of Spanish, the influence of the Spanish language in its own various forms is strong. To do full justice to Latino English is beyond the scope of this book. But some basic observations are possible.

At the start of the twenty-first century, Americans of Hispanic ancestry have become almost as numerous as African Americans. A 1997 U.S. Census Bureau estimate identified about 30 million Americans — more than 11 percent of the total population — as being "of Hispanic origin." That is almost as many as African Americans, who numbered about 35 million, 13 percent of the total. But of the Hispanic Americans, nearly half were born outside the United States. Thus it is not surprising that in the 1990 Census, three-quarters of Hispanic Americans said they spoke Spanish at home, and half of them said they did not speak English very well.

Nor is it surprising that much of the Latino population is concentrated in a few states, especially the four that border on Mexico — California, Arizona, New Mexico, and Texas. California alone has more than one-third of the entire U.S. population of Hispanic ancestry, and Texas has one-fifth. There are also significant populations in Florida, Colorado, New York, New Jersey, Illinois, and Massachusetts.

Some Latinos in each area speak only Spanish, and some speak only English, but the majority have at least some command of both languages. The result is a wide range of styles in both the Spanish and the English of Latinos. Some speakers are such newcomers to English that their English is simply English with a Spanish accent. But many others are native speakers of English, and their way of speaking is not simply that of a foreigner trying to speak English.

Amid these complexities, the most fundamental fact about Latino English dialects is that — though they sound Spanish-accented — they do exist independent of Spanish. Like Bostonian, African American, or Standard English, they have their own rules and patterns. Some of the manifestations of Latino English in fact seem in opposition to those of Spanish, as if the speakers wished to distance themselves from a foreign accent.

Of the different Latino populations in the United States, the largest is Mexican Americans or Chicanos. *Chicano* is simply an adaptation of Spanish *Mexicano*, meaning "Mexican," so both *Mexican American* and *Chicano* have the same meaning. As with *Hispanic* and *Latino*, however, there is divided usage and preference for one term or the other within various communities. *Chicano* emphasizes the uniqueness of the culture and its language, while *Mexican American* emphasizes its participation in the larger American culture.

Not surprisingly, most Latinos in the states bordering on Mexico are Mexican American. Because they are the most numerous of the Latino groups, and because Chicano English has been well studied, we will take it as an example of Latino accents of English.

One of the basic characteristics of Chicano English is just what you would expect from a Spanish accent: substituting the "s" sound for the "z" sound. This occurs everywhere: not only in words like *zoo*, *crazy*, or *haze*, which are spelled with a *z*, but also in the many words where the "z" sound is camouflaged with an *s* spelling: *his*, *hers*, *days*, *easy*, and *wise*, for example. In Chicano English, then, a sentence like "His days are easy" would sound like "Hiss dayss are eassy."

But at least a few Mexican Americans do the opposite, converting every "s" sound to a "z" sound, as in "I won the raze" and "This is my houze." That's even more un-Spanish than Standard English.

Another notable pronunciation of Chicano English is the substitution of the "ch" sound for "sh," so that *shoe* sounds like *chew*, *shop* sounds like *chop*, and *dish* sounds like *ditch*. That's what you'd expect from Spanish, which has a "ch" but not a "sh" sound. However, Chicano English just as freely goes in the reverse direction, changing "ch" to "sh" so that *check* sounds like "shek"; *child* sounds like "shayld"; and *preach* sounds like "preash." In fact, Chicano English allows either sound on all *ch* and *sh* words. So for example *shop* and *chop* can both be pronounced as either *shop* or *chop*. The word *Chicano* itself follows this pattern and has a double pronunciation in Chicano English, sometimes starting with a "ch" sound, sometimes with "sh." That's not what Spanish would do.

A third important trait of Chicano English is changing long vowel sounds to short vowel sounds. *Need*, *keys*, and *feel* become "nid," "kiss," and "fill," for example; *mail* becomes "mel"; and *school* is "skul." (A Spanish accent would cause the opposite to happen, making short vowels long.) When these vowels are followed by *l*, as in the case of *feel*, *mail*, and *school*, similar shortenings can be heard in other dialects of English, and it has been argued that those other dialects learned the shortening from Chicano English. In any case, those pronunciations aren't what you'd expect from Spanish.

Experts have offered a number of possible explanations for these un-Spanish sounds of Chicano English. One explanation, at least for the switching of the "ch" and "sh" sounds, notes that a similar thing happens in the Spanish dialects spoken along the Mexico-United States border, dialects of Spanish that are different from those spoken elsewhere. Another explanation maintains that those who speak with Chicano pronunciations are demonstrating their fluency in English, or their difference from Mexican immigrants who don't speak English, by distancing their speech from Spanish. Whatever the reason, those pronunciations make Chicano English something in its own right.

Other pronunciations in Chicano English are what you would expect from a Spanish accent. For example, the "j" sound becomes a "ch" in the middle or at the ends of words, so *judge* is "jutch," *teenager* is "teenacher," and *language* is "langwich." And some vowels become more Spanish. The vowel of *duck* and *drugs*, which is also the vowel in the first syllable of *money*, in Chicano English becomes an "ah" so that those words are pronounced "dahk," "drahgs" and "mahney."

Chicano shares with African American English the tendency to lose consonant sounds at the end of syllables, so, for example, *want* becomes "wan'" and *friend* is "fren'." But in Chicano English the only consonant sounds lost are "t" and "d." So there is a contrast with African American English in words like *friends*: African American drops the "s," making the plural "fren," which is the same as the singular, while Chicano drops the "d," making the plural "frens."

There is one pronunciation trait that is apparently unique to Chicano English speakers who live in California: "short e" pronounced as "short a" when followed by the letter *l*. So *bell* becomes "bal," rhyming with "pal"; *elevator* becomes "alevator"; and *L.A.*, the widely used abbreviation for *Los Angeles*, is "allay."

Perhaps the most prominent feature of Chicano English, however, is the overall lilt of the voice throughout each sentence. Chicano speakers are likely to raise the pitch of the voice at the beginning, or middle, or end of a statement more often than speakers of other kinds of English.

Pronunciation is it. Unlike African American English, there is much less in the grammar or the vocabulary of Chicano and even Latino English to differentiate it from other varieties of English. Of course, speakers of Latino English who know Spanish may use Spanish words in place of English. Indeed, those who are fluent in Spanish will sometimes go back and forth between the two languages in what is known as "code-switching." Here is an example recorded by Joyce Penfield in El Paso, Texas:

> Fuí ayer con el doctor. Boy, they certainly make money. Me cobró twenty dollars. Fíjese a two minute visit y con trece pacientes en el office. Thirteen times twenty — son $260. Además de lo que le pagan en los hospitales. Híjole! Porqué no me hice doctor instead of accountant? Además del puro mirar las cifras I'm getting blind. Qué barbaridad!

This translates as:

> Yesterday I went to the doctor. Boy, they certainly make money. He charged me twenty dollars. Imagine a two minute visit and with thirteen patients in the office. Thirteen times twenty — it's $260. Besides what they pay him in the hospitals. My goodness! Why didn't I become a doctor instead of an accountant? From looking at these figures I'm getting blind. How ridiculous!

As this example shows, code-switching is not a blend of the two languages but alternation between one and the other, often in the middle of a sentence or even a phrase like *el office*. It's a fascinating study in its own right, but it's not the same as Chicano English, which is indeed a dialect of English.

There are other varieties of Latino English, too many to be discussed in this book. Notable examples are the Cuban-influenced English of Florida and the Puerto Rican- and Dominican-influenced English of New York City and its vicinity. Each is just as complex and systematic as all other varieties of Latino and American English.

American Indian English

American Indian or *Native American*? Yes, once again it's necessary to confront the question of the proper designation for an ethnic group. *Indian* derives from Columbus' mistake in thinking he had reached India when he made landfall on his westward voyage from Spain. If anyone has a right to claim ancestral Americanness, it is those people that Columbus called *Indians*. In very recent times, therefore, there has been an inclination to call them *Native Americans* instead.

Yet this newer term hasn't met with universal acclaim. There's the problem that "native American" can also mean anyone of any ancestry who was born in America. There's the problem that Columbus' mistake has a head start of five centuries of customary usage. Most important, there's the problem that many in the designated ethnic group consider Native American a term imposed on them by outsiders, however well meaning. So this book uses the traditional and still generally accepted designation *American Indian*.

When the first speakers of English arrived in North America, there were perhaps as many as 1,000 different American Indian languages spoken on the continent. Some belonged to larger families of languages, like the Algonquian languages near the Atlantic coast, but many were unrelated to the others. None, of course, were related to English. Even today, despite centuries of decline in Indian populations and the dominance of an English-speaking culture and government, it is still possible to hear close to 200 American Indian languages within the United States, including some as widely spoken as Navajo with about 150,000 native speakers, Ojibwa with more than 40,000, Cherokee with more than 20,000, and Lakota (Sioux) and Muskogee (Creek) with about 6,000 each. A survey in the 1980s estimated that one-quarter of American Indians do not speak English at all. But of course that means that three-quarters of them do.

With such diversity of native languages added to the location of Indians in scattered reservations and communities, and with cultures so diverse that they are recognized as separate nations, any generalizations about the particulars of American Indian English must be suspect. To have one model for American Indian English would be as surprising as to have one model for a pan-European language — though that would be easier, since most European languages are related, and many American Indian ones are not.

So a proper discussion of American Indian English would have to go community by community, treating each separately, with attention given to both the native language spoken by the Indians and to the variety of American English spoken by others in the area. Surprisingly, however, there do seem to be a number of tendencies that distinguish American Indian from other varieties of English.

One is a tendency to use present tense where others would use past. This happens especially when referring to something habitual, as African American English does with *be*. Researchers Walt Wolfram, Donna Christian, William Leap, and Lance Potter noted these examples in two Puebloan communities in the Southwest:

> They all speak in Indian when we first started school.
>
> Kids now go bowling, but we don't have that during our time.
>
> Well, now they are, but before they aren't.
>
> We were very poor when we were young. When they give us a nickel that means a lot, and nowadays the kids don't want a nickel.

Similar use of the present tense has been noted in American Indian English in other parts of the country as well, and as far back as several centuries ago. It may have arisen in the Indians' first contacts with speakers of English, when there was a tendency for each group to simplify its language in early attempts at communication.

Another characteristic of some varieties of American Indian English is a slower pace. Speakers may talk slowly and pause to allow themselves or their listeners to consider what they are saying. One Southwestern Indian said his most difficult adjustment to an off-reservation college was to learn to "talk without thinking."

The manner of speaking in some American Indian languages is also different from what is typical for English. Such languages incline to brevity of expression, inviting listeners to join in rather than remain silent, and they often use figurative language. These characteristics may then be adopted into American Indian English. One example illustrating this was written by a Northern Ute fourth grader:

Autumn is like a million of colors

floating in the air

But such characterizations can easily become overgeneralizations; this haiku-like description could well have come from many other ethnic groups.

So each Indian community deserves its own attention if we are to determine exactly what American Indian English means in any particular case. Consider, for example, the Lumbees of Robeson County in southeastern North Carolina. There are nearly 50,000 of them, the second-largest group of American Indians in the eastern United States. The Indian language they once spoke has been extinct for so long that no one knows what it was like; they speak only English. But researchers Walt Wolfram and Clare Dannenberg have found that the English they speak is unique. In many ways it is like that of their English-speaking white and black neighbors as well as residents of nearby Appalachia and the Outer Banks. But the Lumbee don't sound exactly like any of their neighbors, because no one else has their particular combination of sounds, grammar, and vocabulary.

For example, like local whites and African Americans, Lumbees may call a refrigerator a *kelvinator.* Like local African Americans, Lumbees may call a turtle a *cooter.* Like residents of Appalachia, they may use *chawed* to mean embarrassed. Also like residents of Appalachia, they may start *it* and *ain't* with an "h" sound, as in *hit hain't.* Unlike their immediate neighbors, but like residents of the Outer Banks, they pronounce the "long i" sound in words like *I, high,* and *tide* as "uh-ee," as if the words were spelled with *oi,* as in *hoi toide.*

And the Lumbee also say things that no one else does. Lumbee English includes "I'm been there" or "We're been there" instead of "I've been there" and "We've been there." There are also a few Lumbee words not known to any of their neighbors. *Lum,* meaning "a Lumbee person"; *on the swamp,* meaning "in their neighborhood" (since it's swampy); *sorry in the world,* meaning "doing badly"; and *ellick* meaning "coffee."

The Lumbees know that their language is different and are proud of it. They say that they "talk Indian," which means both that they have a unique way of speaking and that they keep their word.

Yiddish English

Yiddish is just one of the many languages that gave an accent to the English of the immigrants who spoke it, an accent that their native-born children sometimes learned but often shed as they assimilated to their American localities. So why single out Yiddish English for special notice? Why schlep it into this chapter?

There are two interrelated reasons why it stands out. First, there has been a large Yiddish-speaking community in the United States for more than a hundred years. At one time it numbered in the millions; even today it's more than a hundred thousand. Second, this community is in New York City, the nerve center of American communications, where speakers of Yiddish and Yiddish English have played a prominent role for the past century. As a result, Yiddish English has had a strong influence on theater, the mass media, and all of American culture, both high and low. So what's not to like?

Yiddish is, of course, the historic language of much of the Jewish population of eastern Europe. Although it is written with the Hebrew alphabet, it is a close relative not of Hebrew but of German. Yiddish-accented English consequently sounds much like German-accented English, with *w*'s sounding like *v*'s in its strongest form: "Vot do you vant?" In New York City, Yiddish English also is a part of the "Noo Yawk" accent. That's the amalgamation of English, Irish, and Italian sounds on top of which Yiddish was poured during the great immigrations a century ago.

What the rest of the country hears in Yiddish English is "Noo Yawk" with special vocabulary and tone of voice. In vocabulary, Americans can thank Yiddish for our ability not just to *schlep* but to *kibitz*, *kvetch*, and *nosh*, for example — words that mean "drag or carry," "chat or look on," "complain," and "snack," respectively (though without the extra dose of feeling that the Yiddish words provide). Thanks to Yiddish, Americans now have an extra repertoire of complimentary and uncomplimentary names for people — *mensch* and *maven* among the former, *klutz*, *nebbish*, and *schlemiel* among the latter.

Just as notable as the vocabulary of Yiddish English is the tone of voice that can turn a statement into a question. For example:

Moishe walks into a post office to send a package to his wife. The post-master says, "This package is too heavy, you'll need another stamp." Moishe replies, "And that should make it lighter?"

Other Ethnic Varieties

By far the majority of those who immigrated to the United States brought with them languages other than English: Dutch, German, Italian, Norwegian, Polish, Russian, Chinese, Japanese, and Vietnamese, just to mention a few not already covered in this chapter. In each case, where there were enough speakers of a particular language to form a local community, that community would develop its first-generation English with an accent. The second generation would be likely to let that accent go as they assimilated into mainstream American culture, but some traces of the original accent might remain even when these descendants spoke only English. Stories like those of Latino English could be told of many of these ethnic communities, and some have been mentioned in this book in the discussions of particular places.

Definition

A little old lady gets onto a crowded bus and stands in front of a seated young girl. Holding her hand to her chest, she says to the girl, "If you knew what I have, you would give me your seat." The girl gets up and gives up the seat. The girl then takes out a fan and fans herself.

The woman looks up and says, "If you knew what I have, you would give me that fan." The girl gives her the fan. Fifteen minutes later the woman gets up and says to the bus driver, "Stop, I want to get off here." The bus driver tells her he has to drop her at the next corner, not in the middle of the block. Her hand across her chest, she tells the driver, "If you knew what I have, you would let me out here." The bus driver pulls over and opens the door to let her out. As she's walking out of the bus, he asks, "Madam, what is it you have?" "Chutzpah," she replies.

— Jewish Humor webpage

Every language has its variations, even the silent language of the deaf. American Sign Language uses the shape and movement of hands and arms to convey its messages, and researchers recently have found considerable variation across the country in many of the common signs. A five-year national study conducted by Ceil Lucas and others at Gallaudet University found thirteen different signs for *early;* eleven each for *arrest, cereal, cheat,* and *faint;* six for *microwave* and *perfume;* five for *banana, chicken, computer, thief* and *tomato,* just to mention a few.

What's more, many of the different signs had their own variants. There were four different signs for *cake,* for example, and one of them had nine variants of handshape and movement. The researchers did not find regional correlation with this variation; multiple varieties of signs were found everywhere they looked, in Boston, Maryland, Virginia, New Orleans, Kansas, Washington State, and California. The one consistent difference they found was between younger and older signers: the young used signs where the old would use fingerspelling.

It would appear that there is even more variation in sign than in spoken language. Perhaps that's because more of the body is used for signing than for speech, providing more opportunity for difference. Or perhaps that's because signs are more symbolic than speech, and it's easier to come up with different symbols than with different sounds. But it is further evidence that wherever humans communicate, they have a variety of ways.

IN THE MOVIES

What we learn about other varieties of American English often comes from the movies. Sometimes it's an authentic type of language; sometimes it's a stereotype. Writers, directors and actors know that they can use dialect in a variety of ways: to enhance the setting of a film and give it a feel of authenticity, to define a character's background and personality, or to contrast one character with another. Some actors are cast in their native tongue. Tommy Lee Jones, for instance, hails from central Texas. In most of his roles he speaks his home-grown Texas accent. Holly Hunter also comes by a Southern accent naturally, having grown up in Georgia.

But it is the business of actors to change like chameleons to fit the parts they play. Just as they often wear costumes different from their civilian ones, so they must often put on accents. Learning to do this is part of their craft. They may be helped by a dialect coach who gives crash lessons in how to sound like where they're supposed to be from. Of course, an individual actor's ability to master accents varies, and sometimes even within the same movie an accent can wax and wane mysteriously.

Fortunately for the actors, most of us do not need a precise portrayal of a regional or ethnic way of speaking to get absorbed in a movie. As long as the actors can attune their tongue and lips to the most salient sounds and words, that is enough to make the movie work. In the movie *The Big Easy* (1987) Dennis Quaid, a native of Houston, Texas, plays Remy McSwain, a police detective working in a corrupt department. Quaid puts on a New Orleans accent somewhat removed from the real thing, but by peppering his dialogue with telltale locutions like referring to the woman from the D.A.'s office as

"Chere," French for "Dear," he is able to evoke the city's Cajun culture for most viewers. And while some New Orleanians complained that the movie did not have much authentic local speech — one native quipped that the movie has "A city full of people who sound as if they've just returned from Blanche DuBois' summer home" — it comes off just fine for the rest of us.

Similarly, in *Coal Miner's Daughter* (1980), Sissy Spacek (from east Texas) plays country singer Loretta Lynn, Levon Helm (from Arkansas) plays her coal-miner father, and Tommy Lee Jones (from Texas) plays adolescent Loretta's wild and much older boyfriend and eventual husband. All these characters speak with strong Southern accents but do not make much of an attempt to reproduce the South Midlands speech of the Kentucky hills where Lynn grew up. No matter. Their broad Southern is like moonshine that makes us feel as if we're down in the hollow too.

Sometimes the accents in a movie can be flatly wrong and still evocative. For example, you might enjoy Lena Olin as the wife of a baker in Detroit's Polish community and Claire Danes as her daughter in *Polish Wedding* (1998). Just don't take them as realistic. Their accents are suggestive of Central Europe, with rolling "r"s and throat-clearing "ch" sounds, but they bear little resemblance to the English spoken in such Detroit neighborhoods.

Or consider Alfred Hitchcock's classic *The Birds* (1963). It is set in California. All of the characters have unremarkable neutral speech, as might be expected for California — except one. When Rod Taylor's character arrives at the small town on the northern California coast where the birds will eventually attack, he encounters the proprietor of a general store, a local who speaks with the Down East accent of Maine, somehow transplanted a continent away. For a movie audience, this is a cue of a scenic and psychic shift. We are no longer in Los Angeles, where life is hectic and sophisticated. We are out in the country, where life is calm and simple — at least for now.

In most cases, however, we take it for granted that an actor in a regional movie will at least try to use an appropriate regional or ethnic accent. But it was not always so. The first talking movies, in the 1930s, used the language of the stage, and the American stage was inclined to a formal semi-British style of speech. Actors adopted British vowels and dropped their "r"s after vowels (as in "hahd" for *hard)* in the manner of British and some Eastern American speakers. It was closest to cultivated Eastern New England, but with added British touches like the emphasized "t" between vowels in words like *British*. The accent, still used by Americans who want to put on British to do Shakespeare, was called "Transatlantic," because, as the author of *Teach Yourself Transatlantic: Theatre Speech for Actors* (1986) explains, it is "the kind of speech that might be heard somewhere in the Atlantic Ocean exactly halfway between New York City and London." On the Titanic, perhaps?

So the formal speech you hear in an early movie wouldn't be the natural speech of any American locality. The setting of a movie and where its actors were portrayed as coming from rarely made a difference. Even then, though, there were occasional movies that made some use of regional accents. In *Gone With the Wind* (1939), for example, British actress Vivien Leigh put on a strong Southern accent as Scarlett O'Hara, although Clark Gable made no such concession in the role of Rhett Butler.

Over the years, the American accent in the movies became more distinctly American and less British. As a measure of the Americanization of movie talk, researcher Nancy Elliott studied the gradual increase in pronunciation of the "r" sound after vowels, the typical Northern and Western "General American" pronunciation as contrasted with the "r"-dropping of the South, New York City, eastern New England, and England. The "General American" pronouncing of "r" (sounding the "r" in *hard*, for example, rather than saying "hahd") increased from 40 percent in the 1930s to 55 percent in the 1940s, 65 percent in the 1950s, 80 percent in the 1960s, and more than 90 percent in the 1970s. In the 1930s and again in the 1950s, women dropped their "r"s more than men. Elliott speculates that this "r"-lessness gave women the edge in "elegance" in the 1930s and 1950s, with the 1940s a time of "wartime equality" of the genders. But "bad girls," for some reason, were especially "r"-less. And exceptionally good girls could be marked by "r"-lessness too; in *The Wizard of Oz* (1939), for example, Dorothy's plain Kansas talk contrasts with the elegant "r"-less Transatlantic accent of the good witch Glinda.

From the 1930s to the 1950s, Elliott reports, men in the presence of women adapted to the women's elegant "r"-lessness (a notable

John Wayne: Hardly ever

exception being Johnny Weismuller's Tarzan), while keeping their "r"s when talking with the boys *(haRd)*. John Wayne, a man's man, hardly ever dropped his "r"s. The elegant Fred Astaire, on the other hand, "hahdly" ever pronounced an "r" after a vowel.

And Westerns, by and large, were not marked by "r"-dropping or other attempts at "Transatlantic" accents. The exceptions were dudes from the urban East, or even Brits, whose accents marked them as greenhorns.

By the 1970s, elegant or not, the British-influenced stage accent had almost vanished from American movies. British actors playing Americans now had to adopt "r"-pronouncing American accents. And Americans in British movies had to use generic American accents. Andie MacDowell, for example, is from "r"-dropping South Carolina, but when she played the American love interest in the British comedy *Four Weddings and a Funeral* (1994), she assumed an "r"-pronouncing "General American" accent.

Unfortunately, sometimes the use of dialect in movies gives dialect a bad name, since it can be used to stereotype narrowmindedness and ineptitude. Consider the implied message in *The Big Green* (1995), a family-oriented Disney movie. The setting is a small town in Texas. The story is that a bunch of goofy kids, on the verge of going bad because they have low self-esteem, find themselves by playing soccer. To do this they need a coach, and an exchange teacher from Britain, an attractive young woman, steps in to show them the way. The local sheriff, played by New Yorker Steve Guttenberg, starts out with a Southern accent so thick that the kids call him Deputy Dawg. But as he gets involved with soccer (and with the British coach), and thus overcomes his cultural limitations, his accent fades away. Although some of the parents speak Southern, the children have no trace of it in their speech, implying that their horizons are not as limited as their parents'. At the end there is a showdown with a powerhouse team from Austin, whose coach and players speak without a trace of Southern English. The message seems clear — Regional English is for hicks and losers.

It's as subtle and authentic as having the good guy in a Western wear a white hat. Unfortunately such uses of accents are all too common.

Dialect is often used to highlight dramatic tension between characters, and many movies that feature contrasting dialects have become classics. *A Streetcar Named Desire* (1951), a film version of Tennessee Williams' play, is set in New Orleans.

Fred Astaire: Hahdly evah

It matches Vivien Leigh as Blanche DuBois, a fragile Southern belle, against Marlon Brando as Stanley Kowalski, a crude working-class immigrant. The clash of their personalities takes shape in their clashing styles of speaking.

In the Oscar-winning *In the Heat of the Night* (1967), Rod Steiger speaks with a heavy Southern accent in his role as Bill Gillespie, chief of police of Sparta, Mississippi, a small town where a rich white man has been murdered. Sidney Poitier plays Virgil Tibbs, a Philadelphia homicide detective who is visiting his mother in the town and gets involved in the investigation. Confident and righteous in the face of prejudice, Tibbs speaks with an urbane Northern accent but switches to an African-American style of speech when following leads in the black part of town. As they eventually cooperate on solving the crime, Steiger's bigoted redneck sheriff learns to appreciate Tibbs' intelligence and investigative skill, and Poitier's Tibbs comes to appreciate Gillespie's moral courage.

Another Oscar winner, *Midnight Cowboy* (1969), pairs up another odd couple: John Voigt's naive Texan Joe Buck and Dustin Hoffman's sleazy Ratzo Rizzo. Buck leaves his home state and travels to New York City, imagining he will make a living off his sexual prowess as a gigolo. He finds New York less than hospitable, however, and ends up befriending Rizzo, who lives in a condemned apartment building. Voigt's Southern and Hoffman's native New York talk do much to make the movie.

New York talk also figures heavily in Neil Simon's original *Odd Couple* (1968) and *The Odd Couple II* (1998), both with Jack Lemmon and Walter Matthau. Lemmon plays Felix Unger, a portrait photographer whose fastidious neatness has led to his eviction by his wife. Longtime friend and sportswriter Oscar Madison, played by Matthau, takes him in. Oscar has also been evicted by his wife, but for the opposite flaw, his sloppy manners. The opposing characters are further offset by their language. Lemmon, who had a good Boston prep school and Harvard upbringing, modifies his accent into a cultivated version of "General American," while Matthau's down-to-earth Oscar speaks "Noo Yawk" talk — authentically, too, as Matthau is a native.

In *The Silence of the Lambs* (1991), Jodie Foster as FBI agent Clarice Starling adopts an Appalachian-tinged accent with Midlands pronunciations, like an added "r" in "Warshington." She is the simple girl from the backwoods, intelligent and earnest. She is overmatched but undaunted by the cultivated accent and vocabulary of Anthony Hopkins' evil Hannibal Lecter.

There are many movies that use American regional accents accurately, including some with genuine local speakers. The earlier chapters of this book have toured the actual landscape of American dialects; this chapter concludes with a brief sampling of the virtual landscape of American movies.

The South

As the best known and most prominent of American regional dialects, Southern English is well represented in movies.

Tennessee Williams' plays have pronounced Southern settings, and the actors in the movie versions of his plays of necessity adopt Southern accents too. In *Cat on a Hot Tin Roof* (1958), Elizabeth

Taylor (a Californian) and Paul Newman (from Ohio) do their best to sound Southern. Burl Ives (from downstate Illinois), playing Big Daddy, makes less of an effort.

The Long, Hot Summer (1958), a composite of William Faulkner's stories, is set like the stories themselves in Mississippi. The cast — including Paul Newman and his wife Joanne Woodward, a native of Greenville, South Carolina, display full Southern accents.

Fried Green Tomatoes (1991), based on a novel by Fannie Flagg, is set in Alabama in the 1920s as well as the present day. Mary Stuart Masterson, Mary-Louise Parker, Jessica Tandy, and Kathy Bates all have appropriate Southern accents. Bates grew up in Memphis, Tennessee, and Parker in South Carolina, so theirs come naturally.

Holly Hunter, who was raised in Georgia, plays a Mississippi small-town beauty pageant hopeful in Beth Henley's *Miss Firecracker* (1989). She also has a Southern accent in Ethan and Joel Coen's *Raising Arizona* (1987).

Deliverance (1972) is a dramatization of James Dickey's novel about a canoe trip in a Southern wilderness that becomes a nightmare. The cast includes Burt Reynolds, a native of Georgia, and Ned Beatty, a native of Kentucky. But they are the urbanites out for the weekend, so their speech is less Southern than that of the ominous hillbillies they encounter in the backwoods. Dickey, a Georgian himself, is the Southern-accented sheriff who enters the scene at the end.

In *The Apostle* (1997), Robert Duvall, a Californian, puts on a good Southern accent as a Texas preacher who skips town and establishes himself as "Apostle E.F." in Louisiana. As well as starring in the movie, Duvall wrote and directed it. African-American accents are also abundant in the movie, including John Beasley's as a preacher who works with the Apostle in Louisiana.

Duvall also presents a believable Southern accent in *Days of Thunder* (1990), a movie about NASCAR racing, and in the mini-series *Lonesome Dove* (1989) about a nineteenth-century cattle run from Texas to Montana.

Lonesome Dove also stars Tommy Lee Jones, whose Southern accent comes naturally. He was born in San Saba, Texas, in the middle of the state, attended school in Dallas, and then went off to Harvard for college. (His roommate happened to be Al Gore of Tennessee, another state with a Southern accent.) Jones wrote, directed, and

> **Most of the Californians** or New Yorkers that I've met could not distinguish between a Texas regional accent and a Southern one. The only one who struggled was Timothy Bottoms. . . . Early in the movie [*The Last Picture Show*], when he's making out with Charlene Duggs in the pickup truck, he's supposed to say, "Let's do somethin' different." And he refused to do that after many, many coaching sessions to tell him to say "somethin'"; he had to say "some*thang*." "Let's do some*thang* different." And it's in the movie, "some*thang*." It was one of those days I couldn't be on the set, and it snuck by me. And Peter didn't know the difference.
>
> — Gary Chason, assistant to the director,
> in *Texas Monthly* (February 1999)

starred in *The Good Old Boys* (1995), casting himself as a present-day cowboy in his Texas homeland.

Texas accents are carefully modeled in *The Last Picture Show* (1971), Peter Bogdanovich's version of Larry McMurtry's novel about coming of age in a small West Texas town in the 1950s.

Andie MacDowell, who can present a "General American" accent as readily as her native Southern one, has an opportunity to speak Southern in *Shadrach* (1998), a story about a 99-year-old former slave who in the 1930s returns to his old Virginia plantation to arrange to be buried there. In this movie MacDowell takes on a coarser Southern accent than the one she grew up with in South Carolina, portraying, in the words of one commentator, "a beer-guzzling alcoholic mother of a large, unwashed, lice-infested family living below the poverty level."

In *Cookie's Fortune* (1999), Robert Altman's "Southern Gothic comedy," Kentuckian Ned Beatty has a role as a sheriff's deputy, and Julianne Moore, a native of Fayetteville, North Carolina, is a self-centered daughter of the eccentric central character Cookie.

Midnight in the Garden of Good and Evil (1997) is set in Savannah, Georgia. John Cusack (from northern Illinois) and Kevin Spacey (from New Jersey) play the leads with, if anything, even more of an accent than you'd find in Savannah.

To get a taste of Cajun language, watch *Southern Comfort* (1981). In that movie some National Guardsmen on a weekend exercise in a

Louisiana swamp get in serious trouble with hunters. Neither the Guardsmen nor the hunters are Cajuns, but there are Cajun speakers in the local scenes.

The South Midlands

Appalachian coal miners, company operators, thugs, and strikebreakers are heard in director John Sayles' *Matewan* (1987), a 1920s story set in Mingo County, West Virginia, that is based on an actual incident.

Tin Men (1987) is a comedy about aluminum siding salesmen in Baltimore of the 1960s. The lead actors are New Yorkers Danny DeVito and Richard Dreyfuss, but the director Barry Levinson is from Baltimore and takes care to make the setting authentic. "Few movies have ever given such an accurate portrayal of a particular time and place in America as well as this one," comments one reviewer. Michael Tucker, who plays the character called Bagel, is a Baltimore native.

Director John Waters also grew up in Baltimore, as did the transvestite Divine, star of Waters' bizarre *Pink Flamingos* (1972). In that comedy Divine, living in a trailer outside of Baltimore, gets into a vicious competition for the title of "Filthiest Person in the World." Another Waters comedy with Divine and a Baltimore setting is *Hairspray* (1988), about a teen talent television show involved in the controversy over racial integration. Ric Ocasek, who plays the part of "Beatnik Cat," is a Baltimore native.

Yet another Waters movie, *Pecker* (1998), is set in the Hampden neighborhood of Baltimore, but its accents are less than perfect. One reviewer complains that "the people didn't say *Baltimore* the way those characters should say it. It should be 'Baltimere.'"

Boston

Southie (1998) is about a young man involved in organized crime who gets into difficulties when he returns to his South Boston Irish home. Donnie Wahlberg, who plays the lead role, is from that neighborhood himself and gives an accurate rendition of the accent.

Once Around (1991) stars Holly Hunter as Renata Bella, a Boston waitress from an Italian-American family. New Yorker Danny Aiello, among others, has an Italian accent here. Whether it's authentically Boston is another matter.

Blown Away (1994) is a thriller about bombings in Boston, but its most notable accent is the Irish spoken by Tommy Lee Jones.

In *Good Will Hunting*, Robin Williams is supposed to have a South Boston accent, but it's not to be trusted.

New York City

Countless are the movies featuring the stereotypically tough and down-to-earth New York accent, a.k.a. Brooklynese. One who made the accent famous (and over the top) in the movies was San Franciscan Mel Blanc, the voice of Bugs Bunny.

For contemporary New York and New Jersey accents, try *Unmade Beds* (1997), Nicholas Barker's quasi-documentary of four middle-aged people who advertise for partners in the personals columns of newspapers. Much of the movie is their monologues, and two of the characters, Brenda Monte and Mikey Russo, are authentic New Yorkers, playing themselves.

Neil Simon's autobiographical plays have New York accents as well as New York settings. New Yorkese is well represented in their movie versions too, like *Lost in Yonkers* (1993) with New Yorkers Richard Dreyfuss and Mercedes Ruehl.

You can't find much more authentic New York speech than John Travolta's in *Saturday Night Fever* (1977). His Brooklyn accent is as much of his character as his flashy costumes and dance routines. Travolta himself is from Englewood Cliffs, New Jersey, but that's close enough. His love interest, played by New Yorker Karen Lynn Gorney, and other cast members likewise reflect localized New York speech.

You want mobsters? How about *Donnie Brasco* (1997), the true story of an FBI agent who infiltrated the mafia in New York City in the late 1970s. The cast includes New Yorkers Al Pacino, Bruno Kirby, and James Russo.

More lightly, there is *Wise Guys* (1986) starring New Jerseyites Danny DeVito and Joe Piscopo. The plot has accurately been summarized as "Two schmoes tick off the Godfather," and they do it with appropriate New York tough-guy accents. The movie also features Harvey Keitel and Ray Sharkey, both natives of Brooklyn.

In *Cop Land* (1997), corrupt New York cops live in a mob-run town across the river in New Jersey. Sylvester Stallone, a native New Yorker, is the local sheriff who eventually wakes up to the corruption and does the bad guys in. Another native New Yorker, Robert De Niro, is the NYPD Internal Affairs investigator who wakes him up.

An effective way to highlight a New York accent is to place it in a foreign setting. *My Cousin Vinnie* (1992), a comic drama, gives New Yorkese a starring role as Joe Pesci and Marisa Tomei speak thick New York accents in a small Alabama town and courtroom. One of the many memorable linguistic moments occurs as attorney Pesci baffles the courtly Southern judge by referring to the "yutes" charged with murder. That translates as *youths*, of course.

New Yorkese is highlighted in reverse when Steve Martin and Goldie Hawn, alias Henry and Nancy Clark from Ohio, visit New York City as *The Out-of-Towners* (1999). They are more believably non-New York than Jack Lemmon and Sandy Dennis, who starred in the first version of the movie in 1970. Dennis in particular came from "Ohio" with a Brooklyn accent.

The romantic comedy *A Walk on the Moon* (1999), set in the 1960s in a Jewish resort in the Catskills, offers plentiful authentic New York speech. New Yorker Diane Lane plays the lead role of restless housewife Pearl Kantrowitz. Liev Schreiber, who plays her husband, also grew up in New York, as did many of the rest of the cast, including the outspoken mother-in-law Tovah Feldshuh.

Accents from across the river in New Jersey, as well as New York City, are heard in Susan Skoog's *Whatever* (1998), a comedy — or drama, or tragedy, whatever — about a teenage girl coming of age in 1981.

North North Central

Fargo has already been mentioned as a movie permeated by the distinctive pronunciation and phrasing ("oh, yah") that can be heard in Minnesota and its northern neighbors. If anything, the Northern accent is overdone for effect, but what an effect. The writers and directors, Joel and Ethan Coen, know this language well, having grown up in Minneapolis.

Genuine Wisconsin accents are thick and plentiful in Chris Smith's documentary *American Movie* (1999) about Mark Borchardt's three-year struggle to make his low-budget horror film *Coven* (pronounced "coe-ven"). The setting is Menomonee Falls, northwest of Milwaukee, and the filmmaker and actors are all local with local accents. Listen, for example, to Uncle Bill's pronunciation of *okay* as he says it again and again in 30 takes of a short scene.

California

There's no need for a guide to movies with California accents — almost anything with a Los Angeles setting will do, as long as the actors don't make a point of sounding like they're from somewhere else. The lighter side of the city is heard in movies like Steve Martin's *L.A. Story* (1991) and a tougher side in ones like *Freeway* (1996) with Reese Witherspoon as a no-nonsense teenage survivor. The youth culture is celebrated in director Amy Heckerling's movies *Fast Times at Ridgemont High* (1982) and *Clueless* (1995). The first is down in the valley (the San Fernando Valley), the second up in the hills (Beverly Hills). Heckerling herself is from New York City, but you don't find New York accents in these movies, except for Cher's father in *Clueless*, played by Brooklynite Dan Hedaya, who also is the corrupt and heavily New York-accented Detective Vincent Della Pesca in *Hurricane* (1999).

African American

Just as African American English is the best known of American ethnic dialects, so it is the most plentifully portrayed in American movies. Those with all-black casts often offer "Spoken Soul" in rich variety. There is the movie of Alice Walker's *The Color Purple* (1985), for example, starring Danny Glover, Whoopi Goldberg, Margaret Avery, and Oprah Winfrey in an early twentieth century Southern setting. There is Toni Morrison's *Beloved* (1998), set in southern Ohio in the mid-nineteenth century, with a cast that includes Oprah Winfrey, Danny Glover, Thandie Newton, Kimberly Elise, and Albert Hall, all with appropriate "Spoken Soul." Contemporary African-

American "sistas" are portrayed in *Waiting to Exhale* (1995) and *How Stella Got Her Groove Back* (1998), dramatizations of Terry McMillan's novels.

Spike Lee's movies use authentic African-American and New York City accents. You can hear them in *Do the Right Thing* (1989), *Jungle Fever* (1991), *Malcolm X* (1992), *Crooklyn* (1994), and *Summer of Sam* (1999), among others.

Both Chicago and a Mississippi plantation figure in *Down in the Delta* (1998) with Alfre Woodard, Al Freeman Jr., Mary Alice, Esther Rolle, Loretta Devine, and Wesley Snipes using a variety of styles of African-American speech.

Hurricane (1999), the story of boxer Rubin "Hurricane" Carter who spent twenty-two years in prison after being framed for murder, has a variety of examples of African American English, from one extreme to the other. One extreme is the language of the ghetto streets. It is spoken by teenager Vicellous Reon Shannon as Lesra, the youth who comes to live with three Canadians, happens upon Carter's book, and enlists the Canadians in the effort to free Carter. The other extreme is Denzel Washington in the starring role of Carter. Even in his toughest moments and angriest dialogue, Washington's speech has just a flavoring of African American pronunciation, all the while maintaining the dignity of bearing and speech he displays in his other movies. There are also a number of other minor characters who use African American in the realistic setting of Paterson, New Jersey, which is not far from New York City and depressingly corrupt and crime-ridden.

For a rich sampling of the strongly African-influenced Gullah speech of South Carolina and Georgia's Sea Islands, see *Daughters of the Dust* (1992), an evocation of Gullah culture in 1902.

Just as white actors from the South, New York City, Boston, and other notably accented parts of America can leave their regional speech behind to talk neutral American English when the script calls for it, so there are numerous African Americans who can assume a neutral dialect when portraying a character not particularly associated with African-American culture. Sidney Poitier was one of the first to have such roles. Denzel Washington is another as comfortable in Shakespeare (*Much Ado About Nothing*, 1993) as in the streets of Paterson.

American Indian

Although there are numerous Westerns with caricatures of Indians, in recent movies a number of American Indian actors have had roles that allow them to use Indian speechways without the old stereotypes. In Kevin Costner's *Dances with Wolves* (1990), for example, Graham Greene, an Oneida Indian, has the impressive role of Kicking Bird. Chief Dan George has a central role in *Little Big Man* (1970) as Old Lodge Skins, Dustin Hoffman's Indian grandfather. And Russell Means, founder of the American Indian Movement, is the voice of Powhatan in Disney's *Pocahontas* (1995).

In Jim Jarmusch's *Dead Man* (1995), Johnny Depp plays William Blake, a naive white man in the late nineteenth century who goes to the Pacific Northwest in search of a job and ends up wandering the woods with an Indian portrayed by Gary Farmer. Farmer as "Nobody" thinks that Depp is the poet William Blake. The movie respectfully portrays the Indian's visions and religious outlook.

There is also one recent feature film written, directed, and acted by American Indians: *Smoke Signals* (1998). Based on a short story by Sherman Alexie, this is a comedic drama about two young Indians living on a present-day reservation in Idaho who travel to Phoenix on a family errand. Their speech has similarities to the North North Central of whites who live in the same part of the country.

DIALECTS 2100

At the turn of the next century, what will American dialects look like? And will there be any, or will we all sound the same?

The second question is easier to answer than the first. Every language known to man and woman, or at least every language used by man and woman as their primary means of communication, varies from place to place and community to community. Sometimes we imagine that the classical languages, at least, were fixed and unchanging, but scholars of such languages as ancient Greek, Latin, and Chinese know better. Over the course of time, for example, Latin changed so much that it became separate languages, each with its own variations: Italian, French, Spanish, and Portuguese among them. And those weren't even descended from classical Latin, the language of great literature and oratory, but from "vulgar" Latin, the everyday language of ordinary people.

So we can be certain that there will be variation and change in American English a century hence, just as there is now. And whatever technological advances come along, however wired everyone becomes, we can be pretty certain that people will still form communities of communication, and American English will still vary from place to place. It's possible, of course, that the communities might be virtual and the places might be in cyberspace, but it's hard to imagine that even highly wired humans would do entirely without bodies or homes or places on earth.

We can also predict that there will be stability in American English a century hence, just as there is now. Human language is as remarkable for its stability as for its variation. The word *fish*, for example, is pronounced with approximately the same sounds, and approximately the same variation in the vowel, as it was in England more than a thousand years ago. The language of a community can be more stable than the people are. Americans are getting more and more mobile, but the speech patterns learned by the children who grow up in a particular community remain relatively stable, because the children as they grow up generally follow the norms of the community even if their parents are from elsewhere.

Aside from grand generalizations, is there anything particular we can reasonably predict for American English in the year 2100? Yes, if we assume that trends of the past will continue into the future. One important prediction is that the United States will continue to exist in something like its present-day configuration. Such a prediction made in 1900 would have come true in 2000, so perhaps we can accept it for another century. Another prediction is that the South will continue to have a sense of itself as different from the rest of the country, a difference expressed linguistically in the Southern accent. There was a Southern accent in 1900, there is one today, and the South is prominent enough both geographically and in the minds of Americans from all regions that it seems likely to be with us in 2100.

As more and more Northerners become "sunbirds," staying in the South during the winter or taking up permanent residence there, further Northern invasion into Southern speechways may well occur. The erasing of much of the Southernness of southern Florida is already one example. But it would take a more massive and sustained Northern invasion than any since the Civil War to overcome such a strong regional way of speaking as that of the South.

About the distinctive speech of smaller localities it's harder to be confident. Will at least some residents of Boston, New York, Philadelphia, Pittsburgh, New Orleans, and other such places still want to flaunt their distinctive local styles? "Noo Yawkese," at least, seems likely to be preserved, if only to play a starring role in stereotypes of tough city dwellers in the movies and television. Survival of the others will depend on fad and fashion.

During the twentieth century there was also one major change in American English that seems irreversible. Although we still think of British English as classy, we have lost our desire to imitate it or even to pay much attention to it. As late as the mid-twentieth century, even if we were losing our inclination to speak that way, we admired the courageous, cultivated declarations of Winston Churchill and Queen Elizabeth. At the end of the century British English failed to cause such excitement, and sometimes it just sounded silly, whether it was Prince Charles making naughty talk on his cell phone or actor Hugh Grant bumbling and blinking. The movie *Notting Hill* illustrates the relative position of American and British English at the most recent turn of the century. Grant, with his nice little accent and manners, managing a nice little bookshop in a tony little corner of London, is overwhelmed by American star Julia Roberts. In real life Roberts grew up in Smyrna, Georgia, but she long since discarded her Southern accent in favor of a robust "General American." The message of the movie is that even a star is just another person when it comes to love. After the necessary misunderstandings and complications, Roberts and Grant become a happy couple at the movie's end. She loves him, but she shows not the slightest interest in changing even one syllable of her American English to sound like him.

At the start of the twentieth century, the British Empire dominated the English-speaking world. At the start of the twenty-first, American culture and language — everything from Coca-Cola to rock music to the expression "OK" — is washing over most of the world. It's hard to predict the politics of a hundred years from now, but the relative size of the British Isles and America makes it difficult to imagine that the former could regain their influence over the latter. Americans, then, at least outside the South and the Atlantic coast, are likely to look west rather than east for their "normal" speech.

Finally, it is almost certain that in the year 2100 American English will have pronunciations that would sound funny to us today, just as we certainly will sound funny to our descendants a century hence. And it is certain that there will be new words unfamiliar to us, not just on a national scale but also in particular localities, as new occasions, objects, and attitudes come along. Just listen.

Word Index

Subject Index